ROBLEY D. EVANS.

From a photograph taken on the bridge of the battle ship Iowa.

A SAILOR'S LOG

Recollections of Forty Years of Naval Life

By

ROBLEY D. EVANS
Rear-Admiral, U. S. N.

ILLUSTRATED

New York
D. Appleton and Company
1901

TO

MY WIFE,

WITHOUT WHOSE INSPIRATION AND ASSISTANCE
IT WOULD NOT HAVE BEEN WRITTEN,

THIS BOOK IS DEDICATED.

CONTENTS

iii

A Sailor's Log

iv

Contents

v

A Sailor's Log

Contents

LIST OF ILLUSTRATIONS

ix

Before spinning the yarn of my forty years in the navy, it seems only proper that I should give a short history of my life before entering the service.

A SAILOR'S LOG

CHAPTER I

LIFE IN VIRGINIA BEFORE THE WAR

BEFORE spinning the yarn of my forty years in the navy, it seems only proper that I should give a short history of my life before entering the service.

I was born in Floyd County, Virginia, August 18, 1846.

My father, Samuel Andrew Jackson Evans, M. D., was a graduate of the University of Virginia, and named me, his first son, after Doctor Robley Dunglison, who had been his instructor and dear friend. The home of my parents was in the mountains of Virginia, which, at the time of my birth, were almost as wild and rough as the partially settled mountains of the West. We did not have savage Indians to contend with, but we did have their savage white brothers.

As a means of livelihood my father followed his profession of medicine, and he was the only doctor in a circuit of twenty or thirty miles. For pleasure he owned slaves and farmed, and when requested to do so, represented his constituents in the State Legislature. The life of a doctor under such conditions was a very hard one, particularly in the winter season. Frequently he had to be in the saddle all night, facing the storms of snow and rain, to help some sufferer who could only offer his thanks as pay, for most of the people were very poor. It was this exposure that finally cost my father his life in the prime of his manhood and usefulness.

My first distinct memory of myself is when I was about four years old. I had rather long, light-coloured curls, was sturdy in health, and wore a blue velvet suit, with a feather in my cap for ornament. On hiring day, when the slaves were assembled at the court-house to find employers for the next year, I wandered about the village streets and considered myself of importance. At this time I rode from my home to the schoolhouse every day, a distance of five miles; and while I can recall the way the teacher used to thrash the boys, first sending them to cut the birches, I can not recall that I ever learned anything.

When I was six years old I was the happy possessor of a gun, a pony, and a negro boy. The first I learned to handle with considerable skill, was devoted to its use, and in all my life since have found both health and pleasure from the hunting habit formed at that early age. The pony, as I now recollect him, seemed bent on breaking my neck; and the coloured lad, my constant companion, taught me, among other things, to smoke and chew tobacco. He impressed on my mind many superstitions and dreadful ghost stories, some of which I remember to this day. The pony had one marked characteristic which I can also recall. He would go beautifully as long as I was going his way, but any attempt to send him over a road he did not wish to travel led to trouble. He would turn round

and round and buck a few times, to rid himself of his
mount, and, failing in this, lie down in the road and
roll over. I managed, however, to get to the court-
house on most days, and had much pleasure and comfort from his ownership.

Like most Southern children, I was brought up
and cared for by a " black mammy," and I certainly
loved her dearly. She was a short, thickset, very
black woman, much the shape of a flour barrel. In
addition to the care of four of us, she had had eighteen children of her own; but with it all she always
had time to comfort me when I was in trouble, which
I must say was frequently the case. No matter how
busy she might be, she could make the time to coddle
her young master and comfort him in a way that no
other could. The memory of her corn bread and fried
chicken lingers with me after all these years. She was
freed in the early days of the civil war, and spent the
rest of her life in the city of Washington. She died
in the Howard Hospital at the good old age of one
hundred and two years, and it was my great pleasure
to know that in her last years I had given her every
comfort that she could desire, and so paid off a small
portion of the debt I owed her. My grandmother had
given her to my mother as a marriage portion, and
the faithful old soul had lived her life in our family
connection.

Life in the mountains of Virginia in my early boyhood days was very different from any I have ever
known since. The country was thinly settled, and the
people were as a rule poor, but what they had they
freely shared with their neighbours. Their hospitality

was great and sincere. They were honest, hard-working people, who insisted on straight dealing, and they sometimes took the law into their own hands to enforce their ideas. There were two things one must not do—steal horses or interfere with his neighbours' slaves. Churches and schools were few and widely distributed. In place of the former we had the " circuit rider," who came and made himself at home almost as a member of the family, until his duties were performed, when he passed on to some other farmhouse, and so in turn visited the whole section. In the summer time camp meetings were organized, and then the horsemen and horsewomen gathered from all the surrounding mountains and enjoyed themselves in a very sensible way. Most of them prayed and sang until they were tired, and then withdrew to their tents and ate and drank the good things that had been prepared for them. Wheeled vehicles were not in use to any general extent for pleasure purposes, as the few roads we had were mere trails fit only for horses. Sometimes the camp would be made near a smooth stretch of road, and after the ministers and the shouters had done their work the young men would have their innings and speed their favourite horses; certainly there could not have been found a more healthful recreation or a happier way of passing a week during the heat of the summer.

In the fall of the year, when the tobacco had been cured and the apple crop gathered, the overseer on my father's farm usually fitted out an expedition for Lynchburg. This consisted of a number of six-horse wagons, sufficient to carry the tobacco and such other things as were to be sold. When all was ready the start was made, and this starting was quite an occasion. Every man, woman, and child wanted something from town, and the list was never completed until the train was some miles on its way. I can recall now the joy with which I made one of these trips. I had a comfortable place in one of the wagons when I wanted to ride there, or I could mount my own pony. At night we camped by the roadside, and after supper listened to the songs of the teamsters and helpers until bedtime. Early daylight found us under way after a breakfast of fried bacon and chicken, and such corn bread as one can never have now, because such corn meal as we ate in those days is no longer made. When we arrived at our destination the tobacco was soon weighed into the warehouse, the apples and chickens and bacon sold, and then we enjoyed the shopping until our money was gone. My wants were few—a pair of high winter boots with red tops, a saddle for my pony, and a few pounds of powder and shot and half a dozen boxes of caps. Then we came home with our long list of things for the winter—everything from the family groceries to the Christmas presents for the slaves, down to the last pickaninny of them all.

I remember well what a great joy the harvest season was to me as a youngster. After following the cradlers, splendid great black fellows, giants in physique, until noon, the cradles were laid aside and the men gathered under the shade trees for their midday meal. Then the man who had led the gang had an extra glass of apple-jack to encourage him for the afternoon's work, also a few kindly words of encouragement from my father, if he happened to be present. That leader seemed to me one of the greatest men in the world! My particular duty and pleasure during these harvest days was to carry a basket lined with raw cotton in which I gathered the eggs of the Bob White. As the nests were cut over by the cradlers, the mother birds left, never to return, and I at once gathered the eggs and put them under sitting hens to be hatched out. There was one particular clover field which was the favourite nesting place of these birds, and of course my particular delight. I once gathered one hundred and twenty eggs in this field, and succeeded in hatching most of them under a hen in the barn. When the small birds had got rid of their shells, it was interesting to see the old hen try to manage her unnatural brood. At the least bit of noise the whole lot would disappear, and you might search to your heart's content without finding one. The old hen would cluck and scratch with great energy, but the young birds remained in hiding until all danger was passed. As winter came on, I fed these birds in the barnyard, and they remained there until the spring came, when they disappeared in the grain fields.

The winters were very severe, and, of course, life was mostly indoors. When the river was in condition for such sport, we spent much time in sleighing on it. My father had brought from the East a two-horse sleigh, and in this the family had many jolly rides, particularly on moonlight nights. For myself, I think I preferred to stay in the house, where it was warm, or run away with black mammy to the quarters and hear the negroes sing and see them dance. I don't remember ever having much pleasure in the winter either in my boyhood or since; the mere fact of cold weather is enough to take the pleasure out of life for me. We usually had the house full of company both winter and summer, as we had connections who lived far enough North to enjoy the winters, and others living far enough South to enjoy the summers.

Slaves were not owned in large numbers in the mountain regions of Virginia. There was no necessity for their labour. The amount of tobacco grown was small, and the country was thinly settled. Above all, the people as a rule were poor and did their own farm work. I don't remember how many my father owned. I can recall a dozen or more, and they certainly were a happy lot. I never saw but one slave whipped, and he was struck a single blow with a rawhide on his bare back for having ill treated a riding horse. My father never sold one of his slaves, yet stories were frequently circulated that he was going to do so, and this led to no end of trouble. One winter night we were sitting in the parlour eating apples and black walnuts, which was the habit of all Virginia children in that day, before retiring. There came a knock at the door, and when it was opened one of the negro men named Sambo presented himself covered with blood. He told my father that a robber had thrown a hatchet at him and cut him badly. On examination it was found that Sambo's left hand was in bad shape—two fingers entirely cut off and two others hanging by small bits of skin. His hand was dressed and he was sent off to his cabin; but the next day blood marks on the snow showed his trail, and we soon found a stump on the bank of the river a mile or so from the house, where he had cut his own fingers off. He had missed his hand at the first blow in the dark, but the second time he succeeded. The axe with which the cutting was done was found near by, where he had thrown it. When confronted with the evidence he at once admitted his guilt, and pleaded as excuse that he believed my father meant to send him away from his family; that he had been so informed, and he knew that no one would buy him if he had only one hand. The poor chap learned to chop wood with one hand, and that was his sole occupation as long as I knew anything about him. After my father's death he was sold with the rest of the property, and brought seventy-five dollars.

Of course, no one can defend slavery as it existed in our Southern States, nor indeed in any form; but we must admit that in some ways the results were not wholly bad. No one can deny that in many cases slaves were cruelly treated, but this was not the general rule; it was not the business way of looking out for valuable property, to place it on no higher plane. Slaves, as a rule, were too valuable to be ill treated or neglected. The curse of slavery was to the white race and not the black. The bad effects were felt by the growing generation of whites; but as for the blacks, I am sure their lives were easier and happier then than since they were given their freedom. The slaves on my father's farm did not come themselves from Africa, but I have no doubt their parents, or certainly their grandparents, did. It has been my fortune to see something of the Africans in their own country, and when I compare them, with their brutal habits in their unlimited freedom and self-government, with the black people who were slaves in this country, I must conclude that slavery was not all bad. There was something about it that produced honesty and faithfulness and a race of men who, when their masters were away fighting to keep them slaves, took the same care of the women and children as the masters would have taken of them themselves. Their record in this respect is certainly as fine as anything in history. I believe there is not an authentic case of slaves having ill treated the women and children of their masters during the entire civil war. Imagine what would have been the result if these women and children had been left in the care of native Africans under such conditions!

My father died when I was ten years old, and I found myself the head of the family. In order that we might be near good schools, my mother moved at once to Fairfax Courthouse. There my schooling really began, but only continued for a short time. It was in Fairfax that the farmer said to his Northern friend who was congratulating him on the large size of his farm: " I am not as poor as you seem to think. I don't own *all* that land! " The county was always rich in lawsuits, averaging probably one or two to the acre, and since the civil war it is rich in historical incidents.

CHAPTER II

WITH THE INDIANS AND BUFFALO

In the year 1857 I was invited to make my home with my uncle, Mr. A. H. Evans, in Washington, which I gladly did, that I might have the advantage of good schools. I found this new home a real home, and from my uncle and aunt I received all the loving-kindness and attention that I could have had from my own parents; they treated me as one of their own children, except that they were never as severe with my small faults as they were with theirs. To my dear aunt I owe a deep debt of gratitude for her unfailing love and sympathy, and to my good uncle I owe my position in the navy. He was a lawyer by profession, but at the time of which I write was clerk of the House Committee on Claims and a busy newspaper man.

Soon after reaching Washington I was fortunate enough to be admitted to the public school presided over by Mr. John W. Thompson, who was undoubtedly one of the best teachers Washington has ever known. I think I could have learned a great many things from this good man, but my career in his school was very short. One day, after a smart rainstorm, I was trying to sail a toy boat in a pond in the school yard when one of the larger boys smashed my boat with a stone. I immediately smashed him with another, and he was carried home on a door. I was soon at my home with my books and belongings, and thus ended my public-school life. After a few weeks I was entered at Gonzaga College, preparatory to Georgetown College, and here I was lucky enough to remain until my school days in civil life were ended. In this excellent school I learned, or was supposed to learn, much Greek, Latin, and other things. Afterward, when I went to Athens on a vessel of war, I tried to practise some of my Greek, but only met with indifferent success; the people to whom I spoke were at a loss to know even what language I was trying to speak.

Much of my spare time was spent about the committee rooms of the Capitol, and on the floor of the House, where I made the acquaintance of some of the men who afterward became so prominent in the history of the country; among them I remember particularly John A. Logan and Mr. Maynard, of Tennessee. I also passed many happy hours on the water front, watching the various sailing craft as they came and went. I had never seen salt water, and I don't think I knew a single naval officer; but somehow it came to me that I should like a sea life, and from this time on the idea was never out of my mind. I had about decided to run away to sea, when I made the acquaintance of Mr. Hooper, the delegate in Congress from the Territory of Utah, with whom my uncle was in some way associated. He asked me if I would like an appointment to Annapolis, to which I very promptly replied that nothing in the world would please me so much. In order to have the appointment, however, it was necessary that I should go to Salt Lake City and become a resident. I had four days in which to prepare for what was, at that time, a very long and dangerous journey; but the end of the fourth day found me ready for the start.

When I left Washington, in 1859, by the Baltimore and Ohio Railroad, I carried all my worldly goods in a large, old-fashioned grip sack. It contained, among other things, a navy revolver, which was about half as long as I was, and the ammunition for this weapon. On my person in a money belt I carried two hundred and fifty dollars in gold, and in my pocket a ticket to St. Joseph, Missouri. I can recall after all these years the feeling of loneliness that came over me when I changed cars at the Relay House and headed for the West. The job that I had cut out for myself came to me then with full force, and I felt that the chance of my ever coming back was very small. But youth and health are great things, and I was soon comfortably asleep on one of the seats, happily oblivious of my surroundings. In those days sleepers and dining cars were undiscovered luxuries. Passengers slept as best they could, and snatched their meals from designated stations along the road. Everything went well with me until we reached Davis, in the State of Missouri, where we were to spend the night, as there was no connection on to St. Joseph. Upon reaching the nearest tavern I deposited my travelling bag with the clerk in the office and retired, very sleepy and used up. When I awoke in the early morning I went to the office to get some necessary articles from my bag, but upon trying the key found to my dismay that it would not unlock the valise given me, though it seemed from appearances to be mine. Investigation soon disclosed the fact that an old gentleman who had gone East on a train at two o'clock in the morning had taken my bag and left me his. The proprietor of the hotel wired for the lost article, but without success; so, after waiting over one train, I broke open the bag and found, among other things, half a dozen beautiful fine white linen ruffled shirts—any one of them large enough to make two or three garments for me. Quite a crowd had gathered in the office of the hotel, all hands full of sympathy for the small kid who had lost his outfit. After overhauling the bag, I mounted a chair and disposed of the articles at auction, and realized a sum quite sufficient to replace the things I had lost.

At St. Joseph I met friends to whom I was consigned, and they assisted me in finding a suitable party going my way, and in arranging the outfit. We were a party of six—five for California and one for Salt Lake City. Our wagons were soon purchased and stocked with the necessary provisions, blankets, etc. Then we bought the horses and arms, and in a few days we were ready to start. My riding animal was a rather large gray Mexican mule, which, as it afterward turned out, could smell an Indian farther, and, under the influence of his scent, run faster than any animal in the outfit. I was, of course, a very light weight, and it was all I could do at first to manage the beast. He could outbite and outkick anything that ever came my way. Without intending to do so, I delayed our start one day, and came very near delaying it for all time, as far as I personally was concerned. I had gone to a gymnasium with some other boys of my own age, when one of them did a trick on the horizontal bar which I was invited to imitate. I tried, but brought up squarely on top of my head on the floor. Slight concussion of the brain was the result, and the doctor had me in hand that night and part of the next day.

We finally ferried over the Missouri River and pulled out for our long trip over the prairies. Each member of the party had his particular duty and work to do, and each one had to do it to the satisfaction of the guide in charge, one Bromley by name. As I was very young and small, I was assigned to assist the cook in preparing meals, and was sometimes sent out after game, but was excused from standing watch at night. Each one had to look after his own animals, arms, etc.

Our journey for the first few days was through the Kickapoo Indian country. We passed through several of their villages, the leading feature of which was the great number of wolfish-looking dogs they had; they were barking and snapping at our horses continually from the time we sighted the villages until we were a mile or so beyond them. These Indians seemed friendly, and, like all others that I saw, lazy and dirty, but picturesque.

After the first week we headed for the South Platte River, and were soon among the buffalo. We found them in scattered herds, and then in a solid mass—the whole country covered with them as far as the eye could reach, literally untold thousands of them. At one time we drove through a herd for three days without ever being out of gunshot of these magnificent animals. Frequently we had to stop and put all our own animals between the wagons to prevent their being run over and stampeded. I noticed one curious trait of the buffalo: they would trot alongside of our outfit for miles, and then suddenly forge ahead and cross our track! They never seemed to care to cross behind us. When the herd was making for water, they seemed to travel in single file, with a fine full-grown bull in the lead. The straight, narrow paths they made led over the top of any small hill or roll in the prairie; and we often saw the leader some distance ahead of the others, standing like a statue on an elevation, looking apparently for signs of danger. We shot many of them, of course, but in most cases only removed their tongues, leaving the rest for the wolves, which in large numbers hung on to the edges of the herd. The usual way of killing them was to ride up fairly close and empty a revolver into the one selected, aiming to strike behind the point of the shoulder blade. In most cases two or three shots were required before blood appeared at the mouth, which was a sure sign that the animal was done for. I used a Colt's revolving rifle, a five-shooter, and with this I was not required to get to such close quarters, a proceeding that my mule always objected to.

In this beautiful valley of the South Platte we passed many emigrant trains bound to the West and Northwest. They were corralled generally, sometimes as many as fifty wagons in one corral, the horses feeding about over the plains during the daytime, but carefully guarded at night, for fear of Indians, who were generally to be found looking for something to steal. The wagons had the canvas covers taken off, and the exposed frames used for " jerking " buffalo meat. Hundreds of buffalo were killed, the hides removed, and the meat cut into thin strips and hung on the wagon frames, where it slowly dried in the sun. Owing to the pureness of the air, no salt was required to preserve it, and meat thus treated would last the emigrants all the way out to the Pacific coast. Our party did not care for " jerked " meat, but we did enjoy many antelope hams, which were cured by simply putting them on the end of a pole fifteen or twenty feet long and exposing them to the sun for a day or two.

All the way up the Platte Valley we met with the buffalo in such vast numbers that the idea of exterminating them would have seemed absurd, if such a thought had entered any one's mind; though they were killed by the thousand, it seemed to make no difference in the size of the herds; but this was only because no careful estimate of the number was made from year to year. As we drove or rode along over the prairie the carcasses of the buffalo covered the ground in every direction as far as the eye could reach. Immense numbers of piles of white bones showed where the animals had fallen in past years, and the thick brown spots indicated this season's work of destruction. In most cases the tongue was cut out, and the rest left to decay or be eaten by the wolves—the hide was not even removed. I came back over this same

route in 1892, and was amazed to find that all these
bones had been carefully gathered up, sent East, and
sold. Where there had been millions of buffalo not a
single herd of the magnificent game animals remained;
all of them had been destroyed, and in a great measure
wantonly.

We crossed the Platte at Thompson's Ford, a hundred or so miles east of Pike's Peak, and struck off
to the northwest toward Chimney Rock and Fort
Laramie. The trail was fairly good, and our journey
most comfortable. We usually made an early start,
and, halting for a rest in the middle of the day,
brought up in the afternoon in time to make ourselves
comfortable before dark—this programme depending
somewhat upon the water, which was a question of
vital importance. Having reached the water, our tent
was soon up, the wagons arranged so as to give as
much protection and shelter as possible, and the horses
secured near by to feed on the luxuriant grass. Then
my part of the work was soon done: coffee, bread, and
bacon or game were served, and after the guard for the
night was arranged we turned in and were soon sound
asleep. I was small enough to sleep comfortably in
the body of one of the wagons, and this was my usual
place. Sometimes I would vary the monotony by rolling up in my blanket and turning in on the grass under
the wagon. When we reached the rattlesnake ground
I broke myself very quickly of this habit, and always
slept in the wagon.

Fort Laramie was reached in due time, and, after
replenishing some of our stores, we continued on our
way. I think it was the second day out from this

post that we had our first serious trouble. In trying to cross a small stream in a marshy place late in the afternoon our leading wagon stuck in the mud, and the united efforts of all hands failed to pull it out. We concluded to sleep over it, and so turned in for the night. At early daylight we found ourselves surrounded by hostile Indians, and they soon relieved us of all further bother about our outfit by chasing us away, taking what they wanted and burning the wagons. We saved some food, all our arms, powder, etc., and all the animals. The Indians made it very interesting for us for ten or twelve hours until we found cover, when we returned the compliment with interest. My old mule with his light mount was easily the fastest animal in that outfit. After standing the Pawnees off for some time and killing a good many of them, we made our way back to Fort Laramie, where we managed to secure one wagon and some pack animals, bought a fresh lot of supplies, and continued on our way.

We had frequent trouble with Indians until after passing Fort Bridger, where, owing to the absence of the buffalo herds, we were comparatively free from them. Once we were ambushed by the Blackfeet, a tribe supposed to be peaceable; but a hunting party of them thought it an easy way to get some fine animals, and so laid a trap for us. We marched into their trap just after daylight in the morning, but as they had no guns, we soon got clear of them, after a hard tussle at close quarters. I was unfortunate enough to get an arrow through the tendon of my left ankle, which penetrated also the ribs of my mule, and made him perform many new tricks, much to my discomfort. After we had ridden a few miles over very rough ground and had sent the Indians on their way much reduced in numbers, we stopped to take account of stock. Bromley, the guide, was the only one besides myself who had been struck; he had an arrow through the skin over his stomach, which at first looked as if it had gone clear through him from side to side. My mule had only three arrows in him, but some of the animals resembled the "fretful porcupine," being struck pretty thickly all over. To get me out of the saddle was something of a job, as the arrow was driven through the buffalo hide of my stirrup and into a rib of the mule. Any approach toward him was enough to make him dance on his hind feet in true circus fashion. A lasso around both of his forelegs finally brought him to terms, and then, the arrow being cut between my leg and his side, I was released from my unpleasant seat. The wound was not serious, having been made with a hunting arrow; but I rode mostly with one foot for a week afterward. A few days later, or rather a few nights, this same gang came very near getting us. We were camped in a grove of cottonwood trees, and had no idea that Indians were after us, though we were on the lookout for them. In the middle of the night a man rode into our camp at full speed and told us of our danger. He was a pony-express rider, and in passing the red devils one of them had struck at him with some sharp weapon and nearly cut his foot in two. His accident saved us from a hot fight, no doubt, and he remained with us until we reached the next express station.

A Sailor's Log

At Fort Bridger we were most kindly received by the officers and men of the Second Dragoons stationed there. We remained several days, to get in good shape for the final lap that was to land us in Salt Lake City. There was a beautiful trout stream running through the fort, and I amused myself by trying to catch fish. I don't recall that I was very successful, though I perfectly remember seeing an Indian catch trout by snaring them. He sat on the bank of the stream, motionless as a statue; in his right hand he held a short rod or stick, from the end of which depended a fine copper wire with a loop in the lower end. He would watch a fish swimming slowly near him and slip the noose over its head and throw it out on the bank. This kind of sport required just the crafty, sneaking traits of an Indian.

From Fort Bridger we made our way to Robinson's Ferry on Green River, where we were destined to make quite a stay. Robinson was a Frenchman, and kept a trading post and ran the ferry over the river. His storehouses contained a vast stock of furs ready for shipment East, and in addition all the articles usually dealt in by Indians and emigrants. Whisky, I think, was the leading article in demand by all parties, and this he had—very bad and in large quantities. Shortly after our arrival we placed all our horses in a corral near the storehouse, and were glad to think they were safe for the time. In the afternoon a party of Bannocks rode up and wanted to swap horses. One of our party went with them to the inclosure to let them examine our stock, but they had scarcely entered before they set up a yell, and away they went down

20

the river, horses and all. The last we saw of them my old mule was leading, and setting a hot pace for the rest. The Bannocks were too strong for us to think of following them, so we decided to remain where we were until some other parties arrived, when we would move on with them, and thus be better prepared to stand the Indians off if they attacked us.

Two days after the stampede Washakie and his band of Snake Indians camped near us, and when we told him, or rather when his old friend Robinson told him, what had happened, he started off with two or three hundred warriors after the Bannocks. At the end of four days he came back with a drove of horses, ours among them, and told us to help ourselves. Of course there had to be a powwow and smoke over his success, and during the ceremony he passed whisky around for all hands to drink with him. When he came to me, after looking at my small frame, he took the powder measure from his belt, filled it, and gravely handed it to me with the remark " Little Breeches, drink that." I was known on the plains as " Little Breeches."

During the evening of this powwow many of the Indians were howling drunk around the camp, and, I am sorry to say, most of the white men were in the same condition. I was rolled up asleep under our wagon, when I was seized and thrown on to an Indian pony by a son of the chief Washakie. I promptly slipped off on the other side as soon as I could free myself from the blanket, and ran for the storehouse, where I placed myself under the protection of Robinson. The young Indian came after me and explained that he wanted me to go to his camp with him, and that he meant me no harm. As he was quite drunk at the time, we concluded not to discuss the matter until the next day. The following morning Washakie himself came, and after a long talk Robinson said that I had better go, as the chief had promised to bring me back safely at the end of ten days; that if I did not go willingly he would take me anyhow, and in that case there was no telling when I might get back. It was agreed that if the party had to go on before my return, my belongings should be left at the ferry for me, and that I should finish my journey with some other party. The Indians started up the Green River that afternoon, and had it not been for my fear of treachery I should have enjoyed my ten days among them very much. I learned afterward that Washakie had always been a stanch friend of the white men, and served them well on many occasions. He was very tall—over six feet—and the finest-looking Indian I ever saw. He was most kind and generous to me always, and brought me back at the time he had promised.

While I was with them the Indians hunted nearly all the time, and killed large quantities of game of various kinds. The tribe consisted of about a thousand people, and when we camped their ponies and dogs seemed to cover the country for miles around. The ponies were so well trained that a warrior could walk a few steps from his wigwam and whistle or call his pony from the drove feeding on the prairie some distance away. I belonged to the chief's mess, so to speak, and had to sleep in his tepee, which was the most disagreeable part of my experience; the sleepers were too numerous and the air too foul for comfort. During the day we marched or hunted, and as soon as we were camped I was expected to wrestle with some of the Indian lads of my own age, which always seemed to amuse the chief. I could throw the boys, as a rule, but as their hides were well greased I never could hold them. Washakie taught me to shoot with bow and arrow, and to use the lasso, and as soon as we started put his squaws to work making buckskin clothing for me. These garments fitted me well enough, and were things of beauty, with their fringe and beads.

One incident of this visit I recall vividly. We were camped near the river, where the willows grew plentifully, and, for want of something better to do, I cut one of these and made a whistle. When I walked in among the warriors and gave a sharp blast on my whistle there was a scattering and seizing of arms that caused me some uneasiness. Not one of the tribe had ever seen such a thing, and during the next two days I was kept busy whittling out whistles. It was a curious sight to see grown men, and women, too, for that matter, walking about, solemnly tooting on a willow whistle.

At the time promised I was back at the ferry, and found my party waiting—not so much for me, because I found afterward that they all believed that I was gone for good, but to accumulate force enough to face the Bannocks, who were in ugly mood over the loss of their horses. Before we reached the ferry Washakie had a long talk with me, in which he pointed out the

advantages that would come to me if I would let him
adopt me—the ponies I would own, and that I might
some day even have one of his daughters for my wife;
but Indian life had less charm for me the more I saw
of it. I thanked him as best I could, and was very
glad when we had put the river and many miles of
prairie between us and my Snake friends. The presents he gave me—bows and arrows, pipes, and buckskin clothing—I carried to Salt Lake City, and some
of them eventually back to Washington.

CHAPTER III

IN THE MORMON COUNTRY

AFTER crossing Green River our course lay along Ham's Fork in the direction of South Pass, the highest point of the Rocky Mountains we had to cross. We passed the wreck of the supply trains of our army burned by the Mormons in 1857. The wagons had been drawn up in a circle and there burned—the circle still showing, and dotted here and there with tires and such ironwork as the Indians had not cared to carry away. At one place we struck alkali dust, and as soon as our water gave out we found ourselves and our animals in pitiable condition. Our lips and eyes grew sore, and our tongues swelled until we could scarcely talk. After we had passed the dangerous place we came upon an emigrant who had a barrel of whisky in the tail of his wagon. There was no spigot in it, and he refused to put one in, but after a long, wordy contest he agreed that he would bore a gimlet hole in the barrel, each man should select a straw, and for two bits he could suck all the whisky he wanted without drawing breath. They selected straws very carefully, and I remember how each man held on until he was blue in the face before admitting that his drink was done.

A Sailor's Log

On entering South Pass we camped at Pacific Spring and made ourselves comfortable, as there was no longer fear of trouble with the Indians, and our animals needed rest and grass. The spring covered a space of forty by thirty feet, and the water bubbled up cold and clear as crystal and ran toward the Pacific —hence its name. A few doves or wild pigeons were feeding about the camp. The guide bet me that I could not kill one with my rifle, and this led to my killing my first elk. I was anxious to win the bet, and was following the bird as he flew about on the trees to make sure of a fair shot. In this way I wandered off from the trail into the thick cover on the side of the pass, and was about to fire at the pigeon, when I heard a breaking of twigs near me, but above me, on the mountain. My first idea was Indians, and, standing perfectly still in my tracks, I took a quiet look. Within thirty yards of me was a magnificent animal looking straight at me, his head and antlers only showing through the thick cover. I raised the gun to my shoulder very quietly, and, taking good aim at a spot between his eyes, fired. He made a great bound down the side of the mountain in my direction, and at the same moment I started for camp as fast as my legs could carry me, and did not stop until I got there. Bromley asked me if I had killed the bird, to which I replied that I had not, but I believed I had killed the father of all deer. Up to that time I had never seen an elk. When we reached the spot we found a beautiful specimen, with grand antlers, with a bullet fairly through his brain. I had killed him stone-dead, and he had slid almost to where I stood when I fired. The

bet was called off, and removing the head, we skinned
the game, and the entire party had all the meat they
wanted for several days.

Afterward we saw immense herds of elk, many
thousands in a herd, and we had no trouble in killing
them whenever we chose. We also saw and killed a
number of mountain sheep, a very curious animal with
enormously large horns. The guide told marvellous
stories of their jumping down great distances, landing on their horns, which might, for all I know, have
been true; but I never saw one of them do it. They
were wary and hard to get at, as compared with other
kinds of game, and I never saw much of them—only
for a moment before I fired, and then the sheep was
either dead or off out of sight like a flash.

After leaving South Pass we fell in with a Mormon
train, consisting mostly of women from Wales, bound
for Salt Lake City. These people, who seemed a decent lot, had few large wagons, but appeared to depend
for transportation on a species of handcart, which contained their belongings and were pushed along by the
women. A few wagons carried the provisions, and
these were looked after by the dozen or so men of the
party. All the work was done by the women, which
was a foretaste of what their lot was to be after arriving at their destination.

In the forenoon of a beautiful day we had our first
view of Salt Lake City as we slowly wound our way
down Echo Cañon. The mountains rose to a great
height on either side, and were still surmounted by
the low stone breastworks thrown up by the Mormons to oppose the entry of United States troops two

years before. Through the cañon ran a small but swift stream, and upon this the beavers were industriously building their dams, some of which were really works of art. These curious beasts were to be seen in hundreds—some cutting the logs for the dams, and others using their curious flat tails as trowels to cement the face of the dam with mud. Many of the dams had been cut in order to make the road available, but, when left to themselves, the beavers soon had them repaired. The beavers have disappeared, as have the buffalo and other large game of the West, but in their case the excuse can be made that the fur was used to some good purpose; in the case of the big game no such excuse can be offered: it was in a great measure simply senseless, brutal killing for the sake of killing.

My first impressions of the city and Salt Lake Valley, with Great Salt Lake lying blue in the distance, were very pleasing, and a closer inspection did not change them. The city was beautifully laid out, and the houses were generally of a character to indicate comfort, and often wealth and refinement. The water from a rushing mountain stream had been introduced, and, besides answering for household purposes, it ran through the gutters on both sides of the principal streets, thus insuring cleanliness and good sewerage. Many of the houses had gardens about them filled with vegetables, and the most delicious small fruits. The residences of Brigham Young—he had two—were beautifully constructed and surrounded by elaborate flower gardens, which were kept in the most perfect order.

I made my home while in the city with the family

of Mr. Hooper, who was a Mormon, though not a polygamist. They, as well as the people generally whom I met, were kindly and courteous, and did all in their power to make my stay among them agreeable. Mrs. Hooper was worried for fear that I might be converted to Mormonism without the knowledge or consent of my parents, but I assured her that I felt myself strong enough to stand any amount of temptation in that line, and that I really was not in the least danger.

I had command of plenty of horses, and amused myself by making excursions to Camp Floyd, or Salt Lake, or other attractive places. Frequently I went to the country for a day's shooting, and as game of all kinds was plentiful I made very good bags. One day, when I had wandered rather too far into the thick woods on the side of the mountain, I had an exciting experience. I had dismounted from my horse and was advancing slowly and quietly through the thick cover, which was so dense that the sunlight was almost shut out, when I saw some distance ahead of me a curious black object. After watching it for some time without being able to make out what it was I gave it one load of No. 4 shot to see what would happen. I was thoroughly surprised at the result. It proved to be a Digger Indian, with a large black felt hat on his head, digging roots. As he straightened himself up he seemed to me ten feet tall, and I lost no time in mounting my pony; neither did he in mounting his. There was no time to explain matters, and I bolted down the mountain road with the Digger in hot chase. He occasionally sent an arrow over me, and generally behaved in a way to hasten me into town in the shortest possible time. As I reached the front gate of Mr. Hooper's house the Indian pulled up about three hundred yards away and sat on his pony, waiting apparently to see what would happen next. He only waited a few seconds when I appeared with my Colt's rifle, and then we had a spirited race for the mountains, only in this case I was the pursuer, and I surely put him to his best speed to escape. I was more careful after that how I shot at things until I could make out what they were.

As a rule, the city was orderly and peaceful. At times the Indians would come in in considerable numbers, and, having filled up with whisky, would proceed to make themselves disagreeable by shooting arrows at people, and misbehaving in other ways. When they got too bad, word would be sent out to Camp Floyd, and the soldiers would come in and run them out of town—generally killing a few. On one of these occasions I was sitting on the front porch reading a newspaper, when suddenly an arrow drove into the weather-boarding very close to me, and before I could move, a second one came and caught me in the shin bone. My double-barrelled shotgun was in the hall near by, and as I came out with it I discovered a half-drunken Digger standing in the middle of the street, laughing at the joke he had perpetrated on me. I don't think he enjoyed the rest of the afternoon much, as the men in the drug store at the corner had him laid on his back while they picked shot out of him until after dark. The next time I saw my friend he looked as if he had had the smallpox. I presented him with five pounds of brown sugar, and watched with interest while he sat on the pavement and ate the whole of it.

As I was to represent Utah in the navy, I felt it my duty to call on Mr. Young, and at the same time I hesitated to do so, because a pony-express horse, which I had borrowed for a ride on the Fourth of July, had run away with me, and before I could stop him had seriously damaged some beautiful flower beds in Mr. Young's yard. However, I did call, and found the Mormon leader a rugged, hard-looking man, but withal kindly in his manner and good enough to wish me success in the profession I had selected. Without entering into the question of how far he was right in what he had done and was then doing—questions now forever settled by the laws of the land—we must admit that Mr. Young was a man of wonderful ability and a natural leader of men. Otherwise he could never have led his people through the tremendous difficulties they encountered, and then made of the desert a flowering garden.

When I had been sufficiently long in Utah to claim residence I began preparations for my return journey. The call of the sea was strong upon me, and I could not resist it even had I wished to do so, which I certainly did not. The sea and the ships were constantly in my mind, and I was anxious to begin. I secured a seat on the overland coach and left for the East about the middle of July, 1860.

We had a pleasant trip, all things considered. Riding on top of a coach is well enough in the daytime, but not so pleasant at night. I was small for my age, and soon found a way of stowing myself so that I could sleep with a fair amount of comfort. But when it rained, which it often did at night, I was most uncomfortable. The choice was between getting wet or being smothered under blankets—and I generally got wet. The coach stations were reasonably close to each other, and we made good speed all the way. As soon as we arrived at one of these stations all hands went for food—generally very poor—and when that was finished, six wild, kicking, bucking mules were hitched up, and away we went at a full run. The drivers were experts in their line, and the mules usually ran four or five miles before they were pulled down to their regular paces. After that, woe to the unfortunate mule that tried to shirk his fair share of the work!

The party was well armed and thoroughly able to stand off any small band of Indians; but the red men as a rule seemed to fancy the emigrant trains rather than the coaches, and we escaped without serious molestation. During the time we were on the South Platte we had one or two very severe hailstorms, which for a time threatened to destroy the whole outfit. When they struck us, usually accompanied by a hard gale of wind, the mules backed up under the lee of the coach, and no amount of beating would induce them to move until the storm had passed; then they would go on as cheerfully as before, the driver launching at them such a volley of oaths and abuse as could come only from the driver of an overland coach. No other human being could match him. The passengers during these storms found shelter as they could, either in or under the coach, or among the mules. At times

A Prairie Storm

the hail covered the prairies as far as one could see to a depth of two or three inches. Some of the hailstones were large enough to disable a man if they struck him on the head.

While we were resting at Mayersville, Kansas, we experienced a wind storm which lingers in my mind, although I have since seen storms of about all kinds and sizes. It came up very suddenly, and we at first took refuge in a long, narrow frame building used as a storehouse. The wind struck this house end on and soon lifted one end a foot or so from the ground. We then retreated behind a stone wall, but the stones began to fly from the top, and we concluded to follow the example of some of the natives and go out on the open prairie, lie down flat on our faces, head to wind, and hold on to the grass as best we could. In this position each one soon had a considerable sand shoal about him. There were several emigrant trains and a band of Indians camped on the prairie, and these were soon off before the wind as fast as they could go. The "prairie schooners," as the wagons were called, would run some distance before the wind, and then, as they got canted one way or the other, would capsize and spill out women and children and whatever else happened to be in them. The last we saw of the Indians, as they disappeared in the clouds of sand and gravel, the men were riding their ponies, shouting and yelling, and the squaws doing what they could to save their belongings. A few days after this we crossed the Missouri River, I found myself again in civilization, and I was soon on a train bound for Washington, where I arrived late in August.

A Sailor's Log

On September 15th I went to Annapolis, passed my examination, and, after a few days' leave, reported September 20th on board the frigate Constitution as an acting midshipman.

I have so far picked the oakum, now let me spin my yarn of forty years of naval life.

34

CHAPTER IV

A CADET AT ANNAPOLIS

I PASSED my entrance examination to the Naval Academy September 15, 1860, and reported, as an acting midshipman, as I have before stated, on board the frigate Constitution—" Old Ironsides "—on the 20th of the same month. The examination, fortunately for many of us, was a very simple one; nothing like the elaborate and trying affair of to-day, otherwise many of us would not have followed the navy as a profession. The candidate had to be sound physically, and have a fair foundation on which to build the education required of a sea officer, who was not in that day expected to be an engineer, a chemist, a scientist, an electrician, a lawyer, an artist, etc., as is the case to-day— only a seaman and a gunner, with the necessary knowledge of things that pertained to the sea. The superintendent, Captain George S. Blake, was assisted by half a dozen officers, selected for their fitness, and as many civil professors. Among the officers were two brothers, C. R. P. and George Rodgers, lieutenants, both of whom made their mark on the service, and wrote their names high up on the history of the navy which they loved so well and did so much to honour. We have never had two officers whose standard of

35

honour and duty was higher or whose conduct reflected greater credit on the country than that of those two. C. R. P. Rodgers was commandant of midshipmen and George Rodgers was captain of the Constitution, and to them I owe everything in my professional life.

We had one hundred and twenty-seven men in the class when we settled down to work, an average lot, from all parts of the country, and representing the various classes of American life—North, South, East, and West. I was the only one from Utah, and I believe the first one ever appointed from that Territory either in the navy or the army. Our life on board ship was pleasant and novel, and our education on the lines that would fit us for the duties we would in the future have to perform. English studies occupied a considerable part of our time, but practical seamanship and gunnery were considered the important things, and they were hammered into us so hard by our honoured captain that we had to learn them in spite of ourselves. Many showed wonderful cleverness, and after a few months the class standing in seamanship placed the men about as they have since stood in the service.

The Constitution was moored at the end of a long, narrow wharf, which was the only means of approach unless by boat, so that the class was completely isolated from the older classes. We never came in contact with them except when on shore for drill, or on Saturday, when we passed their quarters on our way to the town on liberty. All our recitations and most of our drills took place on board ship. Under such conditions the disgraceful hazing, which later on gave the Naval Academy such a bad name, was impossible, even had the temper of the midshipmen been such as to tolerate it. At the time of which I am writing hazing was absolutely unknown, and I am sure that any attempt to practise it would have led to a duel behind old Fort Severn. It was not until we reached Newport, and the senior classes had been ordered into service, that this brutal, and I must say cowardly, practice took root and grew until it was a disgrace to all those engaged in it. By some means the classes entering after 1862 got the idea from West Point, and in their zeal to emulate really went far beyond the practices of that excellent institution, where hazing of a certain kind was a tradition, and considered necessary to the discipline of the cadets among themselves. With us the proper class distinctions and respect were traditions which did not require hazing to enforce them. I remember very well, one Saturday afternoon, two of us, both very small, were passing the quarters of the first class on our way to town on liberty, when two seniors thought it would be good fun to put us down on the grass and sit on us. They promptly carried out their plan, and sat on us five minutes or so and then let us go. We returned to the ship mad all over, and in a few minutes we swarmed back with most of our class, and there was a beautiful fight which resulted in many black eyes and the destruction of much furniture in the first-class quarters. This was about the nearest approach to hazing we ever had.

The discipline was strict on board ship from the start, and we were expected to observe the regulations

4

as soon as they had been made clear to us. I had formed a warm friendship for a young fellow from Mississippi named Baldwin, and he somehow became involved in a quarrel with a man twice his size; the quarrel soon led to a fight, and the large man attempted to strike Baldwin with a camp stool, when I grabbed him from behind, preventing the blow, and thus myself became part of the row. The next morning I was sent for on the quarter-deck, and, after having the Articles of War read to me and receiving a long lecture on the enormity of my offence, was locked up in a dark room in the wardroom. Some one had reported that Baldwin had a knife in his hand during the fight, and that I called out to him to use it and that I would help him. After being locked up I made up my mind that my time had come, in view of the many offences mentioned in the Articles of War for which the punishment was " death or such other punishment as a court martial may inflict." I wrote a hurried note to my uncle in Washington to come at once if he wished to see me alive, as I was sure that I was soon to be hanged at the yardarm. He answered that discipline was good for me, and that he would wait a few days, or until sentence was pronounced. After three days' confinement I was sent for by the commanding officer, and told him exactly how I became involved in the fight, when I was at once sent to duty, and some one else took my dark room.

On board ship we had our hammocks to sleep in instead of bunks, and our messing was regulated just as it would have been on a cruising vessel. In fact, we lived under service conditions; and while it is now the fashion to decry such training in favour of barracks on shore, I have yet to be convinced that for the conditions then existing it was not the best. Many officers of that school have achieved great success both afloat and ashore, and have certainly met all the requirements of the service as fully as those of the new school can ever meet the requirements that will face them. Our first impressions of the service were received on board ship, and the discomforts of ship life were met and overcome in a way that made such discomforts and even much greater ones seem very trivial afterward. We grew into ship life gradually and naturally, and our knowledge of the ship and all her parts was complete; such knowledge can be acquired in no other way, and while many able officers hold that this is not a matter of importance on this point, I have also still to be convinced of the soundness of their reasoning.

During the winter of 1860–'61 the anxious faces of our officers foretold the storm of war that broke so suddenly in April of the latter year. It was a time of great suspense for all hands; naturally the greatest strain came on those in authority, but the midshipmen had their loads to bear as well. Many of us came from the South, and as the States one after another either seceded or threatened to do so, we had to make up our minds what we were going to do. Conferences were frequent and serious, but never in one of them was there a disloyal word uttered. Every man followed the example set by the Southern men among the officers. So long as we were inside the academy limits, or until our resignations were accepted, we were officers of the navy and would behave as such. Lieutenant Hunter Davidson, afterward the torpedo expert of the Confederacy, was probably more responsible for this position than any other man, though both C. R. P. and George Rodgers were constantly giving us good advice.

During the month of April, 1861, our studies were practically suspended, and preparations were made to defend the academy and the ship Constitution in case of attack. Drills were constant, and every precaution taken to give the enemy a warm reception in case he came. A Confederate cavalry company was organized on the north bank of the Severn River, and for several days they drilled in plain sight of the ship; but when a few boats were sent after them they disappeared, and the next soldiers we saw wore blue uniforms. We had been told that the Confederates in Baltimore had organized an expedition and were coming down in steamers to capture us. A bright lookout was kept for them, and one dark night, about two o'clock in the morning, the lookout reported a large steamer coming in from the bay. General quarters were sounded, and in a few minutes we were ready; and there we stood waiting for the word to fire. The cabin bulkheads had all been taken down, and four thirty-two pounders run out the cabin stern ports and loaded with grape and canister.

The steamer slowly came on until she could be plainly seen with the naked eye moving up directly astern of us, as if to avoid our broadside and carry us by boarding. Captain Rodgers's clear voice rang out: " Ship ahoy! What ship is that? " The gun captains had the guns trained on the mass of men we could now see crowded about the decks and not more than three hundred yards away. Twice more the clear voice rang out: " Ship ahoy! keep off, or I will sink you! " and then a voice we all recognised answered: " For God's sake, don't fire! We are friends! " It was the voice of our chaplain, who had been North on a short leave, and on his return found Colonel B. F. Butler and the Eighth Massachusetts Regiment at Havre de Grace, Maryland, blocked in their effort to reach Washington.

Colonel Butler had seized the ferry steamer Maryland, and, embarking his regiment on board of her, sailed for Annapolis, fortunately bringing with him our chaplain—I say fortunately, because he seemed the only one on board who knew enough to answer the hail from the Constitution, and in a few seconds more we should have opened fire, and no one can doubt what the result would have been. The splendid record of this fine regiment would never have been written; it would have ended there and then, and what one may fairly call the variegated career of General Benjamin F. Butler would have been very short and inglorious.

As soon as the character of the strange craft was satisfactorily established, she was directed to haul up alongside of us, which she did, and remained there until daylight, when the midshipmen were landed under arms, formed with those on shore and marched to the wall in the vicinity of the gate leading to the town of Annapolis, and there deployed in line of battle to cover the landing of the Eighth Massachusetts. We stood in this position until the last soldier was ashore and the regiment had formed line in rear of the midshipmen's quarters and stacked their arms, when sentries from our battalion were posted and the rest of us returned to our quarters. Not a shot had been fired by either side, though the excitement was intense, and there was a readiness on both sides to fight. Both parties hesitated to fire the first shot, and the Confederates contented themselves with pitching stones over the wall, which we caught and tossed back. The newspapers gave graphic accounts of how Butler and his men had recaptured the Constitution and the Naval Academy! They never fired a shot nor saw a rebel to shoot at. The magazines of the Constitution were mined, and she and her crew would have been blown to atoms before surrendering if the rebels had attacked her.

Everything was now made ready as soon as possible, and the ship hauled out into the bay and prepared to transport us to some Northern port. The midshipmen on shore gave up their quarters to the officers of the Seventh New York Infantry and the First Rhode Island Artillery under Colonel Burnside, these regiments having arrived immediately after the Eighth Massachusetts. Our routine was entirely broken up, and our time given to guard and picket duty, until all preparations had been made for our trip North, when orders were given to assemble ready for embarkation. Then followed a scene which those who participated in it can never forget or recall without a tendency to moist eyes. The good fellows from the South who had determined to go with their States said good-bye

to their classmates, and as the rest of us formed ranks
to embark, Captain C. R. P. Rodgers stepped out to
say a few words to us before leaving the dear old
Alma Mater. After a strong effort he managed to say,
" My boys, stand by the old flag! " and then broke
down. We were all in tears, and only braced up when
we heard the men of the Seventh New York cheering
us, which we returned in a feeble sort of way—scram-
bled into the boats, and two hours later were once
more on board " Old Ironsides." That was the last
we saw of the Naval Academy at Annapolis until after
the civil war had done its work. The army took possession, repaired the railroad and locomotives, and
after a month or so of hard work reopened communication with Washington.

The Constitution was towed to New York, from
there to Newport, Rhode Island, where she was anchored in Brinton's Cove, off Fort Adams, and all the
senior classes were ordered into active service. My
class, now about seventy strong, was the only one
left, and we were anxious, of course, to join the
others; but we had not yet sufficiently advanced to
make us of much value. Once more we settled down
to routine and hard work. Fort Adams was unoccu-
pied, so we were transferred there, where we could
have roomy quarters and convenient recitation rooms,
and at the same time man the guns in case of need.
It was all a lark to most of us, and the time given to
study did not amount to much. The officers soon
found that, if we were to do any serious work, proper
quarters would have to be provided; and as the idea
of a return to Annapolis was abandoned, the Atlantic

Hotel, in the heart of Newport, was secured on long lease, duly fitted for our accommodation, and there we were marched, bag and baggage.

In the meantime, steps were taken to quarter the new class, a very large one, which had been appointed. The Constitution and the Santee, which had been sent North for the purpose, had been moored at suitable docks built on the inside of Goat Island in the inner harbour, and the sloops of war John Adams and Marion were anchored near them, to be used for practical seamanship and gunnery drills afloat. This made the most complete outfit in ships the Naval Academy had ever seen and the most useful.

That master of his trade, Stephen B. Luce, had charge of drills afloat, and scarcely a day passed that we were not under his watchful eyes at some sort of practical seamanship. Every Saturday we went outside in one or other or both of the ships, and then the work was most thorough and complete, each midshipman in turn taking charge of the deck for different evolutions. On our way in, in the afternoon, we could generally tell when our work had been satisfactory; if it had not been, the ship was sure to fetch up hard and fast before we reached our anchorage, anchors carried out, and the vessel hove off, properly berthed and everything made snug and shipshape, before we could leave her. For all this work we had only midshipmen—no man to help us. Everything must be done with our own hands, and thus we learned, and learned thoroughly, what a man had to do in every position on board a sailing ship, from passing a close reef to sweeping down the quarter-deck.

Loss of Discipline

We learned how to do it ourselves, and how to make others do it under our instruction, and many of us still cling to the notion that there could not have been better training. If the weather happened to be such that we could not get under way, we sent down yards, masts, and rigging, and proceeded to refit everything. Before the year was out there were very few in the class who could not, with their own hands, do any job of work required of a petty officer or seaman.

The quartering of the senior class on shore and all the others on board ship had a very bad effect, and it was years before the academy recovered its normal condition. All the traditions of the school, the discipline among the classes themselves—which was, and always must be, dependent on traditions and customs —were lost sight of, and, as I have before said, hazing took root on board the Constitution and Santee. It took twenty years to break up this unnaval practice, and even now it occasionally shows its ugly head, generally with the result that some promising youngster has to be dismissed and thus lost to the service.

CHAPTER V

THE EARLY DAYS OF THE WAR

As soon as war was an assured thing, my family demanded that I should resign, come South and fight for my State; but it did not seem to me that this course was imperative. My next younger brother enlisted at the age of fourteen in the Washington Artillery, and went to the front under Pelham; so that there was one member of the family on each side, which was a fair division if he saw his duty in that way. I was much assisted in these dark and trying days by the advice of Captain Rodgers, who pointed out to me very clearly what my duty was. I concluded to stick by " The Old Flag," and let my family ties look after themselves, and so informed my mother, who was much grieved and shamed by my determination. She finally wrote my resignation, sent it to the Navy Department, where it was accepted, and without previous warning I found myself out of the service, despite my determination to stay in.

What to do under such conditions was a serious question to me, and I was again assisted to the right course by Captain Rodgers, who telegraphed to Washington, explaining matters. I was out only about twenty-four hours, but they were very unhappy ones for me, and I was relieved when my reappointment came by wire. My mother, thinking she had finally disposed of the matter, went to Richmond to nurse my brother, who had been badly wounded, and there waited for me to join her. She was naturally much disappointed at the result of her efforts, and wrote me a very severe letter, which she sent through the lines by a blockade runner, who mailed it. When it came to me it showed no signs of having been opened, but I found that it had, and many parts of it underlined with blue pencil. Many of my letters during the war mailed in the same way had been similarly treated, showing that in my case at least the post-office officials had their eyes on me.

My brother fought gallantly, was twice wounded, and served to the end of the war. As soon as he could make his way North he came, and never showed any bitterness over my course. The other members of my family did not behave in quite the same way, but after some years my mother changed her views, and fully forgave me before she died.

In June, 1862, we started on our first real practice cruise, using for the purpose the sloop of war John Adams. We were crowded into her like sardines in a box, and had no end of hard work, with whatever we could find to eat, and all in all about as little comfort as a set of youngsters ever experienced; but we made great headway in learning our business as seamen. The ship was uncomfortable, as all her class were, but at the same time seaworthy and safe. She would run well when off the wind, but with everything braced sharp up when there was any sea on she would butt three times at a sea and then go round it. Before the wind she rolled so that all hands had trouble in sleeping at night; but with all her defects she carried us safely as far south as Port Royal, South Carolina, and brought us safely back to Newport.

On our way South we stopped a few days at Hampton Roads and Yorktown, where we had a chance to see the effects of the war. At Yorktown, particularly, we were much interested. The rebel General Magruder had just evacuated the place, and was retreating up the peninsula, closely followed by the army under General George B. McClellan. The wells had all been poisoned, and the roads in many places mined and torpedoes planted, so that we had to be very careful where we went and what we did. However, midshipmen are notoriously hard to kill, and with the assistance of the cavalry escort which was kindly furnished us, we managed to escape without damage except by falls from the cavalry horses, which all hands seemed determined to ride. Horseback riding was not a novelty to me, and I contented myself with going as quietly as I could in a wagon.

At Port Royal we saw Admiral Dupont's splendid fleet, comprising many of the finest ships in the navy, fresh from their encounter with and complete victory over the rebel forts. Among them all, the Wabash seemed to me the most perfect; she flew the admiral's flag, and on board of her I had the pleasure of again meeting Captain C. R. P. Rodgers, who was fleet captain to Admiral Dupont.

I shall always remember an incident of my visit to this ship. As we went over the side, a large black bear stood on his hind legs at the gangway, among the side boys, hat in hand, and saluting each officer as he went on board. I saw him as I came up the side, and not proposing to give him a chance at me, jumped for the main chains and went over that way, much to the amusement of the officers. A short time after this his bearship came to grief, and had to be sent on shore. He was very fond of alcohol, and, having filled up and become ugly, turned into the bunk of one of the lieutenants, who, finding his bed occupied, turned in somewhere else until his time came for duty. The quartermaster being sent down during the night to call the lieutenant, and getting no answer, undertook to awake him by shaking him, which so enraged the bear, in his half-drunken condition, that he bit the quartermaster so badly that he lost one of his legs.

During this cruise the midshipmen were stationed as a crew for the vessel, and did all the work of the different ratings. When off Hatteras on our way North our efficiency was thoroughly tested. At about ten o'clock the ship was struck by a sudden heavy squall, accompanied by rain and hail. All hands were called to reef topsails, the watch on deck having successfully handled the light sails. We were close enough to the Diamond Shoal to make haste a matter of importance, and the officers hustled us up without much ceremony. The topsails were quickly reefed, and I had just secured the lee earing on the main topsail yard when I heard the order, " Hoist away the topsails!" I was straddling the yard at the time, and just about to swing to the foot rope and lay down from aloft; but I changed my mind very suddenly, and instead hugged that topsail yard until I am sure you could have found the marks of my arms on the paint. It was as black as a pocket, raining in torrents, and as the yards were braced up the topsails filled and the ship made a butt at a heavy sea. I thought my time had come. I reached the deck, however, in safety, only to be properly dressed down by the officer of the deck for being slow in laying down from aloft! We were back at Newport again in September, better for our work, and ready to enjoy the short leave that was then given us.

My family had all gone South, and it was a question what I should do with myself; but as my uncle's house in Washington was in charge of a housekeeper, I concluded to spend my time there, which I did very pleasantly. The good woman who had charge of the house called me one night to inform me that there was a burglar in the cellar, and would I put him out? I was not anxious for the job, but my position as an officer forbade my declining; so with a small revolver in one hand and a lighted candle in the other I sought the burglar in the coal cellar. I had hardly entered the passageway leading past the door of the room in which he was located when a large chunk of coal whizzed past my head, and very close to it. I dropped the candle, which fortunately went out, putting us on more even terms, and after ten minutes I turned my man over to the police with a bullet through his thigh. I learned that night not to hunt burglars with a lighted candle; experience sometimes teaches things in a very forcible way.

My Rebel Brother

During this leave I had a curious meeting with my rebel brother, whose command was operating on the Virginia side of the Potomac, a few miles away. I went one evening to an oyster house with a friend to eat some raw oysters. The place was one that all of us had known and frequented for years. As I entered the door I observed a tall, handsome young fellow who was finishing what he had ordered, and at the same moment I saw him give me a quick glance of recognition. He drank up his glass of beer, and then walked briskly out of the place, while I called for oysters on the half shell, and ate them very slowly. My brother knew what I would do, and he did not hesitate the least bit in his movements; but I had some very serious thinking to do while the man opened oysters for me, and I must admit that I ate more oysters than I wanted.

I could have gone to the exact spot where my brother's skiff was hauled out, but I was giving him all the time I could to get there ahead of the provost guard. Finally, my friend asked me if I were going to eat all night, when I paid my shot and we went out together. I asked if he had recognised my man; he replied that he had not, and then asked me in turn what I was going to do about it. Before I had time to reply, a squad of the provost guard came by, and to the officer in charge I reported that there was a rebel officer in the city—that I had seen and recognised him, and knew him as such. At first he seemed disposed to arrest me, but at last concluded to go after the real offender. After the war, my brother told me that he just managed to escape, and that he had concealed his boat at the spot where I imagined it was. As a result of this incident I was twice arrested and taken before the provost marshal on suspicion of holding intercourse with rebels. The last time I told the officer confidentially who the man was I had reported, and after that I was not annoyed.

Part of my leave I spent in a trip to the Army of the Potomac, to get an idea of how they conducted their business. I had a pass, and was described as an aid to the wounded. The horse I rode was hired from a livery stable, and came near never reaching its owner again. I soon saw enough to convince me that the army would not suit me; that it was not to be compared to the navy for comfort or for getting results. The army seemed to be continually fighting and killing people, without arriving at any satisfactory conclusion as to who was whipped, both sides frequently claiming the same fight. There was much straggling in the rear of the army, and several times on my way back to Washington I was asked for my horse, and was once shot at because I declined to comply with the request. When I finally recrossed the Long Bridge into Washington I made up my mind that I had learned all I wanted to know about the army.

October, 1862, found us all back at Newport, and once more settled down to hard work and study. The demand for officers was so great that the class was divided into two sections, and the instructions arranged so that the first section could be graduated in the following June. It was not my good fortune to be one of this first section; but I lost nothing by this, as we shall see later on.

Under Discipline

There was in this section, however, one of whom we were all very fond—the young Frenchman, Pierre d'Orleans, Duc de Penthièvre, who preferred to acquire his professional education under American auspices. He was a fine, manly young fellow, known in the class as "Pete," and you might expect to find him mixed up in all the class scrapes and troubles. I remember him particularly as a cunning hand with the small sword, and a generous giver of very good French chocolate, an article which he consumed and gave away in enormous quantities.

During the winter of this year I again made acquaintance with the dark room on board the Constitution. Two of us were walking about during the evening in the park opposite our quarters, when I saw a watchman sneaking through the trees to catch some fellows who were violating regulations. The chance was very tempting, and without waiting to count the cost I landed a good-sized stone fairly behind the watchman's ear, sending him to the hospital for repairs. Unfortunately for me, there was a citizen near by who gave the commandant so good a description of me that I was sent for the next morning, and promptly sent on board ship and locked up. This was bad enough in all reason, but I soon made it much worse. The officer of the day, wishing to show proper respect for a senior, smuggled me a novel and a candle, and, having arranged my blanket so as to shut out curious eyes, I read my novel in peace until the sentry, a sailor with a cutlass, pried the blanket to one side. I blew the candle out at once, and then arranged the spring in the candle-

5   53

stick so that I could shoot the candle out when ready. Then I lighted it again, and taking a position favourable for my purpose, I waited for the sailor; and, as he again cautiously pried the blanket aside, I fired the candle through the opening. Unfortunately, it struck Jackey in the eye, and thinking that his head was shot off he bolted from his station.

In a short while the commanding officer was on the scene, and then an end was put to my sport. I was marched out, the room searched, the door boarded up solid, and the key again turned on me. This time there was not the least semblance of fun about it. For two weeks I was kept locked up and then released; but for several days I could not do anything, as the light hurt my eyes dreadfully. It seemed to require a very practical demonstration to convince me that I had to do what I was told. This last experience went a long way in that direction.

CHAPTER VI

FIRST ACTIVE SERVICE

THE first section of the class was graduated in June, 1863, and at once ordered into service. The second section was distributed among the three practice ships, which were to take the junior classes out for the summer. I was one of five who were detailed as watch officers for the sloop of war Marion, as the Navy Department was unable to spare a sufficient number of watch officers for all the ships. We had a captain, of course, an executive officer, and a navigator, and five first-class men in the wardroom. Our crew consisted entirely of midshipmen, who did all the work usually done by sailors, including scrubbing the decks and cleaning the ship. We were to cruise along the coast, making Newport our headquarters, while the other ships went abroad.

The first night out we were beating clear of Block Island. I had the deck, when, at 2 A. M., with a good stiff breeze, the captain ordered me to tack ship and shorten sail in stays. The helm was put down and I was getting on famously, when the quartermaster stepped out from the wheel and reported, "Wheel ropes carried away, sir!" In turn, I reported to the captain, "Wheel ropes are carried

55

away, sir!" His reply was, "Well, wheel ropes carried away, what do you do?" and as far as I could see he paid no further attention to me until the ship was close hauled on the other tack, with the light sails furled. Then, in a quiet, kindly way, he pointed out to me where I had been wrong, at the same time commending my general work. And so it was during the entire cruise: every man of us had to rely on himself; but at the same time a careful, conscientious officer was watching us and correcting us when we went wrong. Many officers in the service to-day remember gratefully the summer cruise of the Marion, Captain E. O. Mathews commanding.

In the course of the month of July the rebel cruiser Florida appeared off the coast, and the merchants of the exposed cities cried out for protection. The Marion was sent out, among other ships, to look for the privateer—an old-fashioned sailing sloop after a modern steam sloop of war! At the same time several vessels were chartered in New York, guns and men tumbled on board, and sent out to cruise off the coast. In one of these I served.

Captain J. W. A. Nicholson was ordered to command a new steamer, the Governor Buckingham, built by Mallory. He had only one officer, a volunteer acting ensign, so he applied to Captain Mathews, who told him that I could be spared, and could perform the duty of watch officer. The following day I received a telegram from the Department appointing me an acting lieutenant, and ordering me to report to Captain Nicholson for duty, which I did at once. The captain seemed somewhat surprised at my youthful appearance, but nevertheless directed me to find a crew for the Buckingham, get the guns on board, coal, and prepare for sea, and report to him when everything was ready. He was serving as one of the officers of the yard at the time. On board the receiving ship I was abused by the executive officer because I did not have the proper papers from the commandant, and cursed all over the quarter-deck and into the cabin by the captain, who was a fine old seaman, but dreadfully profane. He finally gave me thirty men, and surely not the best I ever saw!

On board the Buckingham I found a very curious state of things. The contract read that the merchant captain, his officers and crew, were to work the ship during the daytime under the orders of the naval captain, and to feed the officers but not the crew. At sundown the navy men were to take charge of the ship and do all the night work. The engines were to be run by the owners under orders of the naval captain, the navy to furnish the coal. For all this the Government was to pay one thousand dollars per day.

As soon as I had my crew on board I hauled the ship into the ordnance dock, took on three small guns and the necessary ammunition, and at once anchored off the yard and began coaling. We had only taken in a few bags, when one of the men, a little the worse for liquor, concluded that I was neither old enough nor large enough to make him work; on the contrary, he would show me a thing or two. I landed on top of him from the deck above with a heavy brass trumpet, and he was convinced of his mistake in less than half a minute. I tied him up securely, bandaged his head, and locked him up in a coal bunker. Early the next day I reported the ship ready, and that afternoon we sailed in search of the Florida. Several chartered vessels went on the same mission about the same time, and one of them, the Ericsson, was fortunate enough to sight the privateer about fifty miles northeast of Sandy Hook. She was also fortunate enough to get away from her when the Florida gave chase! She steamed much faster on the trip in than she did going out. I had expected to be punished for my encounter with the man, but Captain Nicholson considered the peculiar circumstances under which I was working, and dismissed the matter with a caution—not to me, but to the man, who afterward proved himself a very good sort of a chap.

We ran as far north as Cape Sable with the Buckingham, and then cruised slowly back, reaching New York safely after an absence of three weeks, without seeing the Florida, which was no doubt fortunate for us, as we were not fast enough to get away from her, and certainly not strong enough to fight her. But we satisfied the merchants of New York, and that was what it was all about. I had done the duty of executive officer, navigator, and watch officer, besides drilling the men for two hours every day. Captain Nicholson was good enough to commend me for my service. Our acting ensign had been found asleep on watch shortly after we sailed, and was not again put on duty, the captain and I standing all the night watches. One part of the contract I remember was faithfully carried out: I mean the feeding of the officers. I never have lived so well at sea since. Every night during the

The First Command

mid watch a beautiful lunch was served to the officer of the deck, including a bottle of wine if he
wanted it.

After the return of the Buckingham I was sent
back to the Marion, and was then given command of
the yacht America, two guns, and a crew of twenty-
four midshipmen. In company with the Marion we
again sailed in search of the Florida, but failed to come
up with her. I enjoyed every day and hour of my first
command, and never missed a chance to race with anything, from a steamer down to a pilot boat. For some
time I was cruising by myself off Cape Cod and toward the Banks, and while so employed overhauled an
English steamer, the skipper of which was not disposed
to pay much attention to me. Two shells across his
bow seemed to have no effect, but the third, which
landed in his main hatch, brought him to very quickly. On my way back to Newport I sighted a schooner
off Nantucket Shoals, and stood toward her. She
made every effort to escape, but the wind was very
light, and we slowly fanned up on her quarter. I saw
that she was a whaler homeward bound, and the men
of the crew were amusing themselves catching mackerel. I had not, up to this time, shown my colours.
When I hoisted the flag I hailed, "Schooner ahoy!"
"Hello!" came back. "Have you seen anything of
any pirates offshore?" "No; bein't you a pirate?"
The captain had mistaken the character of my ship,
and when he discovered his error promptly swung out
a boat and sent me a mess of the finest mackerel I
ever saw.

We returned to Newport late in September, and

were rejoiced to find that the Navy Department had decided to send us into service immediately. Our educations were not complete, but we knew enough to look out for a ship and stop bullets, which were the important things. We were commissioned as acting ensigns from October 1, 1863.

After ten days' leave I reported on board the United States steamer Powhatan at Philadelphia, where she was refitting for service in the West Indies. I was at once given a watch and division of guns, and two classmates and I composed the watch officers of the ship. Captain William Ronckendorf was the commanding officer, and it has been truly said of him that he could make himself disagreeable in more different ways than any man who ever wore naval uniform. I agree perfectly with the man who said it.

After ten days' hard work we put to sea with a fairly good crew and a large complement of officers, all anxious for active service. Although we had many officers, we were kept in three watches, because the captain would not trust volunteer officers to take the deck. We had seven of these gentlemen, excellent men, who had commanded ships, many of them, before I was born; but they knew nothing of man-of-war routine, and this we had to teach them. Drills were constant—forenoon, afternoon, and generally once during the night. In addition I was made midshipman of the foretop, and spent a good portion of my time aloft instructing the green men of the crew in bending and unbending sails, and the thousand and one things a topman has to know. Every time the men were sent aloft, up I went, day or night, rain or

The Powhatan.

shine. By the time we reached Cape Haytien, which
was headquarters of the Flying Squadron, to which we
belonged, I had about concluded that I at least had
work enough to keep me from rusting out.

Upon our arrival at Cape Haytien the captain reported us for duty as flagship of the squadron, and the
next day we flew the flag of Rear-Admiral James
Lardner, one of the finest specimens of the old navy.
He was the very opposite of our captain—a splendid
seaman, a courteous, kindly gentleman, brave to the
point of recklessness, an honour to the service, and a
man under whom all were glad to serve. Tall and
commanding in figure, with close-cropped, snow-white
hair and mustache, he looked what he really was, the
ideal commander. As soon as he came on board many
of the petty annoyances from which we had suffered
ceased, and we became contented and happy. It is
difficult to convince any one to-day of how completely
the captain ruled things in the time of which I am
writing. There was no law off soundings beyond the
captain's will, unless you had an admiral on board,
when his will became the law. Officers could be, and
to my knowledge were, kept on board for months without ever being allowed on shore, because the captain
thought it was better for them!

Admiral Lardner had some peculiarities which were
striking; anything that savoured of insubordination or
disrespect brought the severest punishment, generally a tongue-lashing the recipient remembered all his
life. To a naturally fluent tongue the admiral added
a vocabulary of oaths so fine that it was musical, and
when aroused he did not hesitate to speak his mind

in the language all seamen understand. At the same time his black eyes shone like fireflies, and his white mustache bristled, each hair standing on end. He certainly was a darling, and much beloved by all of us.

When the Rhode Island was his flagship, Captain Trenchard, who commanded, had a very accomplished steward, a coloured man, who had become so expert in catching flies off the captain's bald head that he was never annoyed by them. Admiral Lardner had for his steward a fine, large, heavy-handed Irishman, who watched the coloured man with great envy while his master, undisturbed, enjoyed his meals. Pat's master thrashed at the flies, and swore roundly as they lighted on his close-cropped hair. The coloured man went on catching flies with a quick, dexterous movement of his right hand until Pat could stand it no longer. Drawing back, he made a vicious swing at a fly, but, instead of catching it, he caught the admiral an awful blow on the back of his head. The admiral, thinking there was a mutiny, grabbed the carving knife, and made after Patrick, who retreated to the spar deck, and there was a hurdle race fore and aft—the officer of the deck and the orderly trying to catch the admiral, who was doing his best to put the carving knife in the back of Pat, who finally escaped, but never bothered any more about flies on the admiral's head.

One of the crew of the admiral's barge, a man the admiral was very fond of, died, and, as a mark of great respect, he went to the grave to see the poor fellow buried. The grave diggers had, for some reason, dug a very shallow grave, which so incensed the admiral that he spoke to them very severely, and not receiving a satisfactory reply, seized a stick and made after them. They ran, but he was too quick for them; he caught them and forced them to return, and while we stood around waiting, made them dig a proper grave in which poor Jack was decently buried.

The duty of the Flying Squadron was to look after the rebel privateers in the West Indies, and see that they did not interfere with the Pacific mail steamers on their regular trips. In order to do this most effectually, some vessel, often the flagship, met the steamer at Mariguana Island, and convoyed her clear of Navassa, where she was left to depend on her heels for safety. The convoying vessel got her mail first, and generally a file of late papers from home, so the duty was considered choice, and all hands were anxious for the job. As soon as the mail steamer was out of sight a cruise around the south side of Cuba was in order, generally including Havana and Key West, and then back to Cape Haytien.

The vessels of the squadron were kept constantly cruising through the Windward Islands and as far south as the Spanish Main, and though we used our best exertions we never came up with a privateer, because none of them visited that part of the world. For several months we cruised constantly, disguised as a Frenchman, and showing French colours to passing vessels, with the idea that we might thus decoy the Alabama within range of guns. During a part of this time we had yellow fever on board, and to get rid of it we steamed out into the trade winds, stopped the engines, put the ship under sail, and slowly cruised around with the wind abeam, until the fever disappeared. The admiral was very fond of sailing, and there was no end to sail and spar drills. He would reef the buckets of our paddle wheels, set studding sails on both sides, and run off to leeward, apparently for the fun of beating back again.

Once we thought we had the Alabama sure. We were anchored at Cape Haytien, when a messenger arrived from the consul at St. Nicholas Mole with word that the Alabama was anchored in that harbour. In a few minutes we were under way, heading to the westward, all sails set, and using pork in our furnaces to get all the speed we could out of the old ship. She really made fourteen knots all the way. On the way down the ship was cleared for action, and every preparation made to fight and fight hard. The admiral did not intend that the Alabama should get away from him, as she had from several others who had sighted her. As we approached the harbour preparations were made for anchoring; men were stationed by both anchors to let go when ordered, but the anchors were lashed so securely that nothing short of an axe could have got them clear. It was the intention, if we found the Alabama in port, to approach her at full speed, and when very close to back the engines and order both anchors let go, which failing, she would, of course, be sunk in the collision that would follow. We stood at our stations peering into the dark as we tore around the harbour at twelve knots, much to the surprise of the people on shore, but there was no Alabama.

The next day we found that an English sloop of war had caused all the trouble. Fortunately for her, she had gone out in the afternoon for target practice, and remained outside overnight. If she had been anchored inside, nothing could have saved her, as the admiral had made up his mind what he was going to do, and would not have waited to ask any questions. We agreed among ourselves that the captain of that ship ought to buy a lottery ticket!

Our men were kept on board so long, and we were so steadily under steam, that they became very irritable and ugly. Fights were of daily occurrence, and some of them serious. If a deck hand interfered in any way with a man from the engine room, there was a fight on the spot; and even the firemen fought among themselves on the slightest provocation. The heat seemed to make them particularly ugly. Several men lost their lives in this way, and the admiral finally went to St. Thomas to give shore liberty to the crew.

When we arrived we found the English Flying Squadron in port, but while the feeling against them was very bitter, we did not consider it a good reason why our men should be kept on board; so the starboard watch, consisting of one hundred and fifty men, were sent on shore for twenty-four hours. It was only a few hours before word came off that there was trouble ashore, and later a letter from the English admiral, saying that our men were rioting with the English sailors, some of whom had been killed. Admiral Lardner directed the captain to send the other watch on shore. And then there was a fine time, sure enough! The Danish garrison was turned out and attempted to arrest some of the leaders; but they were soon driven back into their forts, and the English and our men went at it again. The native negroes all sided with the English, and our people had them to contend with as well. Just before sundown the general recall was hoisted as a signal for all hands to repair on board, and such boats as we could man were sent in charge of officers to bring the men off. I was sent in the admiral's barge, the crew of which were picked men, and I anticipated no trouble with them; but on nearing the landing, where two or three hundred men were fighting with such weapons as they could find, I heard the stretchers begin to rattle in the bottom of the boat, the oars were tossed, and before I knew what had happened every man of the crew was out of the boat and into the fight, stretcher in hand. I followed, also armed with a stretcher, a very handy piece of white ash, and soon had my boat nearly loaded with men. But, unfortunately, I saw one of our men with three or four natives after him, and went at once to his assistance. As I grabbed him by the arm one of the negroes struck at my head with a broken oar, but only hit me across the shoulders, which probably saved my life. I was knocked down, of course, but quickly regained my feet with a fine round stone in my hand, which I planted squarely in the negro's mouth, and he gave no further trouble. By midnight we had our people on board, and found that three had been killed and many more or less seriously wounded, while the English were in about the same fix. Some of the rum mills on the water front were badly wrecked. After this experience our men had no more shore liberty until we got back to the United States.

Many years afterward I visited St. Thomas, and at the best hotel I saw a coloured porter without any front teeth, who told me, when I asked him what had become of them, "A little Yankee midshipman hit me in the mouth with a rock!" He was my friend with the broken oar.

During the time we were lying at headquarters the watch officers had a peculiar duty to perform in addition to their regular work. The officer who had the first watch at night was obliged to be ready for duty at four the next morning. As soon as the men had had their coffee, he left the ship with two boats and the fishing seine, and was expected back by eight o'clock, with fish enough for the whole crew. The fishing ground was five or six miles away, and to get to it we had to find our way through a tangle of shoals and coral heads, but once on the ground we could fill both boats with tarpon or other splendid fish at one haul of the seine. Usually we reached the ship just in time for breakfast, and then went on duty for four hours, which made a pretty long forenoon of it. However, we were young and strong, and could stand almost anything.

One morning while exercising at sail drill, we had a sad accident, which was long remembered by the whole crew. We had two brothers on board, one a seaman about twenty-three years old, and the other a landsman about eighteen; both excellent men, very active and promising. The younger one missed his footing in the foretopmast rigging, and fell to the deck and died in a few hours. We were quarantined at the time, and could not bury his body on shore; neither could we buy screws for his coffin when we found that there were none on board. The coffin had to be nailed up, which was anything but a pleasant performance, as the carpenter, a little nervous, I suppose, hit the coffin lid much oftener than he did the heads of the nails. I never understood why the captain insisted on burying the body in a coffin, but he probably had a reason of his own which he did not confide to us.

Just before sundown two boats were called away and dropped to the gangway—one for the body, and the other to tow it out to sea, where it was to be buried. All hands were called to bury the dead, and I was ordered to take charge of the boats when everything was ready. The coffin was placed on the quarter-deck, the officers and men paraded, and the captain had pronounced a few words of the burial service, when a loud, prolonged squeak was heard, and the lid of the coffin slowly raised several inches. It was the most terrifying sound I ever heard in my life, and the effect was startling; most of the men bolted forward, and the officers were very pale. I was standing near the head of the coffin, and my legs were only prevented from carrying me away by the fact that my hands were firmly gripping the spokes of the wheel. The trouble was soon manifest: the gases formed in the body had caused it to swell and lift the lid of the coffin, and the nails in drawing out made the awful noise that had so startled over three hundred men.

There was some delay in getting things ready again, and when I finally left the ship with a crew of petty officers, towing the boat with the body in it, the moon had risen. Out over the bar we went, pitching into rather a rough sea until I thought we had reached the right spot, when the boat was hauled up alongside and the body consigned to the deep. Then we started back for the ship. We had gone only a few hundred yards when the men fell into a perfect panic; some of them even dropped their oars overboard, and all hands stopped pulling, their faces white and terror-stricken. The stroke oar, a splendid specimen of manhood, fairly shook as he said to me, " He's coming, sir! " I turned, and looking out to sea, was not surprised at the condition of the men, for I was horrified myself at what I saw. The coffin was standing upright in the water, and as it rose on the seas it seemed, in the moonlight, to be making great jumps after us. It certainly was a most nerve-shattering sight, especially after the unpleasant scene on board ship. There was only one thing to do, and after quite a struggle with the men we pulled back, knocked the head of the coffin in and allowed it to sink. It was the most uncanny job I ever did in my life, I think, and I was glad when we were back on board and the boats hoisted up. No real danger could have frightened any one of the crew; they were a splendid, manly lot, and showed great spirit when in action; but just a touch of the supernatural, the least bit, and they were ready to hide their heads in the bottom of the boat.

Havana was, for some reasons, the most pleasant port to visit on the station; we got fine cheap cigars, and sometimes good meat there, but we hated it more than any place we had to go to, because the people were so bitter against us. The Southerners who lived there were not so bad, but the Spaniards were almost unbearable. On several occasions we found blockade runners anchored in the harbour, and their crews would pelt our boats with lumps of coal as we passed

back and forth, all of which we could avoid by pulling
a bit farther away; but the abuse on shore we could
not avoid, as we were obliged always to land in uniform. Under such conditions collisions were frequent,
and as a rule we were content with the way we came
out of them. In the matter of coal we were held
strictly to the law, while the blockade runners were
allowed great latitude, and in consequence were very
successful.

In 1864 Jeffrard was ruler of Hayti, and his iron
hand was felt by all classes. He was thoroughly hated
but at the same time feared by the people generally.
Revolutions, shootings, and hangings were the order
of the day; the people seemed happy, and appeared to
enjoy all these diversions. The ordinary routine was
somewhat varied during one of our stays in Cape
Haytien by the discovery of a gang of cannibals, who
occupied a strong position in the mountains near the
Old Castle. Jeffrard went after them, captured the
whole lot, brought them to Cape Haytien, where they
were confined for a few days, and then shot. It was
reported and believed at the time that several barrels
of human flesh had been captured with the prisoners,
and that some of it was produced in evidence before
they were shot. The favourite morsel was said to be
the palm of the hand. If one could judge from appearances, we were sure Jeffrard made no mistake in shooting this lot, for they certainly were the worst-looking
cutthroats we had ever seen.

During the month of October, 1864, a rumour
came that we would soon be ordered to the United
States for more active duty than we had been having

in the West Indies. The next mail brought the order, and all hands, from the admiral down, were as happy as boys out of school. Our preparations for departure were quickly made, and we said good-bye to the West Indies, yellow fever, rebel sympathizers, heat, filth, and hard service—the whole outfit—without a single pang. The old ship seemed to know that she was homeward bound, and did her best. Early in November we anchored in Hampton Roads, and as soon as possible all hands, as they could be spared from duty, sought the dissipations of the city of Norfolk, which at that time was not the best place in the world for those wearing United States uniform. However, we did manage to enjoy a good square meal and the conversation of people of our own race. Only those who have served away from home can appreciate what all this means, and how we enjoyed it.

Soon after our arrival, Admiral Lardner was detached, and left the ship with the respect and affection of every officer and man aboard. A few days later Captain Ronckendorf was sent to other duty, and Commodore Schenck took his place. In our new commander we had one of the ablest men of the navy, and one who soon endeared himself to all on board. He found a splendidly drilled crew and a ship thoroughly organized in every department and detail, and he showed his appreciation of it all. Our men were all long-service men, and there was not the demoralization that always comes with a draft of new men to be whipped into shape with a lot of old ones. I am sure we did not require a dozen men to complete our complement.

We lost one man in a curious way. We had
among the crew a "bounty jumper"—so called because he had drawn a bounty on enlistment and then
deserted. In fact, he had repeated this trick a good
many times before he finally fitted into his place on
board the Powhatan. He was a plausible sort of a
chap, and had made himself a favourite with the men
on board to such an extent that the petty officers
had made him caterer of their mess, and had given
him quite a large sum of money with which to
buy stores. When we anchored, well up toward the
middle ground, a number of bumboats came off to
trade with us, and when they left it was soon discovered that the "bounty jumper" had gone with them,
taking all the mess money. A boat was soon ready
to follow them, manned by a crew of petty officers,
as they would be sure to pull harder than any others
in the ship. I was sent in charge of the boat, and
soon picked out the canoe containing the deserter by
the frantic efforts she was making to escape, which
she finally did, owing to the long start she had. All
the canoes, half a dozen or more, landed at the same
place five minutes ahead of me, and in the semi-dark-
ness I could not see where the men disappeared. I at
once notified the guards about the fort of what had
happened, and asked the officer of the day to order
the man's arrest, which he did. Then I went back to
my boat, and found that the crew had been looking
about, but found nothing of importance. Just as I
was about to shove off, a tall, powerful boatswain's
mate said: "Let me look under this wharf, sir; it is
low tide; he may be there." Off he went, and was gone

Homeward Bound

five or ten minutes. I could hear him occasionally
splashing around, but not making noise enough to indicate any trouble. Finally, he came back, reported,
"He's gone, sir!" and I returned to the ship at once.
The next morning the body of the man we had been
looking for was found under the wharf with his throat
cut from ear to ear, and no money on his person. His
was one of the vacancies we had to fill from Norfolk.

CHAPTER VII

THE FIRST FORT FISHER CAMPAIGN

ADMIRAL PORTER assumed command in November, and at once began assembling a powerful fleet. Every preparation was made for active service. Boilers and machinery were overhauled, magazines, shell rooms, and storerooms replenished, and constant target practice was had with all guns. By the end of November the largest fleet ever seen under the American flag was assembled in Hampton Roads, all classes, from the largest monitor to the small gunboat, being represented. Our destination was a secret, carefully guarded; but we surmised from what was taking place that some important move was contemplated, and in this we were not mistaken. It was evident from the daily target practice that the admiral meant we should hit something when the time for action came, and the landing of the men on the beach for drill was an indication of possible shore service.

The Ticonderoga, anchored near us, was firing at target one morning, and making such good practice that we were all watching her with great interest, when one of her pivot guns, a large-calibre Parrott, was fired. There was a terrific report, as if the shell had burst at the muzzle of the gun, a great cloud of smoke, and then something struck close to her, making a great splash in the water. At the same time, or shortly afterward, the shot she had fired fell near the target. About two feet of the muzzle of the gun had blown off, straight up in the air, and come down within twenty feet of the ship. It was the most curious of the many accidents we had then and afterward with the Parrott rifles. This particular gun, though two feet shorter than it was intended to be, was continued in service, and did good work.

Early in December the troopships arrived—thirteen thousand men under General B. F. Butler—and still our destination was a secret.

About this time I received a letter by flag of truce from my brother, who was serving as a captain of scouts on General Lee's staff, in which he said, "We will give you a warm reception at Fort Fisher when you get there!"—showing that our intended move was not so much of a secret to the rebels as it was to us. The information must have been sent from Washington, as no one in the fleet, outside the admiral's immediate official family, knew anything about it. When I showed the letter to Commodore Schenck, which I was required to do by the regulations, he seemed much surprised, and sent me with it at once to Admiral Porter, who was very indignant when he had read it. For myself, I thought my brother had only made a good guess; there were only a few important places on the Southern coast remaining in the hands of the rebels, and, as our preparations surely indicated an important move, he guessed, and guessed correctly, that we were after the most important of the lot.

Toward the middle of December all our preparations had been completed, and we put to sea under sealed orders. It was a grand sight as we passed Cape Henry; all the water as far as one could see was covered with ships, and among them the flower of the navy. Commodore James Findlay Schenck commanded the third division of the fleet, and flew his flag on the Powhatan. The fleet was formed in three columns, the transports and storeships in the centre.

After passing Cape Henry we experienced beautiful weather, and got around Hatteras in almost a dead calm, much to the delight of the troops, who were dreadfully crowded on the troopships. On December 22d the fleet, having parted company with the transports, anchored in column thirteen miles off the mouth of Cape Fear River, and then, of course, we knew what we had in hand. That afternoon, it came on to blow hard from southeast, and when the sun went down the sight was a grand and threatening one. The seven monitors at the head of the column held on well at their anchors, but would disappear entirely from sight as the heavy seas swept over them. The ships soon began to drag, and all hands were kept on deck during the entire night, ready to do what was possible in case of collision. When daylight came the monitors were still in place, but the rest of the fleet was scattered over a space of sixteen miles, and nowhere could we make out a single transport. At sundown of the 23d the fleet was again anchored in good condition, none the worse for the shaking up it had had; but still we wondered what had become of the transports, as none of them showed up. It turned out later that they were safely anchored well inshore of us, waiting for the stragglers, who had been blown out of place in the gale, to come up.

Before leaving Fortress Monroe, General Butler had proposed a " powder boat," by the explosion of which he hoped to seriously injure the forts on Federal Point, including Fort Fisher. Indeed, he was confident that he would dismount most of the guns and level the works. An old steamer, the Georgiana, had been loaded with several hundred tons of powder, and turned over to the navy to explode at the proper spot. A crew of volunteers, commanded by Captain A. C. Rhind, had her in charge, and on the evening of December 24th took her in for the final act in her career. No man in the navy believed for a moment that she would do much harm, but none of us anticipated how little injury would come from the explosion.

At eleven o'clock that night Admiral Porter steamed about the fleet in his flagship, the side-wheeled steamer Malvern, and made signal: " Powder boat will blow up at 1.30 A. M. Be prepared to get under way, and stand in to engage the fort!" After that there was no sleep for any one; we stood and watched and waited as the hours slowly dragged by. Half past one came, and no explosion, and we were fearful of some mishap; but just as the bells struck two o'clock it came. At first a gentle vibration, then the masts and spars shook as if they would come down about our ears; and then came the low rumble like distant thunder, while the sky to the westward was lighted up for a few seconds, and then great masses of powder smoke hung over the land like thunder clouds. The powder boat had blown up surely, and as the fleet rapidly formed for battle there was great curiosity everywhere to see what the effect had been.

At daylight we were heading in for the fort, and almost in range, when we saw General Butler's flagship coming in at full speed, heading straight at Fort Fisher, which looked to us very grim and strong, and totally uninjured. Everything was very quiet until the general got fairly within range, when there was a flash from the fort and a prolonged roar, and all the guns on that face of the work opened on his ship. If he had had any notion that he could land unopposed he was quickly undeceived, and the way that ship turned and got offshore spoke well for the energy of her fire-room force! The last we saw of her she was running east as fast as her engines could carry her. The powder boat had proved a failure, and the general was grievously disappointed. A rebel newspaper reported that a Yankee gunboat had blown up on the beach and all hands lost.

The fleet stood on in column, the monitors leading until in position, when the leader anchored; and then the rest anchored in succession as they reached their places. It was a beautiful evolution and beautifully performed. As soon as the monitors came in range, all the guns that would bear opened furiously; and as the range was only seven hundred yards, the hits were frequent. The rebels seemed to conclude very quickly that they could do nothing with the ironclads, so they held their fire for the wooden ships. Then the Minne-

The Bombardment

sota took her place, and as her anchor went down her batteries opened, first a broadside from the spar deck, and then her gun-deck broadside roared its Christmas greeting. At the same moment all the rebel guns replied, and the ship was completely enveloped in the smoke from her own guns and the bursting rebel shells. For a moment it looked as if she must be disabled, but then her guns began to speak out with a welcome sound, and we knew she was all right. The Wabash and the Colorado followed the Minnesota, and quickly dropped into their places, opening as they did so with their tremendous batteries. In rapid succession each vessel of the fleet passed them on the off side, firing through the intervals between them, and thus the battle line was formed. At times the shower of shells coming over the vessels engaged gave us a foretaste of what was in store for us, but the losses were wonderfully few.

Just as the Powhatan dropped her anchors an incident occurred which caused much bitter comment afterward. The Brooklyn, the next ship to us in line, was commanded by Captain James Alden, whose conduct at the battle of Mobile Bay had not met the approval of Admiral Farragut. In taking his position in line he held his fire until his anchor was down, when he fired a broadside very smartly, which brought from the admiral the signal, " Well done, Brooklyn!" the only signal of commendation made during the fight. The general feeling was that it was a theatrical performance, and that the signal did injustice to many veteran officers who had handled their ships with consummate skill. However, the signal undoubtedly went far toward removing the stigma of Mobile Bay, and the friends of Captain Alden rejoiced over it.

We had been up, many of us, all night, and our only breakfast had been coffee and hard-tack. As we approached our position Commodore Schenck sent me aloft with a pair of glasses to locate, if possible, some guns that were annoying him. It was a raw, cold morning, and I had on a short double-breasted coat, in the pockets of which I had stowed several pieces of hard-tack. When I had taken my place in the mizzen rigging, just below the top, I put the corner of a hard-tack in my mouth, and was holding it between my teeth while I took a look through the glasses for the guns. I caught them at once, and saw gunners train one of them around until I could only see the muzzle of it, which interested me, because I knew it was pointing directly at us. There was a puff of smoke, something like a lamp-post crossed the field of the glass, and a moment after the rigging was cut four feet below me, and I swung into the mast. I at once thought of my hard-tack, but it was gone, and I never found even a crumb of it. I am sure that I swallowed it whole. When I had reported what I had made out of the battery I was directed to lay down from aloft to my station, which was in charge of the after division of guns; but I hesitated to do so, because my knees were shaking, and I was afraid the men would see it. However, I had to come down, and as soon as I reached the deck I stood up and looked at my legs, and was greatly relieved to find that they did not show the nervous tremor that worried me so. I soon forgot all about it as I became interested and warmed up to my work.

We had only eighteen inches of water under us when we finally anchored and began firing rapidly in obedience to signal from the admiral. There was a wreck of a blockade runner between us and the battery at which we were to fire, and it was soon evident that this had been used as a target and the range was well known. One or two shots were fired in line with it, each one coming closer to us, and then they struck us with a ten-inch shot. Four more followed, each one striking nearly in the same place, on the bends forward of the starboard wheel, and going through on to the berth deck. Then for some reason the shot and shell began going over us, striking the water thirty or forty feet away. Probably the gunners on shore could not see the splash of these shots, and thought they were striking us. If they had not changed their range when they did they would have sunk us in an hour. As it was, we hauled out at sundown pretty well hammered, and leaking so that we had to shift all our guns to port in order to stop the shot holes.

We had damaged the fort to the extent of dismounting some of the guns and burning the barracks and officers' quarters. When the whole line was fairly engaged the sight was magnificent, and never to be forgotten by those who saw it. No fort had ever before been subjected to such a fire, and the garrison could only make a feeble response; most of them were driven into the bombproofs, where they remained until we hauled off for the night. The heaviest losses on our side had been caused by the bursting of the one-hundred-pound Parrott rifles; thirty-five or forty men had been killed or wounded in this way.

The transports in the meantime were got together, and while a slow, steady fire was kept up on the forts by the monitors and a portion of the fleet, the rest of us devoted our energies to getting the troops on shore. The weather was favourable for the purpose, and in one day and night we landed General Butler and his thirteen thousand soldiers with their ammunition and stores. Then for two days more we hammered away at the fort, expecting every hour to see them carried by the army; but we were not to have that pleasure. Some officers and men did get very near the fort, but, without making the effort, the general decided that the works had not been seriously damaged as defensive works, and were too strong to be carried by assault. He therefore asked that we reembark his men, which we did, and he sailed for the North. So ended the first attack on Fort Fisher, which had promised so much to the national cause.

CHAPTER VIII

THE ASSAULT ON FORT FISHER

ADMIRAL PORTER was not willing to give up so easily, and on his representations, concurred in by General Grant, the second expedition was organized. The fleet was ordered to Beaufort, North Carolina, and such vessels as could do so entered the harbour; the rest anchored outside, and all hands worked day and night coaling and filling up with ammunition and stores. Any one who has served on that coast in the winter months will know the difficulties with which we had to contend; to those who have not, no adequate idea can be given. Gales of wind were of almost constant occurrence, and, as we were in the open sea, the vessels rolled so that frequently we had to use life lines on our decks to prevent the men from being washed overboard. On many occasions vessels had to slip their cables and go to sea to ride out the storms.

Notwithstanding all this, in two weeks we were ready to try it again, and this time success seemed to be in the air. That gallant soldier, General Alfred Terry, was in command of the army contingent; his men were enthusiastic and anxious for the fight, and he and Admiral Porter were working in harmony—a fact of itself promising the very best results. It was agreed between the commanders that a naval brigade should be landed to assist the army in the assault, by attacking the sea face of the fort, while the army went in on the northwest angle. Volunteers were called for from the navy for this service, and it was gratifying to see the officers and men come forward, almost in a body, for a job they knew would be a desperate one. So many volunteered that finally a detail had to be made from each ship, and there were many sorely disappointed ones when the names were published.

It was my good fortune to be officer of the deck when the order came on board directing the movement, and so I had my name put first on the list of those who volunteered. At this time there were four classmates on board—Harris, Kellogg, Morris, and Evans. All volunteered, and as only two could go, we agreed that Harris and Kellogg, being in the first section of the class, should have one chance between them, and Morris and I being in the second section, should have the other chance. Harris won his chance on the toss of a penny; but I, being a Virginian and having no particular family ties, insisted that I should go rather than Morris, who came from New York and would be sadly missed if he were killed. To all of this Morris naturally objected, and we seemed a long way from any conclusion, when he suggested that we leave the selection to Lieutenant-Commander George Bache, who was to command the men from the Powhatan, which was done, and Bache selected me.

January 13th found us again in front of Fort Fisher, and this time we came to stay. The fleet opened on the fort, and kept up a constant and accurate fire. We soon found a great difference in the garrison from the one we had fought in the first attack. They stood up and fought their guns most gallantly, and would not be driven into the bombproofs. A division of gunboats was sent close in to cover the landing of the troops, which was done by the boats of the fleet in a sea heavy enough to make care necessary. I was in charge of the commodore's barge, a very handsome, large, able boat, fit to carry thirty-five or forty men. We made the first landing with over two hundred boats, and the sight was a notable one as we pulled in, an occasional shell splashing among us, and the bullets spluttering on the surface of the water.

As soon as the order was given to land we went for the beach at full speed, and, after passing the first breakers, turned our boats and backed them in until our passengers could land almost with dry feet but to get them out of the boats at the right moment was almost impossible. They would wait too long, and as a result most of them were rolled up on the beach by the surf, soaking wet. But once on shore it was glorious to see how they knew their business and the way they did it. As soon as they got their feet they spread out into a skirmish line, and the rifles began to crack. When I came in with the second load those on shore had captured some cattle, and were skinning them, and did not seem the least bit worried by the fire of the skirmishers, only three or four hundred yards away. Before dark we had all the men landed, and enough ammunition and stores to make them safe and comfortable in case it should come on to blow. During the night we completed the landing of stores and supplies and some thirty-pound Parrott guns, which were immediately put in position facing General Bragg, who was coming from the direction of Wilmington to re-enforce the garrison of Fort Fisher. The bombardment was kept up during the 14th, while the army got into position for the assault, which had been fixed for the afternoon of the 15th.

The premonitions that men have before going into battle are very curious and interesting, particularly when they come true. We had on board the Powhatan a fine young seaman named Flannigan, who came from Philadelphia. On the night of the 14th of January he came to my room with a small box in his hand, and said to me, " Mr. Evans, will you be kind enough to take charge of this box for me—it has some little trinkets in it—and give it to my sister in Philadelphia? " I asked him why he did not deliver it himself, to which he replied, " I am going ashore with you to-morrow, and will be killed." I told him how many bullets it required to kill a man in action, and in other ways tried to shake his conviction, but it was no use— he stuck to it. He showed no nervousness over it, but seemed to regard it as a matter of course. I took the box and, after making a proper memorandum, put it away among my things. On the afternoon of the next day, when we were charging the fort and just as we came under fire, at about eight hundred yards, I saw Flannigan reel out to one side and drop, the first man hit, with a bullet through his heart. I stepped quickly to his side and asked if he were badly hurt; the only reply was a smile as he looked up into my face and rolled over dead. The box was delivered as he requested, and I afterward assisted in getting a pension for his sister.

January 15th proved a beautiful day for our work, clear and warm enough, with a smooth beach for our landing. At early daylight the whole fleet opened on the fort, and poured shells in on it at a fearful rate. After a hasty dinner at noon the signal was made at one o'clock, " Land naval brigade." In a few minutes we were off, cheered by our shipmates, and pulling for the shore, where we landed unopposed and without serious accident, about one mile and a half from the northeast angle of Fort Fisher. On the way ashore some evilly disposed person fired a shot at us, which struck the stroke oar of my boat, cut it in two, and sent the handle spinning across my stomach with such force that I thought I was broken in two. On landing we were quickly formed in three divisions, with the marine battalion in the lead.

During the forenoon a force of firemen had landed under Lieutenant Preston to dig rifle pits, well to the front, and these were to be occupied by the marines, who were to keep down the rebel fire until the sailors, armed with cutlass and revolver, reached the parapet. When the divisions were formed, we advanced until we reached a point about twelve hundred yards from the fort, where we halted and waited the signal to charge, which was to be the blowing of the steam whistle on the flagship, repeated by other vessels of the fleet. All the guns that we could see had been dismounted or disabled in the bombardment, but after we landed there was one large rifle that opened on us and did some damage.

A Sailor's Log

The shells generally struck short of us, and would then ricochet down the level beach, jumping along for all the world like rabbits. To avoid this shell fire the divisions had been marched by the flank to take advantage of what shelter the slope of the beach offered. It thus happened that the three divisions forged up abreast of each other, and we charged in this formation—three columns abreast, the marines leading. While we were waiting for the army to report ready, our men had a good rest, and seemed to be in excellent spirits. The rebels were firing at us slowly, but doing no damage to speak of. Curious little puffs of sand showed where the Enfield rifle balls were striking, but they only hit a man now and then by accident.

At three o'clock the order to charge was given, and we started for our long run of twelve hundred yards over the loose sand. The fleet kept up a hot fire until we approached within about six hundred yards of the fort, and then ceased firing. The rebels seemed to understand our signals, and almost before the last gun was fired manned the parapet and opened on us with twenty-six hundred muskets. The army had not yet assaulted, so the whole garrison concentrated its fire on us. Under the shower of bullets the marines broke before reaching the rifle pits that had been dug for them, and did not appear again as an organization in the assault. Most of the men and many of the officers mixed in with the column of sailors, and went on with them. About five hundred yards from the fort the head of the column suddenly stopped, and, as if by magic, the whole mass of men went down like a row of falling bricks; in a second every man was flat on his stomach. The officers called on the men, and they responded instantly, starting forward as fast as they could go. At about three hundred yards they again went down, this time under the effect of canister added to the rifle fire. Again we rallied them, and once more started to the front under a perfect hail of lead, with men dropping rapidly in every direction. We were now so close that we could hear the voices of the rebels, and what they said need not be written here. The officers were pulling their caps down over their eyes, for it was almost impossible to look at the deadly flashing blue line of parapet, and we all felt that in a few minutes more we should get our cutlasses to work and make up for the fearful loss we had suffered.

At this moment I saw Colonel Lamb, the Confederate commander, gallantly standing out on the parapet and calling on his men to get up and shoot the Yankees. I considered him within range of revolver, so took a deliberate shot at him. As I fired, a bullet ripped through the front of my coat across my breast, turning me completely around. I felt a burning sensation, like a hot iron, over my heart, and saw something red coming out of the hole in my coat which I took for blood. I knew, of course, that if a bullet had gone through this portion of my body I was done for; but that was no place to stop, so I went on at the head of my company. As we approached the remains of the stockade I was aware that one particular sharpshooter was shooting at me, and when we were a hundred yards away he hit me in the left leg, about three inches below the knee. The force of the blow was so great that I landed on my face in the sand. I got a silk handkerchief out of my pocket, and with the kind assistance of my classmate, Hoban Sands, soon stopped the blood, and again went to the front as fast as I could.

About this time the men were stumbling over wires which they cut with their knives—they proved to be wires to the torpedoes over which we had charged, but they failed to explode. My left leg seemed asleep, but I was able to use it. The stockade, or what remained of it, was very near, and I determined to lead my company by the flank through a break in it, and then charge over the angle of the fort, which now looked very difficult to climb. I managed to get through the stockade with seven others, when my sharpshooter friend sent a bullet through my right knee, and I realized that my chance of going was settled. I tried to stand up, but it was no use; my legs would not hold me, and besides this I was bleeding dreadfully, and I knew that was a matter which had to be looked to. I heard some one say, "They are retreating!" and looking back I saw our men breaking from the rear of the columns and retreating. All the officers, in their anxiety to be the first into the fort, had advanced to the heads of the columns, leaving no one to steady the men in behind; and it was in this way we were defeated, by the men breaking from the rear. Two minutes more and we should have been on the parapet, and then—nobody can even guess what would have happened, but surely a dreadful loss of life. As the men retreated down the beach they were gathered up and put into the trenches to oppose Bragg, and there served until after the fort was captured. Of the eight of us who went inside the stockade all were shot down; one, the colour bearer of my company, was halfway up the parapet when he received his death wound.

When I received the wound in my right knee I began at once to try to stop the flow of blood. I used for the purpose one of the half dozen silk handkerchiefs with which I had provided myself, but I was so tired and weak from loss of blood that I was some time doing the trick. In the meantime my sharpshooter friend, about thirty-five yards away, continued to shoot at me, at the same time addressing me in very forcible but uncomplimentary language. At the fifth shot, I think it was, he hit me again, taking off the end of one of my toes, tearing off the sole of my shoe, and wrenching my ankle dreadfully. I thought the bullet had gone through my ankle, the pain was so intense. For some reason, I don't know why, this shot made me unreasonably angry, and, rolling over in the sand so as to face my antagonist, I addressed a few brief remarks to him; and then, just as some one handed him a freshly loaded musket, I fired, aiming at his breast. I knew all the time that I should kill him if I shot at him, but had not intended to do so until he shot me in the toe. My bullet went a little high, striking the poor chap in the throat and passing out at the back of his neck. He staggered around, after dropping his gun, and finally pitched over the parapet and rolled down near me, where he lay dead. I could see his feet as they projected over a pile of sand, and from their position knew that he had fought his last fight. Near me was lying the cockswain of my boat, Campbell by name, who had a canister ball through his lungs, and was evidently bleeding to death. When he saw the result of my shot he said, " Mr. Evans, let me crawl over and give that —— —— another shot." He was dead almost before I could tell him that the poor fellow did not require any further attention from us.

One of the marines from the Powhatan, a splendid fellow named Wasmouth, came through the stockade, quickly gathered me up under one arm, and before the sharpshooters could hit him laid me down in a place of comparative safety; but a moment afterward the fleet opened fire again, and the shells from the New Ironsides and the monitors began falling dangerously near us. Occasionally one would strike short and, exploding, send great chunks of mud and pieces of log flying in all directions. Wasmouth again picked me up, and, after carrying me about fifty yards, dropped me into a pit made by a large shell. Here I was entirely protected from the rebel fire, and several times called to him to take cover, but he said each time, " The bullet has not been made that will kill me." I was very drowsy and almost asleep when I heard the peculiar thug of a pullet, and looking up, found poor Wasmouth with his hand to his neck, turning round and round, and the blood spurting out in a steady stream. The bullet had gone through his neck, cutting the jugular, and in a few minutes he dropped in the edge of the surf and bled to death. He certainly was an honour to his uniform.

Just as our men began to break, the army made their charge, and were able to make a lodgment on the northwest portion of the works before the rebels, who had taken us for the main assaulting column, saw them. When they discovered them, however, they went at them with a savage yell, and for seven hours fought them desperately, the same bombproof in several cases being captured and recaptured five or six times. A number of sharpshooters remained on the sea face and northeast angle, and shot at every moving thing. No doubt this was owing to the fact that quite a number of marines were scattered about the beach wherever they could find cover, keeping up a steady fire.

After Wasmouth was killed I soon fell asleep, and when I awoke it was some time before I could recall my surroundings. The tide had come in, and the hole in which I was lying was nearly full of water, which had about covered me and was trickling into my ears. I could see a monitor firing, and apparently very near, and the thought came to me that I could swim off to her if I only had a bit of plank or driftwood, but this I could not get. It was plain enough that I should soon be drowned like a rat in a hole unless I managed to get out somehow. Dead and wounded men were lying about in ghastly piles, but no one to lend me a helping hand. By this time I could not use my legs in any way, and when I dug my hands into the sides of my prison and tried to pull myself out the sand gave way and left me still lying in the water. Finally, I made a strong effort, and rolled myself sideways out of the hole. When I got out I saw a marine a short distance away, nicely covered by a pile of sand, and firing very deliberately at the fort. I called to him to pull me in behind his pile of sand, but he declined, on the ground that the rebel fire was too sharp for him to expose himself. I persuaded him with my revolver to change his mind, and in two seconds he had me in a place of safety—that is to say, safe by a small margin, for when he fired, the rebel bullets would snip the sand within a few inches of our heads. If the marine had known that my revolver was soaking wet, and could not possibly be fired, I suppose I should have been buried the next morning, as many other poor fellows were. As soon as I could reach some cartridges from a dead sailor lying near me I loaded my revolver, thinking it might be useful before the job was finished.

When I was jerked in behind this pile of sand, I landed across the body of the only coward I ever saw in the naval service. At first I was not conscious that there was a man under me, so completely had he worked himself into the sand; he was actually below the surface of the ground. The monitors were firing over us, and as a shell came roaring by he pulled his knees up to his chin, which hurt me, as it jostled my broken legs. I said, " Hello! are you wounded? " " No, sir," he replied; " I am afraid to move." " All right, then," I said; " keep quiet, and don't hurt my legs again! " The next shell that came over he did the same thing, and the next, notwithstanding my repeated cautions. So I tapped him between the eyes with the butt of my revolver, and he was quiet after that. The poor creature was so scared that he would lie still and cry as the shells flew over us. As I said before, he was the only coward I ever saw in the naval service.

I persuaded him with my revolver to change his mind.

A Desperate Battle

From my new position I could see the army slowly fighting its way from one gun to another, and it was a magnificent sight. They knew their business thoroughly, these gallant fellows from the Army of the Potomac, and in the end, at ten o'clock that night, won a victory that will live as long as heroic deeds are recorded. I can recall to this day the splendid courage of General Curtis, leading his brigade; he seemed to stand head and shoulders above those around him; and while I looked at him he went down, but was soon on his feet, only to go down a second time, shot in the eye. As darkness approached and the cold began to be felt, our men seemed to fight with more desperate determination, and the advance was more rapid. The Confederates were doing, and had done, all that human courage could do, but they were wearing out, and the arrival of fresh brigades on our side discouraged them.

The scene on the beach at this time was a pitiful one—dead and wounded officers and men as far as one could see. As a rule, they lay quiet on the sand and took their punishment like the brave lads they were, but occasionally the thirst brought on by loss of blood was more than they could bear, and a sound-wave would drift along, "Water, water, water!" and then all would be quiet again. It was one of the worst of the awful features of war. Just as the sun went down, and it did seem to go very slowly that afternoon, I saw an officer coming up the beach dressed in an overcoat and wearing side arms. As he approached me I recognised Dr. Longstreet, and begged him to lie down, as the bullets were singing around his head. He took a canteen off a dead marine and gave me a swallow of sand and water, and did the same for another wounded man. Then, turning his face toward me, he said, " We will have you all off the beach to-night," and was moving on to the front, when a bullet struck him in the forehead. He sprang several feet in the air, fell at full length on his back, and lay quite still and dead. His resignation had been accepted a week before, and as soon as this fight was done he was going home to Norfolk to be married.

After the death of Dr. Longstreet I saw another man coming toward me; but he was taking advantage of all the cover he could get, and arrived without accident. He was a fireman from the gunboat Chicopee, and said he had come after me, but had only a coal-shovel with which to aid me. He said if I could sit in the coal-shovel he could drag me off! The twilight was deepening, and it seemed improbable that a sharpshooter could hit either of us, so I managed to get seated on the shovel, and the fireman, with both hands behind him on the handle, started to pull me off, but had only gone a few steps when a bullet struck him, passing through both arms below the elbows. That ended my trip on a coal-shovel, and I spent the time until dark making my friend as comfortable as possible. Then I heard some one calling my name, and in a few minutes two men came who said Captain Cushing had sent them to find me and bring me off. They had only their hands, but they used them most willingly and tenderly. One would put me on his back and carry me, while the other held me on. When the first one was tired, the two would change places; and thus I was carried, shot through both legs, a distance of a mile and a half.

The outfit for the care and comfort of the wounded consisted of a large fire made of cracker boxes and driftwood, a fair supply of very bad whisky, and a number of able and intelligent medical officers. To the vicinity of this blazing fire I, among a large number of wounded men, was carried, and stretched out on a piece of plank with my head on a cracker box, where I enjoyed the warmth, which was very grateful in the chill of the January evening. My clothing was saturated with blood and salt water, and thoroughly filled with sand. My wounds were in the same condition. A rebel gunboat in the bayou back of the fort was using our fire as a target, and finally succeeded in landing a shell fairly in the middle of it, much to our discomfort. When the shell exploded several men were killed, and the fire blown about over the rest of us. The doctor finally got to me, and after cutting off my trousers and drawers well up on my thighs, split them down the sides and threw them into the fire. Then he ran a probe, first through one hole, then the other, said I was badly wounded, gave me a stiff glass of grog, and passed on to the next man, leaving me practically naked. A brother officer, seeing my condition, took the cape off his overcoat and wrapped it about my legs, and this, with the assistance of the grog, soon made me very comfortable.

About half past nine that night Captain Breese, who commanded the brigade, succeeded in getting a lifeboat in through the heavy surf breaking on the beach, and at once wounded officers were tumbled into her, while the crew stood in the water holding her head on to the seas. My turn came at last, and two friends landed me in the boat with my legs hanging over the stern; then the crew jumped in, the cockswain sat down calmly on my knees, gave the men the word, and out we went through the surf in beautiful style. The boat was from the gunboat Nereus, Captain Howell commanding, and to her we were taken. We found her rolling in the trough of the sea, but the officer of the deck had all preparations made, and we were quickly hoisted up to the davits, and willing hands soon transferred us to the deck. Just as they were putting me on a cot, before taking me below, I saw a signal torch on the parapet of the fort calling the flagship, and a moment later I read this signal: "The fort is O U R—" and then everything broke loose! Nobody waited for the completion of the signal; all hands knew what that last letter would be. There was a great burst of rockets and blue lights, and the men manning the rigging cheered as the guns roared with saluting charges. Long after I was comfortably swung in the wardroom I could hear the fleet rejoicing over the downfall of the great rebel stronghold.

The officers of the Nereus, from the captain down, spent the night doing all in their power to make us comfortable. We had a good supply of whisky and a pitcher of morphine and water, and they gave us plenty of both. Shortly after daylight signal was made to transfer all wounded men on board to the Santiago de Cuba, and for vessels having dead on board to hoist colours at half-mast. I shall never forget the sight that greeted me when I was carried on deck to be put in the boat. The fleet lay just in the position in which it had fought the day before, and it seemed to me that every ship had her flag at half-mast lazily flapping in the drizzling rain. The weather was cold and raw, and all our wounds were stiff and sore, and every movement of those helping us caused indescribable suffering. In the excitement of the charge, getting wounded was fun, but we had a different problem to solve, and it required real nerve to face it.

CHAPTER IX

EXPERIENCES OF A CONVALESCENT

THE Santiago de Cuba was soon loaded to her utmost capacity, and early in the forenoon we started for Norfolk, Virginia. My friends Kellogg and Morris had kindly packed all my traps for me, and sent them on board so that I had a change of linen. The officers of the ship devoted themselves entirely to our comfort. Lieutenant-Commander Farquhar, the executive officer, put four of us in his room and made us feel that everything he had belonged to us. If we had been his own brothers he could not have treated us with greater kindness. Before we passed Hatteras the fresh water ran low, and we had to drink warm water from the distillers, but we regarded that as a small matter so long as we could have a drop of whisky with it.

The chaplain was a good soul, and was unremitting in his attentions to those who needed them. Once, when he came to see us, he said to one who was pretty badly used up, "My friend, you should be very thankful that it is no worse!" To which the officer replied, "I am, but I would be a d—d sight more thankful if it had not been so bad!" This did not evoke a reply from the man of God, who seemed to

100

consider it quite a new view of the situation; but to the rest of us it sounded like good common sense.

After a very comfortable trip, all things considered, we arrived at Norfolk at daylight in the morning, and hauled alongside the wharf at the Naval Hospital. We were landed without delay, and I found myself on a comfortable bed in a large, clean-looking ward. I slipped my revolver under the pillow, and pulling the blankets up about my chin, went to sleep and did not awake until ten o'clock that night. The surgeon in charge and his principal assistant were standing by the bedside, and after a careful examination of my wounds they retired to the end of the room for consultation, when I distinctly heard the senior one say, " Take both legs off in the morning." I did not get much sleep that night, but I did do some very serious thinking.

The following morning the assistant, who was a personal friend of mine, came in, and after a few words of greeting began to tell me how seriously I was wounded, and how dangerous wounds about the knee were. I saw at once that he hated to tell me what he was going to do to me, so to relieve the situation I told him that I had overheard the conversation the night before; that I had thought very seriously of the matter, and that I preferred to die with my legs on; that I was only eighteen years old, and the thought of living my life without my legs was more than I cared to face; that as the legs belonged to me, I thought I had a right to say what was to become of them; and that I asked the doctors to do what they could for me with my legs on, and if I died it was

8   101

no matter. He heard me very quietly, and I thought with sympathy, but when I had finished he said, " You know, Evans, orders have to be obeyed! " Thinking that he had misunderstood me, I went over matters again, and wound up by asking that they put me out on the lawn on a cot rather than cut me to pieces; that I would find some one to take me to a hospital farther North. Again came the reply about obeying orders. Reaching over, I pulled the gun from under my pillow; I told him that there were six loads in it, and that if he or any one else entered my door with anything that looked like a case of instruments I meant to begin shooting, and that he might rest perfectly sure that I would kill six before they cut my legs off. This brought matters to a crisis at once, and in a few minutes the surgeon in charge came in very angry and full of threats. But the result was that they left my legs on, and paid very little attention to me in any way for two weeks, when they found I had fever and must be looked after.

To the wife of the doctor who was going to operate and his little daughter I owe my life. Had it not been for their kindness and care I should undoubtedly have died. It would be difficult to make any one believe to-day the conditions that existed in the Norfolk Hospital at the time of which I write. No doubt the medical officers did the best they could with the tools they had to work with, but the tools were awfully bad. Hospital diet was unknown, and we lived on regular rations—at least I did, until bacon and cabbage knocked me out, strong as I was, and it was then that the doctor's wife and daughter saved me. Such a thing as a trained nurse was absolutely unknown, and there were none of the modern conveniences for handling men in my perfectly helpless condition. No language of man can convey any idea of the quantity and variety of vermin in that hospital. I have lived my whole life in hopes that it would burn down and that I might be there to see the slaughter!

When it was discovered that I had fever I was placed in a room with two other officers—Paymaster Schenck, who had been wounded in the first fight at Fort Fisher, and a volunteer lieutenant named Vassallo, who had been literally peppered in the same fight by the bursting of a Parrott gun which he was firing. Schenck, who was the jolliest, best soul in the world, kept us amused with his stories, and read to us or wrote letters for us when we were unable to do so for ourselves. Erysipelas soon developed in my right leg from the attendant using a dirty sponge, and then came an abscess in the right knee. In the meantime bedsores added to my misery, and all the bones on my right side, hip, knee, and ankle came through the skin. In fact, I was a skeleton, and nothing more. For nurse in this room we had a fine chap named Milligan, an enlisted man, who had been wounded and was convalescent, six feet tall and as strong as an ox, and scrupulously honest, but he knew nothing about nursing. Milligan had a pass-book, and every third day he would go to Norfolk and buy things for us, generally sugar and coffee and whisky. At five o'clock in the morning he would turn out and make a pot of strong coffee, and each patient would have a cup of it with enough whisky put in to make it bite. Then we would smoke a cigar or two and be ready for what breakfast we could get. Looking back at it now, the wonder is that any of us got well.

After a time Schenck recovered from his compound fracture and went home, and later on Vassallo also. Then I was left alone to watch the trees grow outside my window. As spring advanced into summer one branch spread out and almost covered it. I amused myself by sketching this branch each day when I was strong enough to do it. Often I was too weak to lift my hand, much less use a pencil. Several times the doctors gave me up, and though they never told me so, I knew when they thought I was going to die by the appearance of the chaplain, who never hesitated to tell me that I was dying, and also just where I was going to bring up after I was dead. Fortunately, I did not believe him in either of his statements. One of them was clearly wrong, and the other has yet to be decided.

The Powhatan came to Norfolk early in February, and I then heard for the first time an accurate account of our losses in the Fort Fisher fight. All the officers from our ship had been wounded, and out of the sixty-two men in my company fifty-four had been either killed or wounded. The naval brigade as a whole had been fearfully punished, but we did what was expected of us —drew the garrison away from the point selected by General Terry for his assault, thereby aiding the army to get in.

Early in June my wounds had healed, and I made up my mind to get away from the hospital if I could.

After Fort Fisher.

A Difficult Journey

I told Milligan, who was a carpenter by trade, to go to the carpenter shop and make me a stretcher narrow enough to go in the aisle of a car, and to use a hammock to cover it. When he had done it he managed to get me on the stretcher and cover me with a sheet. Then I sent for the surgeon in charge, who was so surprised that he fell in with my plan and allowed me to go, or rather to be taken, to the Bay Line steamer for Baltimore. In fact, he sent Milligan with me to take care of me until I reached my home, which was then in Philadelphia. I have sometimes thought the dear old doctor was very glad to get rid of me. I was taken across the harbour in a small boat, and nearly drowned in a squall that struck us on the way; but we managed to make the steamer finally, and here my troubles began again. The stretcher would not fit in anywhere! Finally, the captain stowed me in the ladies' cabin, where some beautiful rebel girls gave me the benefit of their tongues. I was as patient under this as I could be, and when we got into Chesapeake Bay that night, and they were all very seasick, I had my innings.

On board the steamer I found a company of the Twelfth Infantry, who took charge of me and showed me every kindness and attention. At Baltimore they carried me to the train, but the sergeant in charge of the squad concluded that I could go more comfortably by boat through the canal, so took me there and saw me snugly berthed before he left me. At Philadelphia my uncle, who had returned from the South, met me with a fireman's ambulance, and I was soon comfortably housed and cared for by loving hands. In taking me into the house, on account of a sharp turn in the stairs, the stretcher had to be shoved out of a second-story window, which alarmed Milligan very much, but did not worry me, as I knew nothing about it.

My convalescence was slow and very tedious. My right leg had been allowed to contract to such an extent that I could not get my foot to the ground, and the tendons of my left leg had healed into the wound in that leg and seemed very much too short. When I stood on my left foot my heel would not come to the ground, and when I tried to force it down the pain in the calf of my leg was very severe. However, I stuck to it, and after a few months the left leg worked fairly well. Then I went to duty at the Philadelphia Navy Yard, where I remained only a short time, when I was ordered to ordnance duty at the Washington yard.

CHAPTER X

SEA SERVICE IN THE ORIENT

THE desire to get back to sea duty was very strong, but my condition absolutely forbade it. I could not use my right leg, and was compelled to walk with crutches. The idea came to me that my right knee could be broken again, and my leg set at such an angle that I could walk on it. I returned to Philadelphia and consulted Dr. Samuel Gross, who made me very happy by saying that he would undertake the job. I was soon under chloroform, and the operation successfully done. An instrument was put on my leg by which it was hoped that the motion of my knee might be restored, and I was cautioned to work it every day for that purpose. It caused me great pain, and after torturing myself with it for a year and a half, without any apparent benefit, I buried it in the Indian Ocean.

The question of my promotion now came up, and the Medical Board promptly had me placed on the retired list, on the ground that I could not perform all my duties at sea. There was nothing for it but to go to Congress for relief, which I did. Being the only officer in the navy retired for wounds received in battle, I was put back on the active list, and shortly afterward advanced some thirty numbers, in company with three other classmates. This advancement was the result of being selected by a Board of Admirals, no one of whom I knew; nor did I know a single member of Congress, Senator or Representative, at the time, yet my promotion caused me no end of trouble. I have always supposed that it was made purely on my record, as I knew nothing about it until I was sent for at the Navy Department and there told of it. The following extract from the report of Lieutenant-Commander James Parker, who was the senior officer on shore in the attack on Fort Fisher, was a matter of pride to me as a young officer, and is of interest in this connection:

"Acting Ensign (Regular) R. D. Evans was wounded in the leg just after reaching the end of the palisade; he bound up the wound with his handkerchief, and then pressed on until he fell with a second wound in the knee joint.

"From all I can learn, his bravery and determination to enter the fort were equalled by few and excelled by none.

"He now lies in a critical state at the Naval Hospital, Norfolk."

After I had been confirmed as a lieutenant, the question of sea service once more came to the front, and I determined to settle it once for all by going to sea and making the effort to do all the duties required of me. Captain Daniel Ammen was going out to China in command of Admiral Rowan's flagship, the Piscataqua, and to him I applied. He very kindly asked for my detail to his ship, and my orders were made out immediately.

The Piscataqua was fitting out at Portsmouth, New Hampshire, and I reported on board of her in October, 1867. After several weeks' delay, we sailed from Portsmouth for New York, where the ship was docked and some necessary work done to complete her. She was a new ship, and this was to be her maiden voyage. Toward the end of November we were finally ready for sea, and anchored off the Battery, New York, to await our orders. A violent northeast gale came on, with a heavy snowstorm, and in the midst of it the apothecary thought it a good time to kill himself, which he did by taking poison. Then the ship walked away with her anchors during the night, and in the morning we had two large schooners under our bows with their chains and our own beautifully twisted together—so effectually, indeed, that it took us all day to clear them. The decks were covered with snow to an average depth of two feet, and this was frozen as hard as a nail, so that there was not much comfort on board. However, there is an end to all things, and at last, having buried the apothecary, who had caused so much trouble, we put to sea.

In the wardroom we had a splendid mess of twenty-three members, and in the steerage we carried nineteen midshipmen, just graduated from Annapolis, many of them being older than the watch officers. Admiral Rowan and Captain Ammen were well known in the professional world as officers of great ability and reputation, without superiors in any service.

As we passed out by Sandy Hook, the caterer of

the midshipmen's mess appealed to the officer of the deck to detail some men to find their mess stores, which he did, and two barrels of potatoes were dug out of the snow, all frozen hard; and these were the only food that the youngsters had provided to last them to Rio. Captain Ammen gave them a barrel of peanuts, which, with ship's rations, was all they had to rely on. Both the admiral and the captain were officers of the old school, and believed in old-time methods.

The midshipmen were stationed in three watches and were sent aloft whenever the men went up, and were expected to call the officers of the relief watches and light their candles. The war had broken up many of these old customs, and this was the first effort to renew them. Of course the youngsters kicked hard, but the routine was carried out to the end of the cruise, much to the benefit of all concerned. Quite a number of the nineteen are still living, all distinguished as excellent officers, and if you should ask any one of them he would tell you that this first cruise was the making of him. The captain carried a case of beautiful duelling pistols which he thought his young officers might want to use.

The Piscataqua was one of those long, narrow productions so much in fashion about the time our civil war closed. She had many bad qualities, but no good ones. She did, however, serve as an object lesson to show the naval constructors what bad work they were doing, and helped them to something better. She could carry sail well off the wind, and made good speed when pressed, but on the wind she could do nothing. As a steamer she was a notable failure.

In Rio Harbour

When forced, she could do twelve knots in smooth water, but while doing it she would fairly shake the teeth out of your head. If it had not been for the strong diagonal bracing of the hull the stern would have dropped off before we reached our destination. Fortunately for the comfort of all hands, we sailed most of the time, and thus avoided the excessive vibrations caused by the screw, which at times really prevented any one in the after part of the ship from sleeping.

We stood well out to the eastward, and carried good winds down to the line, where Father Neptune had a hard job, as we were all green hands to him, except a few of the older men. After the usual visit— dirty soapsuds for shaving and much salt water for ducking—he gave us certificates, and we steamed for a few days before we caught the welcome trades. Once we got them, however, we held them almost to our anchorage in Rio Harbour, where we arrived January 15, 1868, thirty-one days out from New York.

Rio was, comparatively speaking, free from fever at the time of our visit, and we enjoyed it to the utmost. The opera, in which Aimée was the star, was very good; the restaurants gave us fine food after our sea grub, and the suburbs were charming. When we had been in port a few days a Russian practice ship came in filled with midshipmen. They and our youngsters fraternized on shore, and that evening owned the largest theatre in the city. A party of fifteen or twenty midshipmen in Russian uniform took charge of the stage and ran the performance to suit themselves, which did not please the audience; and the result was

111

that all the morning papers had hard words for the Russian ship and her crew. During the forenoon of the following day all our midshipmen were sent for by the admiral and quarantined to the ship. He was the only one who had detected our gang in the Russian uniforms.

Leaving Rio January 29th, we ran down to the " roaring forties " and squared away for the Cape of Good Hope. During this trip we had a good chance to see what the ship would do running in a hard gale, for we had nothing but gales all the way over. We found that she ran fairly well, but was most uncomfortable, rolling from thirty-seven to forty-five degrees, and keeping it up for days without a let up. We fairly rolled our way to the Cape, arriving at Simon's Town February 19th. We had tried the " brave west winds," and were ready to admit that they were all that had been claimed for them, and as much more as anybody wanted to say; and the seas that came with and were made by them were worth a trip around the world to see. Coming as they did all the way around Cape Horn and across the South Atlantic, they acquired a force and grandeur never seen in any other part of the world. At times our big ship would settle down between two great mountains of water, and one involuntarily held his breath for a moment until she climbed the side in front of her; and then, as she settled down again, the great white-crested following sea raced after her, looking as if it must board her and sweep everything before it.

Each day at noon we threw overboard a bottle tightly corked, and containing the latitude and longitude, with the request that the finder send the slip of paper to the Navy Department at Washington, giving the location where the bottle was found. This was done in order to help, if possible, in determining the force and direction of ocean currents. In the afternoon we usually amused ourselves fishing for albatross. We used a blunt-pointed hook, which generally caught under the projecting bill, and by keeping a steady strain on the line the beautiful bird was landed on deck unhurt. Some of those we caught measured ten feet from tip to tip. After robbing them of a few feathers, and placing about their necks a brass shield with the date and name of the ship, we threw them overboard to rejoin their companions.

The anchorage in Simon's Bay was at times very uncomfortable, owing to the heavy sea that set in when the winds blew home, which they frequently did. It was selected in preference to Cape Town because at that season of the year the prevailing winds were supposed to be more favourable for boating, but we all agreed that it was rough enough where we were. Frequently all hands in a boat would land or reach the ship thoroughly soaked with salt water.

The trip around to Cape Town was a very delightful one, and I made it several times. Part of the way we drove on a beautiful firm beach, and then took the road over some picturesque mountains, where the scenery was very characteristic of South Africa. We usually rested and had breakfast at the Halfway House, and then jogged along slowly through the grape district, stopping now and then to enjoy the delicious fruit, or maybe a glass or bottle of the excellent wine made hereabouts. On arriving at Cape Town, we always went to the Royal Hotel, where we were well treated, and found the food most enjoyable after our sea fare of hard-tack and " salt horse." Once I joined a party for a trip to Table Mountain, from which we had a magnificent view of all the surrounding country and the coast for many miles. For once in my life I drank Bass ale when it was perfect—all the surroundings conspired to make it so. I was dead tired when lunch time came, and the ale was brought on, not too cold, with cold roast beef and cheese. I have often said that it was worth the price of this trip to know how good ale could be when it was at its best. We left Simon's Town, after a stay of ten days, with sincere regret, and started for our long and tedious run across the Indian Ocean.

We could not carry coal enough to steam the whole distance, and therefore relied on our canvas, which made the trip pleasanter and more interesting than it would otherwise have been. Officers and men soon shook down into their places, and the healthy rivalry that does so much to make our service what it is showed itself. Each watch was ready to wager anything that it could make sail or reduce it to a squall in half the time the other could, and the gun divisions had the same feeling. We were drilled constantly, as the admiral would not tolerate any but the very best work, particularly with the guns. He had a fashion of coming out of his cabin in the middle of the night and, without previous warning to any one, ordering the alarm for general quarters sounded. On such occasions he would order a shot or shell fired from each gun in the battery, carefully taking the time himself, and the last one to fire usually heard some very plain words from him.

One night I was the officer of the deck when he had an exercise of this kind, and one of my guns fired the first shot. It was fired just as I reached the gun and before things were ready, and caused considerable trouble by parting side tackles and other gear. Several minutes elapsed before another gun was fired, and the officers of the other divisions claimed that my gun captain had obtained his cartridge by unfair means, while I myself was satisfied that the gun had really been fired before the magazine was opened; but of course I said nothing about it, and stood up for my man, praising his promptness. After a few days he told me all about it: he had the cartridge in his hammock, where he had carried it since the last exercise, determined to be among the first. The powder boy swore that he got the cartridge from the powder division and carried it to the gun and handed it to the loader. He even remembered particulars: how the man in the powder division had said to him, " You are pretty d—d quick this time! " How could you doubt such evidence? Of course, it was all right, and the gun had been properly loaded and fired.

After a very pleasant run across the Indian Ocean we passed Java Head and hurried on to Singapore, where the Hartford was waiting for us to relieve her; and it was here that we had the first news of Admiral Bell's death. He had been drowned at Osaka, in Japan, while attempting to cross the bar in his barge.

The sea was breaking very heavily, and, before leaving the ship, the danger was pointed out to him; but the ministers were in peril on shore, and he decided to take the chance, and so lost his life. The boats of the ship were prepared as soon as he shoved off, so confident were the officers that he would come to grief, and the moment his barge was capsized they were hurried to the rescue, and succeeded in saving most of the crew.

Singapore proved a charming place to me. The people were most hospitably disposed, and the mode of living well suited to the climate. For the first time in my life I tasted real curry. Of course I had eaten the rice paste, served in the United States with its offensive hot yellow gravy, but here in Singapore we had the real thing—fresh curry powder each day, rice that was like a pile of snow flakes, Bombay duck, a flat, dried fish baked crisp, and Borneo red fish. When prepared like this, one has the finest breakfast dish in the world, and one that can be had only in the tropics, because only there can the fresh curry powder be obtained, and without that you can't have real curry. We also had for the first time the mangosteen, which some one has described as strawberries and peaches and cream mixed; but the description only gives a faint idea of the excellence of the fruit. Of course, all other tropical fruits were in abundance, and the people of Singapore knew how to serve them. All our spare time was given to enjoying the hospitality which the people were most lavish in extending to us, and we went on our way to Hong-Kong with much regret and many hopes that we might soon be back.

Chinese Pirates

We had been sent to the East with orders to punish the natives of Formosa for their ill treatment of some shipwrecked Americans, and we were all ready for the job—organized, armed, and equipped; but before we arrived the affair had been settled by Admiral Bell, so we were saved the trouble. A large force had been landed, and a fight resulted, in which Lieutenant-Commander Mackenzie had lost his life, he being the only man killed.

When we arrived at Hong-Kong piracy prevailed to such an extent that the admiral sent Cushing in the Maumee to look after the pirates and break them up. As this was a good chance for service, I volunteered for the trip, but Captain Ammen decided that I was wanted on board the flagship, and my application was returned to me disapproved. I had settled the question of being able to do all my duties at sea by this time, and was very anxious to have this cruise on a small, lively vessel to clinch the matter; but it was not to be. I argued and begged hard, but the captain maintained that my services were required where I was. Cushing went after the pirates, and in a few days they began to arrive at Hong-Kong by the dozen. He found, as we all suspected he would, that every Chinese junk was a pirate when it suited the owner to be so. The war junks were the worst of the lot. So Cushing ran in everything that he came across, and only stopped when the authorities asked that he be recalled, as he was capturing the entire Chinese merchant fleet. China had no navy then outside of her fleet of junks, armed with old smooth-bore guns and stinkpots. Her ports were all fairly well defended by forts, and on these she relied for protection.

Hong-Kong I found an ideal place for defence. The English certainly showed their wisdom in selecting it as their base of supplies in China. When we arrived there it was garrisoned by two English and several Indian regiments, all excellent troops, and kept up to the highest standard of efficiency. Socially, Hong-Kong was the best place on the station, but only endurable in the winter months; in summer the heat was intense, and all sorts of sickness prevailed, including the plague. The fine race track at Happy Valley and the resort on the signal station hill, particularly the latter, were patronized by all hands. Two Chinamen with a sedan chair would trot you up to this place about as fast as a horse could go, and in a cool evening a visit and dinner here were sure to be enjoyed. There was one hotel in Hong-Kong at this time, and it was anything but good; but the English Club was excellent, and always open to us. The custom of inviting newcomers to visit the large business houses had not yet died out, and there was, in consequence, no demand for large hotel accommodations. The roads were excellent, as is always the case in places under English control, and I made many excursions in the suburbs either by chair or wheeled vehicle.

The Chinese population seemed happy and prosperous, but given to gambling to an extent that I never saw before. I often visited the gambling shops frequented by the high-caste Chinese, and was much interested in watching the play. Fan-tan was the game, and it was not unusual to see a Chinaman bet his wife after having lost everything else. Judging from the appearance of the women, the only wonder was that the banker could place a value low enough on them. Like all Chinese coast cities, there was a large fishing population; by that I mean people who lived and had their homes on the water, the women and children not being allowed to visit the shore except at certain specified times. The men were allowed to land where they had employment, but not otherwise, except at stated times and places. When they had landed the boats were shoved off and went about their business until time for the men to embark, when the boats were allowed to come in and take them off. The water police were expected to look after all these people and keep them in order. My observation was that the water population was justly noted as expert boatmen and thieves. You could trust yourself in one of their boats in any kind of weather, and be very certain that they would steal from you every movable thing on your person. On one occasion they stripped the copper off one entire side of a Pacific mail steamer in one night, while she was lying at her dock, and not a soul on board heard even a suspicious noise.

When bad weather came many of these *sampans*, as they were called, were wrecked, and many lives lost. To prevent the loss of life as much as possible, all the children had small wooden buoys made fast to their bodies. I once saw an entire family driven overboard in a curious way. A Chinese bumboatman brought to our ship a very large monkey, or ape, which he offered for sale. It was a ferocious-looking beast, very wild and vicious; but the maintopmen concluded that they wanted him for the starboard gangway, and so purchased him. He was brought on board at supper time with a short length of chain and a stout leather collar about his neck. Jacky thought it well to give him his first lesson in discipline, so he ran the chain through a ringbolt in the deck, and, having pulled the ape's head close down to it, was giving him a good sound thrashing with a broom handle, when the collar broke, and the ape at once ran up the main rigging and took possession of the maintop. Several men tried to get into the top, but it was impossible for them to do it, so fierce were the attacks of the enraged beast. At last he was allowed to remain in charge with the hope that he would be in a better humour in the morning. During the night, however, he cast loose the bunt gaskets of the maintopsail, and at daylight the officer of the deck found the sail hanging from the yard. Of course, this would not do, and several men were sent up to restow the sail. The ape grabbed the first head that appeared in the top and yanked out a handful of hair, nearly scalping the man in the process. The second man was severely bitten, and the others retreated to the deck. At this time Captain Ammen came on deck, having been aroused by the unusual commotion, and, seeing the conditions, ordered the ape to be shot. While the gunner's mate was getting a rifle, however, the ape walked out on the main yard, grinning defiance to all hands. As soon as he was well out on the yard the braces were manned, the yard quickly swung around, and the beast fell overboard. As soon as he came to the surface he swam to a Chinese boat lying near, pulled himself on board, and was soon in command of the craft. The Chinese family of eight or ten persons never disputed possession for a moment, but bolted overboard and swam for the nearest boat. The last we saw of the captured boat as she drifted off to leeward the ape was industriously throwing overboard everything he could lay hands on.

Our stay at Hong-Kong was not a very long one, but we had sufficient time to make a number of very interesting excursions; two of them I recall. A party of us—youngsters, of course—figured out a scheme by which we could beat the Chinese gambling game known as " fan-tan." Our system was carefully gone over, and the more we examined it the more certain it appeared that we had only to play long enough in order to amass great wealth. Finally, we made our plans to go to the Portuguese city of Macao, some fifty miles away, and clean out the gambling shops there first, as they were reputed to be more wealthy than the Chinese dens in Hong-Kong, and wealth was what we were after. Some of our shipmates heard of our scheme, and, being convinced of the soundness of our system, intrusted us with various sums to be invested for their interest—the foundation of their fortunes, as it were. Four of us finally set out on this important excursion, reached Macao safely, and, having secured comfortable rooms at one of the best hotels, began our breaking process on one of the large gambling houses. For a time we did well, and it really looked as if we were going to get the best of the game; but the banker eventually struck the weak point in the system, and we went home at 3 A. M. with just money enough to pay our hotel bill and our fare back to Hong Kong.

We did not hear the last of that expedition for many a long day.

Quite a party of us, young and old, went to Canton, and there spent several days looking over that interesting old city. There were no hotels, so we chartered a flower boat, in which we were fairly comfortable at night; the days we spent sightseeing. I was most interested, I think, in the capital punishments as illustrated in the Temple of Horrors by full-sized wax figures. There were hundreds of them, and the authorities had certainly exercised great ingenuity in devising plans for making the victim suffer for long periods of time before actually ending his life. The theory of them all seemed to be that an offender should be made to suffer for his offence, and finally to pay the penalty of his life for the crime he had committed; but the first idea was that he should suffer, and suffer long and cruelly. In carrying out this idea they had certainly shown wonderful ability, and had drawn freely on the experience and practice of all the nations with whom they had come in contact. Among all the punishments illustrated there was not a single one shown that caused instant death to the victim. The one most in use was that by which the suffering was the longest drawn out.

I was also interested in meeting, in the heart of the city, in one of the narrow streets where two chairs could scarcely pass each other, a young man with all the outward signs of a Chinaman except the colour of his skin, and yet who was evidently an Anglo-Saxon. He had the dress of the country and the long pigtail hair of a Chinaman, and was talking fluently with the natives

in their own dialect, but he was, in fact, a young
Catholic priest. I found afterward that there were a
number of them, not only in Canton, but in other Chinese cities, living as this young man was among the
people, really one of them. They encountered untold
hardships and privations, but they met with success
in their calling, and the progress of so-called civilization in the East is marked by their graves. Their
right, moral or legal, to do the things they were doing
is a question each man must settle for himself; but
that they caused much trouble and the loss of thousands of human lives is a fact that can not be disputed.
How many souls they saved is a question that can be
settled only at the last roll-call. That the Catholics,
however, lived nearer the people and had more influence with them for good or for evil than any other denomination, was plain to me. I am not a Catholic.

Before returning to Hong-Kong we desired to
smoke opium Chinese fashion, that we might know
from practical experience what the sensation was like.
We borrowed a few Chinese experts from the flower
boat of a nobleman lying near us, and after due preparation proceeded to smoke. The expert who was giving me his attention prepared a small pill of the opium
mixture, and placed it over the pin hole in the pipe,
which takes the place of the ordinary bowl. When
I had managed to get the large stem of the pipe into
my mouth, he applied a red-hot iron to the opium,
and the smoking began. I inhaled three whiffs of the
smoke, which was all the small pill produced, and
then I was very sorry I had done it. All the fine
dreams and hallucinations which I had been led to

expect and did really expect to experience, were missing, and in their stead I was genuinely seasick—nauseated until I could neither eat, sleep, nor stay awake. The sensation lasted for several days, notwithstanding the large amount of strong tea and coffee I drank, not to mention other liquids. I was quickly and thoroughly cured of my desire to smoke or take opium in any form.

After a short stay at Hong-Kong we proceeded on our way up the coast of China, bound to Yokohama, Japan. We stopped at Amoy, where I had the pleasure of meeting an old friend, a missionary, who had been my rector in Washington. I called on him and listened to a very eloquent sermon on Sunday. The small chapel was well filled with the foreign element of the settlement, and they appeared to enjoy the sermon; while the native converts, four in number, worked the *punka* from the outside of the building, and fanned us while we prayed. Afterward we dined at a comfortable stone house, on a bluff overlooking the sea, where the converts were again in evidence, this time serving the table in a most beautiful and noiseless way.

CHAPTER XI

STORMY DAYS IN JAPAN

Upon our arrival at Yokohama we found most of the American squadron, as well as a fair number of war ships of other nations, assembled. The Stonewall had crossed the Pacific under command of that excellent seaman Captain George Brown, of the navy, and was waiting to be turned over to the Tycoon; but he was engaged in a deadly struggle with the forces of the Mikado, and no one could foresee how the great revolution of 1867 would terminate. The throne of Japan, and, as it afterward turned out, the fate of the country, hung in the balance, while Japanese soldiers fought in the streets of Yeddo, and unsuccessful officers promptly committed *hara-kiri*. The vessels of the squadron were at once put in condition for active service, owing to the avowed purpose of the Mikado to drive all foreigners out of Japan when he had subdued the Tycoon. Admiral Rowan was not the man to allow American interests or citizens to suffer, and his recent experience in the civil war fitted him admirably for the important position he was filling. Nearly every officer under his command had had war service, and all were ready for any job that might turn up.

We were deeply interested in our surroundings, but found it difficult to take seriously the war performances of the Japanese. Their army was organized as it had been for a hundred years, and commanded, as had been the custom, by the Damios, or feudal lords, each one supporting and leading his particular band of followers. They were armed with every conceivable kind of ancient weapon, and all wore the long, heavy Japanese sword, the officers being each provided with two. The Mikado had one or two batteries of Whitworth field guns, but their use was little understood. All were in the ancient uniform of Japan, and presented a curious contrast to the nut-brown Confederates and blue-coated Federals, whose sharp work we had been accustomed to see. The Japanese navy was entirely in the hands of the Tycoon, and consisted of a few old-fashioned sailing craft, under the command of Admiral Ennymoto, a lion-hearted old seaman, who was sure always to give a good account of himself. The officers generally were brave and courteous, but, as military men, about one hundred years behind the European standard. The enlisted men were brave, barbarous, hardy little brown chaps, capable of vast improvement.

Under the circumstances it can be readily understood why the Stonewall, a modern ironclad built by the French for the late Confederate government, was regarded with so much anxiety, and so eagerly sought by each side in the war. It can also be seen why we, fresh from the greatest war of modern times, should feel little concern over this Falstaffian array of Japanese braves. If the Mikado succeeded in securing the

A Threatened Attack

Stonewall, his avowed purpose was to drive the foreign ships out of Japanese waters, and we all hoped that he might get her in order to try the experiment— otherwise our sympathies were all with the Tycoon and his brave old admiral.

While the fighting continued in and about the city of Yeddo, a large foreign fleet was kept constantly in Yokohama Bay. When the Tycoon's forces were cleared out of that vicinity, the danger became even greater, and the number of foreign ships was increased. We were told many times of what the Mikado meant to do to us; but as he had failed to do any of these things, we naturally grew incredulous, and maybe somewhat careless. At last, however, news came through the American minister that sent a thrill of excitement through the entire foreign fleet. The Japs, so the story ran, had prepared a very formidable boat expedition in Yeddo, and were coming down on a certain night to cut out the Stonewall and carry her away. Their preparations were reported to be complete, and there was to be a very large force employed. On receipt of this news most of the foreign ships got under way and anchored well out in the bay, where they would be free to manœuvre when the dreaded ironclad should attack them. Admiral Rowan, who had spent many days within four hundred yards of Fort Wagner in Charleston Harbour, in the New Ironsides, believed in fighting at close quarters; and therefore, after clearing his ships for action, anchored them about the Stonewall in such positions as could best command the approach to her, and at the same time be ready to sink her if the

Yeddo force really succeeded in gaining possession of her.

When it was dark all the American ships went to general quarters and prepared for battle. The men stood by their guns ready to open fire, while a sharp lookout was kept for the hostile Japanese boats. An officer was sent on board the Stonewall with orders to remove parts of her machinery, so that she could not get under way, and then to take station on her turret and signal the approach of the boats, when the fleet would open with grape and canister. I remember well how this officer felt as he sat on top of the turret, torch in hand, waiting to make the signal. There was an open scuttle near his feet, which he was prepared to use quickly at the flash of the first gun. Fortunately for all concerned, the authorities saw what our preparations meant, and wisely determined to wait until they could gain peaceable possession of the vessel, which they eventually did, after giving suitable guarantees for her conduct.

When conditions permitted, we started for the south, intending to stop at such Japanese ports as we were permitted to visit *en route*. These were Kobé and Nagasaki, and three miles inland was our limit, which rule also applied at Yokohama. From Kobé, our first stopping place, I visited Osaka, a newly opened port, and the place where Admiral Bell had lately lost his life.

Dr. H. S. Pitkin, one of our assistant surgeons, and I obtained three days' leave, and thoroughly enjoyed every hour of it. There was not such a thing as a hotel known at Osaka, but we managed to find two rooms in which we could sleep and store our plunder; the days we spent cruising about over the queer old town, buying such curios as struck our fancy. Lacquered ware, rare and old and valuable, was offered to us at every turn for almost nothing. We were among the first visitors, and the market had not yet been spoiled by the rich globe-trotter. The simple and honest natives offered their goods to us at the same price they sold them to their own people, and I am sure our customs officers would have grown green with envy if they had seen the things we purchased, which, by the way, they never did.

Pitkin was an enthusiastic collector of coins, and during our first day's ramble we came across an old Japanese merchant who had followed the same line all his life. He showed us his collection with great pride, and well he might, for it was one of the finest in Japan, containing about one thousand coins, a few of them dating before the time of Christ. The old man had no intention of parting with them at any price, but the doctor wanted them and wanted them badly; in fact, had made up his mind to have them. That night we counted up our funds, and found that we could spare one hundred Mexican dollars for the purchase. The next day we made the offer, which was politely refused. Then we stacked the silver dollars up in ten piles, and then in twenty, and then scattered them about, making them ring as much as possible. Meanwhile the merchant eyed the money, and each time we stacked it up we could see a change in his face. In the end the silver won the day, and the coins, case and all, were taken to our rooms, where the old man went over them for the last time, and tearfully left us in possession of what it had taken him a lifetime to collect. We could exchange our silver for Japanese gold, weight for weight, at that time. What we had offered him was probably more money than he had ever seen before at one time. The value of the collection was very great. It is now the property of one of our leading universities.

On our arrival at Nagasaki, which we reached by way of the beautiful inland sea, we found the city crowded with Japanese troops of the Mikado party. The English flagship was present, and there was much excitement over the killing of two of her men. A party of soldiers had found them on shore somewhat the worse for liquor, and at once cut their heads off, left their bodies in the gutter, and put the heads on the curbstone in front of the consul's house. The admiral demanded immediate satisfaction, which he of course received; but as the same thing was liable to happen to any foreign officer or man who was caught on shore at night, the prospect was not pleasing. The governor of the province represented to Admiral Rowan that our officers would be safe if they wore two swords—that all Japanese officers wore two, and that only enlisted men were one-swordmen. The admiral replied that he could arrange matters in a simpler and more satisfactory way, and immediately issued an order that all officers visiting the shore should wear in their belts a loaded Remington breech-loading pistol, and if upon meeting a Japanese soldier he carried his hand to his sword hilt, they were to shoot him at once. This was done because the sword was never unsheathed except for use; a Japanese who drew his sword and returned it without drawing blood was disgraced. A copy of this order, with a letter of explanation, was sent to the governor, and though we remained many weeks in Nagasaki, none of us were ever molested.

The contrast between the Japanese and their neighbours, the Chinese, was at this time very striking and vastly in favour of the former people. Since then it has become even more marked. The leading characteristic of the Japanese was honesty. It was in striking contrast with the trickiness, not to say dishonesty, of the Chinese as a race. During my whole stay in Japan I was constantly tramping about the country, shooting or wandering over strange cities, picking up curios here and there. In all my experience I never had anything stolen from me, though at times I intrusted articles of all sorts to the first small boy I met on the street, to be delivered to my boat or at my hotel, often miles away. Every article was promptly and carefully delivered. If such an experiment had been tried in China, everything would have been stolen.

When out shooting I generally had with me a Japanese lad of eighteen or nineteen years of age, and we frequently went far beyond the three-mile limit which was supposed to fence us in; but uniform kindness and courtesy were what I always received from the people among whom I found myself. A few words of explanation from my faithful boy always secured such food as they had, and frequently quarters for the night. The houses even of the poorest classes were always scrupulously clean, while those of the Chinese were exactly the opposite. The Chinaman was a dandy in dress, but personally vilely dirty, while the Japanese was plainly dressed, but in person as clean and neat as soap and water could make him. The Chinese had a certain shrewd imitativeness which was much misunderstood, and even taken by many persons for an indication of genius. The Japanese, as a people, had the genius of progress and expansion, with the result that in thirty years from the time of which I am writing they have advanced by steady strides, until they hold a proud place among the leading nations. In that short space of time they have organized an army which is second only to the German in its general staff, and armed as well as the best. Its fighting ability was shown in a winter campaign against the Chinese, which elicited the admiration of all military critics. At the same time their navy became the wonder of modern times in its phenomenal development. It is true that the magnificent ships were, many of them, paid for in borrowed money or bonds; but the way they fight their guns and handle their fleet will prevent any sudden foreclosing of mortgages by foreign countries. To-day they have as fine docks and dockyards as any nation, and can build and arm their own ships. When one thinks that all this has been done in less than thirty years, the conclusion can not be avoided that Japan has broken the record in expansion, and must be seriously considered in any future settlement of the Eastern question.

I had occasion to witness some of the capital punishments of Japan. When we first visited the country

An Execution

the theft of more than thirty dollars' worth of anything was considered sufficient ground for beheading the thief. I saw one of these executions when four men had their heads cut off for various offences. One of them was a young boatman who had often served me in my shooting trips about Yokohama Bay. The execution ground was a cleared space in the edge of a wood on the side of the public road four or five miles from Yokohama, and was in no way screened from the view of the public. When I arrived on the spot, about sunrise, everything was in readiness for the execution. Four small pits were dug in the ground and the earth excavated from them neatly levelled off, and a bucket of water placed near each. The judges who sentenced the men to death sat in a row in front of these pits and about fifteen feet away. The executioner, who had cut off more than one thousand heads, was in attendance, and very proud of his sword, the keen edge of which he examined from time to time. The hilt was carefully wrapped with very fine white linen.

The populace—men, women, and children—stood about the inclosure and conversed in low tones. The four condemned men were brought to the spot, and quickly seated opposite the pits with their legs crossed under them tailor fashion. The executioner advanced to the man on the left of the line, held the heavy, keen-edged sword over his neck for a moment, and then, bringing his left hand up to the long hilt or handle, gave the sword a sharp, quick, downward jerk toward him and the man was dead. The head fell into the pit, the trunk dropping forward; the blood from the body was discharged into the same place. Stepping quickly to the second man, his head dropped off the same way, and so on to the third and fourth. The four men were dead inside of two minutes after they were seated near the pits. Then an attendant stepped up to the first pit, took the head by the hair, dowsed it into the bucket of water, which removed all blood stains, and then held it up, the face toward the judges, who nodded in token that the man was dead. The head was then placed on a post by the side of the road, as were the others after each had been subjected to the inspection of the judges, and here they remained under guard for three days as a warning to others. The bodies were doubled up, placed in coarse bags, and buried on the spot. The whole job was businesslike and quickly performed.

If there is anything in public executions calculated to deter others from committing crime, Japan certainly has the correct method. What I saw on this occasion was in striking contrast to the hanging method as practised in most of the States in America. These poor Japanese convicts were killed as quickly as possible, and that they experienced no pain was evident from a glance at the dead faces, each one of which bore a smile. The mode of execution was meant to be quick and merciful, just the opposite of the Chinese method. I could not help thinking that it was far ahead of our practice, where a poor devil is sung over and prayed over for days, then marched to the scaffold, offered time to address the few newspaper correspondents and prison officials present, and then choked to death. Electrocution, which is now the legal process in some States, is more

Indifference to Death

merciful, but even the electric spark is slow in producing death when compared with severing the spinal column by the keen edge of a Japanese sword in the hands of a man expert in its use. The interval between the time when the man is in full possession of all his faculties and when he is stone dead is inconceivably small. When the men who were executed at the time of which I have just written were brought on to the execution ground, the young boatman who attended me so often looked up at me and smilingly said, "Good-bye." The Japanese have no fear of death, and in this one characteristic alone I found them like the Chinese. This young boatman had, while under the influence of too much *saki*, a Japanese liquor made from rice, overhauled a countryman near Yokohama and pulled him from his chair, which he appropriated for himself and rode in it to the city. He was charged with highway robbery, and though I did all in my power to save him he was convicted, sentenced, and executed.

CHAPTER XII

HONG-KONG AND THE PHILIPPINES

AFTER leaving Nagasaki, which we did with great regret, we anchored in Hong-Kong once more. Our men had not yet been granted shore leave generally, and, as this seemed a favourable place for the purpose, they were sent on shore by watches, starboard watch one day and port watch the next, as was then the custom in the service. Naturally, trouble quickly followed. The American Jacky has no love and little respect for a policeman. The absurd-looking Mohammedan policeman of the Hong-Kong force excited his mirth, and when he had secured a sufficient number of drinks he proceeded to have fun with him. In a short time the turbans and clubs were all in possession of the sailors, and it was not until an English regiment had been put on duty that they were corralled on the dock. Then they fought out their personal difficulties, and were brought on board much battered and the worse for wear, but having had, as they claimed, "a bang-up good time." Five or six months more on board ship fitted them excellently for just such another spree, and they had it when the time came. Fortunately, we do things differently now.

Among my other possessions I was the happy

owner of a fine bull terrier—"Jowler"—who could whip any dog in China; at least he had whipped every one that had fought with him. He was a great pet with every one on board ship, from the admiral down, and was really a finely bred, beautifully trained dog. In all the shore riots and pleasures he was an important part. The men would come to the mast and ask for shore leave for him just as they did for themselves. They always saw to it that he whipped everything he came in contact with, man or beast, and the result was that he would tackle a whole menagerie, if the chance offered. After shore leave he generally went into the hands of the doctor, along with Jacky, to have his cuts sewed up and needed repairs made before he appeared on deck.

Our relations with the English military people were strictly official during the earlier days of the cruise, owing to the bitter feeling engendered by the position of the English Government during the civil war; but a hint from their Government changed all this and we became very friendly. They were courteous, hospitable gentlemen, and we enjoyed their mess dinners wonderfully. On their part they always seemed willing to come to us and make a night of it whenever we were ready. On the 22d of February we gave the finest entertainment we had so far attempted, seating over one hundred guests, most of them foreign officers. We broke up at 1 A. M., after a beautiful evening long to be remembered. One of our English army guests jumped overboard and swam ashore, where I delivered his sword and cap to him the next day over a glass of brandy and soda. Long years afterward I met him at the United Service Club in London, old and dignified, and looking as if he had never been young. He did, however, cheer up over another glass of brandy and soda and the old Hong-Kong episode.

From Hong-Kong we ran down to Manila to have a look at the Spaniards and their great Eastern colony. Owing to the size of our ship, now named the Delaware, we had to anchor well out in the bay, and visiting the shore was quite an undertaking; but once on shore we found ourselves well repaid for our trouble.

The city was beautiful, and under Spanish military rule very safe, and on the surface clean and orderly. The *cafés* were excellent, and the music of the bands in the afternoon made the Lunetta a favourite promenade. All Manila turned out to look at each other, in which it did not differ from any other city where people had so little to do. The markets were good, there being at all seasons fine fish and splendid tropical fruits in abundance, principal among which was the mangosteen, that queen of all fruits. The tobacco was of that peculiar light quality which grows on a smoker's taste. We were all slaves to cheroots before the cruise was over.

The Spanish authorities gave us a ball, which was largely attended, and added much to the enjoyment of our visit. We, of course, returned the compliment and had the pleasure of meeting on board our ship not only all the officials and their families, but also some of the better class of natives—*mestizos*, as they are called—who danced and behaved generally most becomingly. The ladies were shod with sandals only, which gave one a good view of their beautiful feet. After a delightful visit of two weeks we again sailed down the grand bay of Manila, little dreaming that an American admiral would one day make it celebrated in the annals of naval warfare by showing to the world what destruction modern ships and modern guns could cause when properly handled.

We returned to Hong-Kong, and, as the hot season approached, retraced our way toward Japan and the north. The two leading elements in all efforts to civilize so-called barbarous natives—cards and whisky—were in full blast in all the ports we visited, except Kobé, where they had not yet had time to take root. One had only to stick to the two long enough and he was sure to be ruined, for the card players were expert and the whisky was bad. My tastes ran rather toward out-of-door sports—boating, shooting, and fishing—and I found my amusement in this line; not that I did not drink and gamble somewhat—I could not afford to be so much out of the fashion—but most of my spare time was given to athletics. The shooting all along the coast was excellent; snipe always on the marshes, easy to get at, and delicious for the table. Golden pheasants were in great numbers only a short distance from Shanghai, and a house-boat party after them was one of the pleasantest sprees one could have. We killed them sometimes as many as one hundred to the gun per day. The natives were not allowed to use firearms, and the game in consequence was plentiful and easy to get.

The trapping of all sorts of wild things by both Chinese and Japanese was very skilfully done, particularly so by the Chinese, who would at any time bring us all the teal ducks or snipe we wanted alive from their traps. They were not yet sufficiently civilized to charge us three prices for things, so that we lived reasonably well at a very moderaate cost. The Japanese caught most of their game with a gum which they called *torri-mouchi*. Even deer were caught in this way; any bird or animal that touched it was sure to stick fast until it was removed by cutting off the foot. I never tried the gum, but I certainly had some wonderful days in Japan with my gun. My favourite sport was snipe-shooting, but I sometimes went after ducks and waders, such as curlew and plover, and when such occasions offered, our wardroom table was sure to be good for some days afterward.

Once only did I meet with any mishap. Two companions, officers of the ship, were with me, when one of them, in his anxiety to kill all the plover that were in a flock, got me in range with them and loaded me up pretty well with shot. Fortunately, none of them struck about my eyes, and half an hour's careful work with a sharp knife removed them all. The officer was dreadfully mortified, and I really believe suffered more than I did. On another occasion the marine officer, a very fat, heavy man, walked into a quicksand while we were shooting snipe and came near losing his life. I found him when he had sunk in up to his armpits, and my boatman and I had all we could do to pull him out.

My boating experiences would make a very long story were I to tell them all. The admiral's barge, a

fourteen-oared cutter, was built at the New York
Navy Yard, and it was soon seen that she was a very
fast boat, both under sail and oars. I was very fond
of racing, and naturally it fell to my lot to take charge
of and train the racing crew. We had plenty of splendid men to choose from, and in a few months I had a
crew that could pull six miles from start to finish
without distress. I used to say that one could crack
walnuts on any of them without marking his skin,
and I really believe one could have done so. They
were a fine, sandy lot of chaps, and were never beaten
while we were on the station, though we challenged
all the ships we met, and raced with all who dared to
accept.

Probably the most notable race we pulled was that
in Hong-Kong on the French emperor's birthday.
The French admiral was determined to take the championship away from us, and to do so had built a
sixteen-oared mahogany barge, which was light and
supposed to be very fast. The crew trained at night,
so that it was impossible to get an idea of what they
were like; but I succeeded at last, by watching them
closely and surprising them in the darkness, in getting a line on them. I was convinced that we could
beat them, and advised all our people to bet that
way, which they did; and as the betting was at long
odds on the French boat, many of us did not have to
trouble the paymaster for months. As the day for
the race approached, the flagships of the different nations—French, English, American, and Russian—were
moored on the course, where all could have a good
view of the race from start to finish. Six boats were

entered—two French, two English, and two American—and the distance to be pulled was six miles, three miles away and a turn. I was lucky enough to draw the position next the starting boat, which insured my getting off promptly at the word. Next to me was the French barge, on which so much money had been bet. She certainly did look very fit and dangerous, but six miles is a long way, and I knew that I had wind and muscle in my boat. The day before the race every man in the Delaware drew all the money that was due him, and bet it, of course. Deck buckets of silver dollars were taken on board the French flagship, sized up against theirs, and placed under guard. Everybody was betting, and all, except our crew, were backing the French boat to win.

The first mile of the course was packed on either side with boats crowded with people and covered with flags, and must have presented a beautiful sight to those who had time to observe it. I was not able to see much of it. I was busy watching that red-coloured French barge, and occasionally glancing at the fourteen hard-set, anxious faces in my boat. At last we were on the line, oars pointed forward, feet firmly braced against the stretchers, mouths shut like steel traps, and every muscle and nerve tense almost to the point of breaking. "Are you ready?" and then "Go!" came from the starter. With one beautiful flash of the oars we all caught the water together, and were off. I could feel my heart thump in my throat as I saw, with one eye, the light French-built boat shoot out half a length ahead of us, and with the other eye the fourteen faces all turned on mine. Three hard,

Midshipman and Captain.

quick strokes had set us going, and for a moment the red barge seemed to be tied to us, so even was our pace; then I could see my starboard bow-oar slowly, inch by inch, dip out ahead of her. About five hundred yards from the start was a bunch of American boats crowded with yelling lunatics, and as I approached them I spoke a word to the crew, signaled the stroke to rise to forty, and before the Frenchman knew what had happened to him he had our wash, and, barring accidents, the race was won. Then we settled down to our long, swinging thirty-two strokes, which were to last the rest of the distance. The French crew began yelling when we passed them, and I believe they kept it up to the finish.

It struck me as about the worst use I had ever known a racing crew to put their lungs to, but it pleased me immensely to have them do it. At the turning buoy we were thirty seconds ahead, and on the pull in we gained one minute. Crossing the finish line, I tossed oars for a second as the gun flashed, and then pulled to the ship at the same racing speed. As I shot alongside, the tackles were hooked and the boat run up to the davits, crew and all. All hands tumbled out on deck, and when the French barge crossed the line our boat was quietly hanging at the davits, as if nothing had happened. It was only a boat race, it is true, but it was a grand one, and we won it. The boat from the Iroquois came in second, so we had all the honours as well as all the money.

While we were anchored at Hong-Kong news came of the sinking of the Oneida, one of our squadron and the " chum " ship of the Delaware. She had been run down by the English mail steamer Bombay in Yokohama Bay and all hands lost; at least so the story ran. Later and more reliable news was to the effect that the ship and most of her officers and men were lost, but that about fifty of them had been saved. We were under way by daylight the following morning, bound for the scene of the disaster. As we entered Yokohama Bay we stopped and lowered a boat, and I was sent to report what I could make out of the wreck. The main truck, the top of the main royal mast, was just awash, and as I held on to it and looked down into the clear water I could see the yards and the neatly furled sails, but nothing else. The ship was resting on the bottom on her keel, upright, the grave of nearly two hundred as brave hearts as ever sailed under the dear old flag.

The court that followed showed clearly how the Bombay had carelessly cut the Oneida down and sunk her, and how her captain had done a thing most unusual for men of his race—sailed away and left the victims of his carelessness to drown. But in drowning they reflected only credit on their country, for they stood at their quarters and went down like men, without a whimper. We buried some of the poor chaps, but most of them were never recovered. The Bombay was fortunately not in Yokohama when we arrived; if she had been there, it would have required hard work to control our officers and men and prevent some sort of a demonstration against her. The Oneida was homeward bound when she was sunk, and her loss cast a gloom over the entire squadron.

My promotion to the grade of lieutenant commander came soon after we reached Hong-Kong, during the first year of the cruise. It was thought at first that I would be detached and ordered to some other vessel, but Admiral Rowan believed in keeping both officers and men in the ships in which they commissioned during the entire cruise when possible, and so I was not disturbed. Captain Ammen, who was respected and loved by all of us, was detached, and came home to be appointed chief of the Bureau of Navigation, and Captain Earl English transferred to us from the command of the Iroquois. He was one of the ablest seamen in the navy, and a prime favourite with officers and men. His tastes were for out-of-door sports, and he and I spent many happy hours tramping over the rice fields of China and Japan in search of game. Our cruise, continued until the summer of 1869, was nearly spent when we proceeded to Singapore, there to await the arrival of our relief, the steam frigate Colorado, Admiral John Rodgers.

CHAPTER XIII

SOME ORIENTAL DIVERSIONS

THE life in Singapore at this time was simply ideal, and I enjoyed it to the full. The climate was hot, but not unbearable, not even hurtful to those who could and would take reasonable care of themselves. No work was done during the heat of the day. One lived his life at night, so to speak, when the cool sea breeze made existence very enjoyable. The temperature varied only a few degrees—about three—during the year, say from one hundred and seven to one hundred and ten. So also at 10 P. M. the temperature ran from eighty to eighty-five during the year. The mornings were fine for sleeping, and if one remained carefully in the shade until late in the afternoon, he could enjoy the evening and night. Our men were thoroughly well drilled, and the admiral therefore reduced the exercises to the minimum.

The Colorado was much delayed in her passage out, so that we remained at our anchorage four months before she appeared. Every day had its pleasures for me, however. We were all invited to dine out every day, and sometimes had two or more invitations for the same day. We dined with all sorts of people, for every one was anxious to have us; native princes, foreign ministers, military messes, and civilians all asked us, and we went to them all, first and last. The governor was most hospitable, and I enjoyed many pleasant evenings with his charming daughters. One of the military bands furnished music every afternoon in the public square, and here we all met for an hour for the latest gossip, after which we drank tea somewhere and then prepared for dinner, which was the feature of the day.

Five of us hired a bungalow on shore, and regularly set up our establishment, which was a very simple one, but at the same time most comfortable and convenient. It was situated on the edge of the jungle near one of the best hotels, from which we obtained our meals. It was, of course, headquarters for all officers when on shore, particularly for those who had to remain ashore all night. We had only five beds, but they were very elastic, and could be made on occasion to hold a great many men. Cobras and tarantulas were very common " varmints," and no one therefore slept much on the floor or porches. Snake-charmers, jugglers, and fakirs generally abounded, and some of them could always be found near our bungalow.

One morning, as five of us sat taking our morning fruit and coffee, the Chinese attendant broke into the room almost paralyzed with fear, screaming, " Cobra! cobra!" In a moment we had located a large, vicious-looking reptile in the back yard, and the happy thought came to some one to send for a snake-charmer and test his qualities on this specimen, which had evidently just crawled out of the jungle. In five minutes, or possibly less, the charmer appeared, and proceeded to do the neatest trick I ever witnessed. He was a Mohammedan, about forty years of age, stripped to the waist, and carrying a sealskin bag with the fur on the inside, in which he had a large collection of cobras and other snakes. He stood quietly watching the newcomer for a few moments, evidently sizing him up, and then, producing a small reed fife, began blowing it, making a sharp monotonous noise. At the same time an assistant some yards behind him beat slowly on a small tom-tom, or drum. The two advanced slowly to the middle of the small inclosure, and when fifteen or twenty feet from their quest seated themselves quietly on the ground and continued their music, or, more properly speaking, noise. The cobra in the meantime was much excited, and showed signs of fight. He rapidly coiled himself, raised a foot or two of his body vertically, spread his hood, and generally looked very ugly. The monotonous noise of the performers continued, and the cobra shifted his position first to the side, and then directly toward the charmers, always watching them closely with his keen, scintillating eyes. After half an hour of this play he was almost between the feet of the Mohammedan, and as he raised himself and spread his hood we all expected to see him strike and end the performance; but instead, the man reached out his hand, slowly seized the cobra by the neck, and, rising with him, held him limp in the air for a moment, and then deposited him in the bag with his other snakes. The Chinaman had in the meantime bolted; nothing could induce him to stay longer in such a dangerous spot. The assistant took his departure, and the charmer, with his bag of snakes, stepped into our dining room for a parting drink.

The unfortunate thought came to one of our men that it would be a good idea to get the Mohammedan drunk to see what he would do; so he prepared a dose for him that was very effective. He poured a good stiff drink of brandy into a beer glass, and then filled it with gin instead of water. The charmer took kindly to the drink, and in a short time rolled out of his chair on to the floor very drunk, and was soon fast asleep. The bag of snakes had not been thought of up to this time, but it also fell, and the inhabitants quickly spread over the floor. In the meantime five American officers took to the table, and drawing their feet up carefully, remained there until the snake-charmer slept off his dose. He snored quietly while the snakes crawled over and around him, but it was a long time before he finally came to himself, secured his pets, and took them away. We did not repeat that experiment.

I went one Sunday to breakfast with an English officer who was quartered some distance in the country among the hills in a very neat one-story bungalow. I arrived early, found my bachelor friend in his bath, and, lighting a cheroot, sat waiting for him to show up. In a few moments I heard a sharp exclamation from him, and on turning my head saw him in his bath dress looking back into the bathroom, which he had just left. He had discovered a cobra, which had been under the tub while he was in it, and was now reared up and looking into the tub. It was enough to give one the shivers to think what a close call he had had. My friend left me for a few moments, and then came back with a mongoose, or jungle cat, which is the deadly enemy of the cobra. The small cat when released seemed to be all tail, but he knew his business, and did it in a way to excite my unbounded admiration. The fight between the two was short, but very exciting. Several times it looked as if the cobra must win, but the cat managed, somehow, to avoid the lightning-like strokes, and finally fastened on the back of the snake's neck and killed it. I looked carefully under the table as I sat down to breakfast, to be sure that I should not have a cobra coiling himself in my lap before I had finished. The bite of this snake is so absolutely fatal that I never cared to take any chances with it.

While we were cruising in the waters about Java and Singapore we saw hundreds of the salt-water snakes said to be so deadly. Sometimes the sea would be dotted with them, swimming with the head well out of water, and diving always on the approach of the ship. Many tales were told of the ravages of these pests, which climbed up the chains or into the ports of vessels at anchor and stung people to death. I noticed that all the fishermen about Singapore carried long, heavy knives, which they told me were used in killing the snakes as the fishing nets were hauled in. We never succeeded in catching one, though we saw thousands of them.

Early in August, 1870, the admiral concluded that we had had enough of Singapore, so we said good-bye to all our friends who had entertained us so lavishly, and sailed for Batavia in the island of Java, where we drank no end of gin, and behaved generally after the fashion of the Dutch. I don't think any of us enjoyed our stay very much, as we were expecting our relief hourly, and took little interest in anything else. But the Colorado would not come, no matter how anxiously we looked for her; so the admiral, who was by this time tired of waiting, steamed over to the Straits Settlement in the Straits of Java, where we learned that she had passed in the day before bound for Singapore. Back we went as fast as steam and sails could carry us, and on our arrival found her there waiting for us.

The transfer of commands began at once and was soon completed, but before we sailed we must have one more boat race. The Colorado had brought out a barge which was considered very fast, and our admiral naturally wanted to have the fastest boat on the station to defend the championship we had held so long. I pulled under the bows of the newcomer and challenged, which was accepted, and a race arranged for the following day. Our racing crew had, of course, grown stale from the effects of climate and want of regular practice, but they were better than the Colorado's by long odds. As soon as I saw the boats in the water I felt a warning of the good licking we got. They beat us twenty seconds in four miles after one of the hardest races I was ever in. The boat did it, for our men were in good shape at the finish, while the other crew was pulled to a standstill. The Daring—that was her name—became afterward the most celebrated man-of-war cutter that was ever in the East. She beat everything she ever raced with, either under oars or sails; even the shell boats of the Shanghai Club could not hold her. When the race was over we pulled alongside the Colorado, and each man shouldered his oar with its silver bands on the blade, marched on board, and deposited it on the quarter-deck as a present to the newcomers. I had our beautiful black gamecock under my arm as a present to the admiral; it was the first time he had ever been in a race without crowing at the finish. Admiral Rodgers ordered a decanter of wine, which was placed on the capstan on the quarter-deck, and my crew drank success to the Daring. The racing days of the Delaware's boat were over, but we felt sure she had a worthy successor.

On August 22, 1870, we broke out our homeward-bound pennant, which was longer than the ship, catted our anchor with three cheers, and stood out of the harbour. Our China cruise was over, and none of us regretted either that we had had it or that it was behind us.

Our run across the Indian Ocean was truly a grand one. We held the trades fresh all the way to Cape Town, where we arrived and anchored without more serious mishap than the loss of a few light sails. After resting a week we again got under way and ran down to St. Helena, and all hands had a chance to see that celebrated and beautiful island. I paid a visit to Longwood and saw the various Napoleon relics, which a major of the French army took great pains to explain to me, not forgetting any of the incidents which reflected discredit on the emperor's English guardians.

Return to New York

Before we left, the mail steamer came in, and the major, taking one glance at the papers, burst into tears. Sedan had been added to the long list of French defeats. I could not help thinking as I walked back to my boat how fortunate it was for Germany that the real Napoleon was dead.

After leaving St. Helena we reached New York in forty-seven days, certainly a fine run for a ship dragging a four-bladed screw. As we entered the Narrows the Guerrière was made out inside the Hook, bound for Brazil. She saluted us with seventeen guns, which was the first intimation we had that Admiral Rowan had been made vice-admiral. Our officers and crew were wild with delight, and cheered until the admiral showed himself on deck. It was a splendid reward for his magnificent conduct during the civil war, and made solely on his merits. At the time it was done he was at sea, out of reach of anything like political influence, and not even where he could be communicated with. Once in our history, anyhow, the man who deserved it was made vice-admiral.

We anchored off the Battery for a few days, and then went to the navy yard, where we got rid of our trash—stripped the ship, put her out of commission, and paid off the crew. My dog "Jowler" was missing soon after the men left, and I never saw him again. Many months afterward I received a note from one of the racing crew begging me to forgive him for stealing my dog, and asking me if I ever came to Brooklyn to come and see him at a certain saloon which he mentioned. He said he loved the dog so that he simply had to have him; that he knew I would not sell him, so he had to steal him.

I was granted a short leave after this cruise, and before it was up was ordered to duty in the Ordnance Department of the Washington Navy Yard, where I had interesting work during the winter. Admiral Goldsborough, an officer of the old school, was in command of the yard, which insured a lively time for all hands; and Commander F. M. Ramsay, the inspector of ordnance, was not noted for allowing those under his command to neglect their work or spend many idle moments.

It was in the course of this winter that I became engaged to Miss Charlotte Taylor, of Washington, daughter of Mr. Franck Taylor, and sister of my classmate, Harry C. Taylor, now one of the most distinguished officers of our navy.

CHAPTER XIV

A NEW VIEW OF ANNAPOLIS

In July of the following year I was married, and after spending the summer at the North, was assigned to duty at that Mecca of young married people, the Naval Academy at Annapolis, Maryland. Things had changed wonderfully since my school days, and during my first year there I found that I had to study nearly all night in order to instruct the midshipmen during the day. I say "instruct" the midshipmen, but there really was very little instruction given them. It required all my time to hear them tell me what they knew or did not know. The system was afterward changed to a much better one, under which really valuable instruction was given. During the second year of my detail I had more leisure, and a fine setter dog and a catboat helped me to bear the most undesirable duty I have ever had in the navy. Wild ducks and quail were to be had, and I thoroughly enjoyed getting them, and did get a good many first and last. I bred and trained my own dogs, and in this training at least I was successful.

It was during this year that the first coloured cadet was appointed to the Naval Academy. He came upon us suddenly, and before we knew it he had passed his examination and appeared in uniform, with a coloured girl as his companion. The place was in an uproar at once, and the excitement among all classes was intense. As I walked along the row of officers' quarters, all the coloured servants were at the front gates discussing the news. When I reached my own quarters my dining-room boy, a small, copper-coloured imp, with his eyes sticking out of his head, said to me, " My Lord, Mr. Evans, a nigger done enter the Naval Academy! " That was what we were all feeling, though we expressed ourselves somewhat differently.

The first consideration was, of course, to see that no bodily harm came to the lad, who had not been wisely advised, and did not behave himself in a way to induce respect from those around him. Our second thought was for the reputation of the naval school, that nothing unworthy its grand record should take place. The great danger was from the system of hazing, which had grown to very deplorable proportions, and which we were bending our energies to destroy. In our efforts to protect the coloured boy we ran into the error of favouring him too much, and he soon came to give himself undue importance. He fancied that he was an issue which the authorities of the school dared not meet—which, though a natural mistake to make, was a fatal one for him in the end. After being dismissed several times by court-martial, and each time restored by the Secretary of the Navy, who could not bring himself to believe that politics had nothing to do with the sentence of the court— how should he, poor man?—the boy was really unbearable.

Coloured Cadets

In the same class was a youngster from New York city, a bootblack by profession, who had been appointed to the academy by Mr. S. S. Cox, who represented a district in Congress. Some of us thought that politics might have had something to do with this appointment. At any rate, the two lads, the coloured representative of the great State of South Carolina and the bootblack from the great city of New York, were appointed to room together, with the result that each succeeded in having the other dismissed in a few months. I well remember one night when I was on duty as officer in charge of cadet quarters, that the coloured cadet was reported as missing. It was in the middle of a cold, raw night, and after a long, careful search no sign could be found of him. I was about to report the matter to the commandant of cadets, when I heard a curious barking among some tall trees in the grounds, as if a dog were tied up. On investigation, I found the missing cadet in the top of a tree, very scantily clad, and barking with all his might because some senior classmen had told him to do it. It was the only time I ever knew him to be really hazed, and it was impossible to punish the guilty ones, because the boy himself refused to assist in any way in bringing them to punishment.

We all breathed easier when the two of them, black and bootblack, departed for their homes. The question of colour was one we were not prepared to tackle, and I don't see that we are any better prepared for it to-day than we were in 1872. The antagonism of the two races seems greater now than it was then.

CHAPTER XV

Two years at Annapolis was all I could bear, and I looked about me for a ship and sea service. The sloop of war Shenandoah, of the Mediterranean fleet, was short a navigator, and the Department was good enough to order me to her in that capacity. I packed up my guns, gave away my dogs, sold my catboat, and with my wife and young daughter sailed on the Cunarder Parthia, Captain Watson. I reported for duty at Gibraltar early in August.

The Shenandoah was a sloop of war built during the civil war. She carried a good battery, could steam about six knots an hour, and roll forty degrees each way twenty times a minute and keep it up for hours at a time. When I joined her she was commanded by Captain Clarke H. Wells, and my old classmate McGregor was executive officer. My duties as navigator were light, and the prospects of a pleasant cruise very promising.

The ship was somewhat notorious for the part she had played in the revolution then being fought out in Spain. She was at anchor in Cadiz, when one of the captured Spanish ironclads came in and anchored. The rebellious crew had murdered all the

officers, and with the red flag flying, and a new crew
of soldiers on board, entered the harbour and threatened all sorts of things under penalty of bombardment. A council of foreign officers was called on
board the English flagship, and it was unanimously
decided to ask the American captain to blow her up
if she should attempt to carry out her threats. Captain Wells accepted this task promptly, as he had himself decided to do it before the council was called. He
got his ship under way, and, anchoring close to the
ironclad, informed her commanding officer that as he
flew no recognised flag he would not permit him either
to get under way or bombard as he had threatened,
and if he attempted to do so he would blow him out
of the water. Wells then opened communication with
our minister in Madrid, and actually held the ship
under his guns until she was turned back to the Spanish navy.

I found a large English garrison at Gibraltar, and
a most hospitable lot they were. Their mess dinners
were very enjoyable affairs, and they seemed more
than anxious always to have our officers as their
guests. I attended one soon after I arrived which
lasted all night. I reached my ship at 4.20 in the
morning. The dinner was given by the officers of
the Thirty-first Regiment, whose mess outfit and plate
were as fine as any I had up to that time seen. The
quarters were comfortable and handsomely furnished,
and the service fully up to the standard of the English
army. The officers were a well-educated and cultured
lot of hard-drinking chaps, who seemed ready for any
sort of a job that might turn up. They owned a fine

pack of hounds, and rode after them several days each week over the rough country beyond the neutral zone. I was cordially invited to join them, but, not wishing to come to my end in that way, excused myself on the ground that I had neither red coat nor spurs.

Toward the end of August the Wachusetts arrived, with directions for Captain Wells to run up to Cartagena to see what was going on, which we did, stopping at various ports on the way. At Cartagena we found quite a large fleet assembled. The Spanish rebels, who held the place and all the heavy works surrounding it, had seized two steamers, merchant vessels, for some imaginary offence, and declared their intention of confiscating them. Admiral Yelverton, of the English navy, commanding the Mediterranean fleet, had notified them that on a certain day he meant to take the two steamers to sea and deliver them to their rightful owners, and that they must not be moved in the meantime. In reply, the Spaniards said that if Admiral Yelverton attempted any such move, they would engage him with their forts and ironclad fleet. We were lying in Escombrera Bay, where we could see every move on either side. The forts frowned down on us from a great height, and as the Spaniards shifted gun after gun to bear on the English fleet, and their ironclads prepared for action, it looked as if we might see some exciting work before the episode was closed. The shores near us were bleak and forbidding in the extreme, not a sign of vegetation anywhere. The only buildings in sight were a few silver-smelting works.

Monday forenoon we tripped our anchor and stood

down toward the entrance of the harbour, so that we might be in better position to witness the fight, which many expected to see. I was not one of them. I knew what the English would do, and I believed the Spaniards would back down when the time came for action. The English fleet was cleared for action and, as we steamed past them, looked very grim and businesslike. Promptly at noon, the hour set by the admiral for the movement, the fleet got under way, the ironclad division formed around the two merchant steamers, their anchors were broken out, and they steamed away to sea with the English flag flying on each of them. As they were escorted out by the ironclads, and gained some distance from the port, a division of English gunboats stood slowly in toward the forts, turned deliberately, and steamed away after the fast-disappearing admiral. The Spaniards stood by their loaded guns. The huge ironclads sizzled with steam and smoked viciously from their stacks, but not a shot was fired. Admiral Yelverton had done his work beautifully.

The Spaniards were wise enough to see that it was not well to monkey with such a buzz saw as the sea power of England. This action of the admiral was much questioned at the time, but was finally approved by his Government, which gave it the stamp of right. He claimed, and the Spanish rebels admitted, that the two vessels, seized from loyal Spanish subjects, were to be fitted out as privateers to prey on Spanish commerce. He further claimed, which was a fact beyond question, that they were to sail under a flag not recognised by any nation, hence they would be pirates, and for this reason he seized them. There seems to have been good ground for his action.

From Cartagena we cruised along the Spanish coast as far as Barcelona, where we found the flagship Wabash, flying the flag of Admiral Case, commanding the squadron. Personally we were glad to see the dear old gentleman, but officially we would rather he had been somewhere else. Whenever a number of ships get together there is always a lot of work to be done by surveys, and the navigators seem to be traditionally the men to do it. We surveyed old stoves, carpets, curtains, pans and pots, until I felt myself quite competent to run a shop in Chatham Street. As soon as we arrived we received notice that the admiral would inspect us in a few days, and that meant incessant work until the inspection was completed. We had in our crew representatives of all the nations of Europe, and some from Asia. It was difficult to make one's self understood without the use of at least two or three languages. This was caused by keeping the ship on the station long after the time of enlistment of her proper crew had expired, and was a most unhappy condition. We were moored in Barcelona Harbour between two ironclads, English on one side of us and Austrian on the other, and we could see that our extra work was interesting them. They watched us all the time, and were evidently very curious to see what the Yankes were up to.

Admiral Case was a great believer in torpedoes, and decided that we should fire one on our inspection. The spar torpedo—" a bag of powder on the end of a pole "—was the kind of infernal machine then in favour; but so far none had been exploded in the Mediterranean, and we were to have the distinction of being the first to do it. We had no torpedoes to work with—only an old-fashioned firing machine and a small quantity of insulated wire; the rest I had to make as best I might. After messing myself up with pitch and soluble rubber for three days, I reported that my torpedo was ready, and the inspection began. Our work was fairly well done, considering the crew we had, but our condition in the mind of the admiral and his official report depended largely on the success of the torpedo. At the proper moment I received the order, " Fire the starboard torpedo! " as if we had a dozen on tap. This was to impress the foreigners, who were watching us intently. Admiral Case had a fine sense of humour.

My pitched-over water-breaker, containing one hundred pounds of old black powder, was launched on the end of a long spar and sunk to a depth of about ten feet. Then I touched the firing key, and there was a real commotion for all hands. The explosion which followed instantly shook the ship—in fact, all the ships in the harbour—quite thoroughly, threw a fine column of water two hundred feet in the air, and covered the decks of the Austrian, who was to leeward of us, with very filthy mud blown up from the bottom. The admiral considered it all very successful, complimented me on my work, and ordered that each ship of the squadron should prepare and fire one torpedo each month. It is hard to believe, in these days of perfect-running Whiteheads and Howells, that I am relating what actually occurred on a United States vessel in

1873. Other nations were no better off than we, if as well.

Before leaving Barcelona I determined to witness some of the shows which amused the people, and as Sunday was the great day for that sort of thing, selected it for my outing. I hope I may never spend another such Sunday. First I visited a combination fight—chickens first, then " bull baiting," and finally a dog fight, each more brutal than the other. The bull baiting consisted in tying a bull to a post in the centre of an inclosure by means of a ring fastened through his nose, and then turning loose on him a number of savage bulldogs. The poor beast was unable to defend himself, and soon succumbed to his tormentors. A lean-looking old donkey was then introduced, and the dogs let loose on him. He evidently had more sense than the bull, for he succeeded in killing one dog with his teeth and two with his heels before they finally pulled him down. I regretted very much that it was not men instead of dogs he had demolished. Then came the dog fight, which was a very noisy affair, not on account of the dogs that were fighting, but by reason of the curs surrounding the pit. Almost every cur had a smaller cur under his arm —smaller, of course, and much less brutal and savage than his master. I fittingly wound up the day by visiting a large gambling hell, where I lost a few pesetas, and was chased out on the roof by a gang of thugs, who seemed anxious to put a knife or two in me. When I reached the ship I felt that I had learned something of Spanish customs, and was impressed with the necessity of a bath, both moral and physical.

Hunting in Morocco

From Barcelona we hurried down to Alicante to see the bombardment of that place by the rebel ships. We were so slow, however, that we arrived the day after the fight. There were no forts to be seen when at daylight the bombardment began; but the people on shore had mounted some heavy guns in a masked battery and served them so well that the fleet was driven off before sundown, with quite a list of killed and wounded. The town suffered somewhat, but no lives were lost. The bombardment was caused by the refusal of the authorities to pay the large sum of money demanded of them by the rebel government.

Upon our arrival at Tangiers, Morocco, the American consul, Colonel Mathews, arranged a hunting party for Captain Wells, and I was fortunate enough to be asked to join it. A tribe of Moors furnished the attendants, three camels carried our tents and mess outfit, and we, four of us, followed on horseback. The attendants, cooks, hunters, etc., numbered about fifty. When we had gone some seventy-five miles into the country we struck the hunting ground and the fun began. I had determined to shoot from my horse, as the cover was very thick and the weather hot enough to make the work of getting through it hard for a lame man. Colonel Mathews assured me that the horse, a thoroughbred Arabian, would probably break my neck if I fired from his back, but I had my own views about that. As we were leaving our camp in the morning for our first day's shoot, two partridges got up under my horse's nose and I downed them both, but a second later found myself sitting on the ground. When I fired I took the precaution to throw both my feet out of the stirrups. The horse squatted down and jumped from under me as if he had been greased, and then ran away. He was finally caught, and, after half an hour's training, stood fire like a veteran. I shot from his back every day while we were out, and I am sure he learned to enjoy it. I certainly did. We were shooting the African red-legged partridge, and they were in great numbers. The Moors were spread out like a picket line, with the gunners stationed along at regular intervals. As the line advanced, the flight of birds was almost constant and the banging of the guns incessant, the Moors acting as beaters and retrievers.

Each morning the camp was sent ahead to a spot selected by the colonel, and when we arrived, generally early in the afternoon, we found everything ship-shape and our lunch ready. Our trip was made during the Ramadan, or lenten season, and the Moors neither ate nor drank from sunrise to sunset, but during the night they made merry. Not so with us, however; we ate, drank, and made merry during the day, and slept during the night when the fleas would allow us to. These little pests were in the sand, and in such numbers and so active that we all bore the marks of them for weeks afterward. Colonel Mathews was a real *cordon bleu*, and the stews he made out of English hare, of which we killed a number, and mutton, were beyond criticism. We were all sorry when our week was up and we had to return to work.

The news of the seizure of the Virginius came about this time, and we received hurry orders to proceed to Nice, our storehouse and headquarters. We were off at once and had a fine run until we passed Port Mahon, when a long swell from the Gulf of Lyons and a rapidly falling barometer indicated trouble ahead. The captain had his family on board, and one of his daughters was to be married to an officer on our arrival at Nice; and as we would probably be hurried away as soon as we could take in stores, without much consideration for the young couple, it was desirable that we should make as much speed as possible. The storm warnings were not heeded, and at sundown we were on our course under all sails and steam. Half an hour afterward I was called on deck to shorten sail, but before I could do anything half the canvas was blown away. We finally got her under storm sails, but she rolled until the side seams were so opened that the water squirted into the officers' bunks in the wardroom. I was on deck, in my double capacity of executive officer and navigator, during the entire night, and I have rarely seen a worse one. The wind blew with hurricane force, and our crew of " dagos " and " rock scorpions " were of little use. Many of the officers had to go aloft to help furl the few sails we had managed to save, most of which afterward blew out of the furling lines and were lost. Our engines were of little use in the heavy sea, barely giving us steerage way, and as a whole the prospect was not pleasing. During the mid watch, about half past one, I was thrown on deck by the heavy lurching of the ship, and had the skin taken off my left knee in a spot just the size of the knee cap. When I had a chance the doctor took a look at it in the wardroom, and before I knew what he was about he clapped a large piece of thick adhesive plaster, which he had melted over a candle, on the raw flesh. It fairly fried me, and caused me intense pain for several days, as well as the use of very strong language.

At daylight the gale blew out, and the ship was really a picture to see. Bits of canvas remained on the yards where the sails had been, and other bits had whipped themselves about the rigging, and all were frayed out, until the Shenandoah looked as if she had been picking cotton. We arrived at Nice, however, after a time, the parson tied the knot for the captain's daughter, amid most beautiful surroundings and distinguished people, and in a few days we reported ready for sea again. War rumours were in the air, and when we said good-bye to our families none of us could even guess when we might see them again. It was a sad time for us all, but the women were so plucky and behaved so well that we were cheered by their example. No weeping and wailing for them—only pale faces and set teeth to show what they were suffering. How proud we were of our American wives!

The admiral sent us to sea as fast as we were coaled and ready to rendezvous at Gibraltar, where we arrived in five days, which was an excellent run for us. The weather tried to make up to us for its hard treatment a few days before, and the wind blew steadily in our favour all the way. Before leaving Nice our cabin party was increased by the arrival on board of the paymaster's wife, who came to look after her sick husband. I shall have more to say about him later on. When we reached Gibraltar war with Spain seemed probable, and orders were received to proceed immediately to Key West. These were somewhat accentuated when the admiral wired to know if there were any further orders, by the answer from the Department at Washington: "Obey your orders at once!" After this the ships got to sea rather promptly, we being the last to start. We ran down to Madeira, where we remained a week, and then headed for St. Thomas, in the West Indies.

The paymaster was very ill at this time and growing worse. Many of us, who knew him well, thought the best thing he could do would be to die—the best for all hands, particularly the wife. The captain, at the instigation of the doctor, purchased a goat, in order that the patient might have the advantage of fresh milk on the passage over. We left Madeira early in the morning, and at eleven o'clock that night the orderly turned me out, saying the captain wanted to see me on deck. I was at a loss to know what he could possibly want with me at that hour, but, supposing it to be something of importance, hurried into my clothes and reported to him on the quarter-deck, when the following conversation took place: "Evans, you know the paymaster is very ill, and may die?" "Yes, sir; I hope he will." "Well, he surely will unless he can have some goat's milk. I have sent for you to ask if you won't milk the goat for us. I know you can do it. So far we have not succeeded in getting a drop of milk from the beast, though she seems to have plenty." To this proposition I was naturally disposed to make a sharp reply, but, having a great regard for the captain, I only said, "I was not aware, sir, that it was any part of the navigator's duty to milk a goat." " Of course not, Evans, of course not; I ask you to do it as a matter of humanity, and to oblige me."

That, of course, settled the question, and down I went to tackle Mrs. Goat. I found her in a very excited state of mind apparently, having butted out the captain's steward and a marine orderly who had attempted to relieve her of her milk. One of them had tried to hold her while the other went for the milk. I remembered how the darkies in my young days had treated a cow under the same conditions, and procuring some warm water and exercising a little patience in the premises, soon relieved her of the milk, which was evidently giving her pain. This I sent to the cabin, and went back to my sleep. At breakfast in the morning the whole mess knew what had taken place, and I was, of course, the subject of no end of chaff.

In the afternoon I was again sent for and requested to milk the goat. I declared I would "be jiggered " if I would; but the captain again persuaded me to do it. This time I found the goat standing on her hind legs, snorting at the steward, who was being unmercifully jeered at by the crew because he failed in all his attempt to produce milk. It now looked as if I would have to go on milking the blessed goat all the way to St. Thomas. However, I found a young marine who seemed willing to assume my duties, if the goat would let him, and I succeeded finally in teaching him the trick of milking her successfully. This was my first and only experience with goats. The paymaster lived to reach the United States, where he died a few months later.

An Inefficient Fleet

On arriving at St. Thomas, we learned that the Virginius trouble was in a fair way of being settled without war. We were, however, to hurry on to Key West, where we had a large fleet assembled ready to fight in case diplomacy failed. The Ticonderoga was in port, just arrived from Brazil, and as soon as coaled we sailed in company and made a good run to the coast of Florida. The force assembled at Key West was the best, and indeed about all, we had. We had no stores or storehouses to speak of at this so-called base of supplies, and if it had not been so serious it would have been laughable to see our condition. We remained there several weeks, making faces at the Spaniards ninety miles away at Havana, while two modern vessels of war would have done us up in thirty minutes. As there was to be no war, the authorities in Washington allowed the foreign *attachés* to come and inspect us, and report our warlike condition to their different Governments. We were dreadfully mortified over it all, but we were not to blame; we did the best we could with what Congress gave us.

We had several weeks of fleet manœuvres, which were excellent both for officers and men, and then, as a grand wind up, a landing drill, which for some reason has become the favourite in our service over all legitimate work. On this occasion we landed about three thousand men, and, after spending an afternoon in a temperature running as high as 130° in the sun, returned to our ships and nursed our blisters for days afterward. I had command of the artillery, eighteen guns, which we hauled about seven or eight miles in the hot sun and through cactus so thick in some places that we had to blow it away with the guns in order to get them through. I found one of the men, an old quartermaster, with his shoes hanging around his neck. He said he wasn't going to ruin his shoes by wearing them over that cactus. Finally, we flanked the position of the imaginary enemy, and, with the expenditure of much old, condemned powder, carried it with a rush. Then we had a brigade dress parade, which would have impressed the Spanish regulars if they had seen it. This done, we went on board our ships, and the doctors pulled the cactus thorns out of us.

The time spent on this drill and the money it cost were not entirely wasted. We learned many things besides how to live on turtle steaks. We of the navy knew long before this that our so-called naval force was a sham, and that the country was absolutely without sea power; but if there were any doubters among us they were convinced. The country at large learned something that shocked the people, and they began to take more interest in our floating defences. We tried all the kinds of torpedoes then known to us, and decided that they were good only for newspaper stories, or to scare timid people with. The much-talked-of Harvey towing-torpedo was towed about for days in an effort to make it strike a ship, but it would not do it. Once it did seem to wake up, and jumped over an innocent tugboat, fortunately without killing any one. Then we ran at a large raft, made of many hundreds of oil barrels securely lashed together, and exploded spar torpedoes under it, producing very beautiful fountains, and knocking the barrels about considerably. This was generally done at very low speed, because most of us could not steam over seven knots; some ships undertook the exercise at speeds as high as ten knots, but they always carried away something when the spar was lowered into the water, and before they reached the target the torpedo had swung alongside, where it could not be exploded without disastrous result. Our gun practice was good, and it was found that the officers could handle their ships in a seamanlike way; but the general conclusion was that torpedoes in their then state of development were a very much overrated weapon. Of course, there were enthusiasts who still believed in them. You can find those who believe that " the earth stands still and the sun do move! "

CHAPTER XVI

A CRUISE TO AFRICA

WAR with Spain being once more postponed, orders were issued for the fleet to disband, and for the various vessels to proceed to their new stations. The Shenandoah was ordered North to go out of commission for repairs, but as my sea service in her had been very short, I was transferred to the Congress as executive officer. I was considered very young for the job, but I was not responsible either for my age or my orders, and neither gave me any concern. W. T. Sampson, who afterward rendered the country such conspicuous service in the war with Spain, had been her executive, and in relieving him I, of course, found a well-organized ship. She had a new crew, composed of merchant sailors principally, who had enlisted at Southern ports for the threatened Cuban war, and they were about as tough a lot of Christians as I ever ran up against; but time and discipline did wonders for them. I was again very fortunate in my captain, as my old Delaware captain, Earl English, was ordered to command us. I reported on board early in April, and a few days later Captain English came with orders to hurry things up as much as possible and get off to the Mediterranean without delay. We did not allow any barnacles to grow on us after this, for we knew how many ships would be pleased to take our place. A week or ten days was all we required, after the order came, to report ready, and immediately afterward we went to sea.

Our run to Madeira was made in good time, considering the fact that we did it all under sail. I asked the captain to allow me to drill the men an hour or so each day with sails and spars, as I considered that the best and quickest way to get them in shape. He was good enough to approve the plan I had suggested, and every afternoon we worked ship for an hour, furling and shifting sails, sending up and down yards, and doing the many small things which, if persevered in, tend to make a seaman. Both officers and men thoroughly enjoyed the work, and the improvement in them was most marked. Upon our arrival at Madeira we received orders to proceed to the coast of Africa, where some of the natives near Monrovia had threatened to barbecue our wards, the coloured American colonists. As soon as necessary repairs could be made we left Madeira for the south.

We found the trades good and strong, and running off before them under all sail was the finest going to sea one could have. We enjoyed the perfect semitropical weather to the full, and arrived at Santa Cruz May 13, 1874. The historical old town was well worth a visit, and we all regretted that the service on which we were bound allowed us to remain only three days, during which time we refilled our coal bunkers and made such excursions on shore as were possible. I organized a party of eleven to visit the village of

Orotava, which is situated in a valley at the foot of Mount Teneriffe, celebrated as one of the most beautiful peaks in the world. The question of how to get there was solved when I had succeeded in chartering three shabby old hacks and six so-called horses to pull them. We were soon started, and, working laboriously up the steady mountain grade, arrived after a while at an elevation of three thousand feet, where we met the rain in tropical torrents. A convenient hole in the roof of my hack let the water through, and I soon had a small river running down my back and into my shoes, which detracted from the pleasure of the trip, but did not destroy it. The rain soon ceased, and there below us lay the city and the harbour completely inclosed in a perfect rainbow, which touched the water north and south. It was the most beautiful picture I have ever seen, painted by the Master Hand that makes no mistakes.

At the little village of Laguna we halted, wet and tired, to get what lunch we could from the scowling gang of Spaniards who surrounded us. The Virginius affair had not made us popular with these cutthroats. The tavern in which we found ourselves was foully dirty, and the food was in keeping; but we managed to make some sort of a meal on salad and eggs, washed down with very warm Bass ale. After leaving this village we found ourselves on a road winding around the side of the mountain, with the sea nearly four thousand feet below us. The scene was wild and beautiful as the sun broke through the clouds which enveloped us. Nature did all she could to make the panorama perfect, but the shadow of Spain was over everything.

The Congress.

Visit to Orotava

Darkness came as we turned into the valley and began the sharp descent to the village, and we saw nothing more until we arrived at the one miserable hotel Orotava at that time contained. After much wrangling and the use of many bad words we succeeded in getting enough cot beds for the party, but it was hours before we were served with dinner, and a very poor one it was when it finally came. When we retired for the night I discovered that one of the sheets for my bed was the tablecloth off which I had dined! This, however, was soon forgotten under the attack of the fleas, which literally swarmed everywhere, and sleep was out of the question. I thought I had seen fleas in Morocco and in Japan, but I was mistaken—it was left for Orotava to show me the real thing. We gave up the beds as a bad job, and wandered about until daylight, when we ascended to the roof of the hotel to watch the sun rise and catch the shadows on the beautiful Peak of Teneriffe. It was a clear morning, fortunately, and as the sun rose we were well repaid for all the inconvenience we had suffered.

After breakfast we strolled for two hours about the village, admiring the splendid flowers, which in their perfection and abundance reminded me of those about Montevideo. The roses were the finest I had ever seen, and I can recall after all these years the appearance of a stone wall which had a cloth of gold climbing over it bearing more than five hundred splendid flowers. After a look at the great dragon tree, which had fallen two years before, having stood the storms of many hundreds if not thousands of years, we started on our return trip. At a point in the road where the view was the most perfect we halted and looked back over the beautiful valley. It was at this spot that Humboldt was said to have dropped on his knees and exclaimed, " I have found the Garden of Eden! " The view, though very beautiful, had changed much since his time. Then the entire country was one vast vineyard—grapevines everywhere; but now only cactus plants could be seen, and they certainly could not be called beautiful. The people had found that cochineal paid better than wine, and did not require anything like so much labour, so they planted cactus and collected and roasted the small red insects. At the time of my visit aniline dyes had entirely superseded cochineal for colouring purposes, and the cactus plants had consequently been left without care to grow as they pleased.

Our run down to Porto Grande was as pleasant as any I ever made, the weather being perfect. Our drills were kept up constantly, and the men showed the good stuff that was in them. The captain was, unfortunately, very sick all the way, and my work in consequence much harder. There were executives in the service at that day, and I suppose they are not all dead yet, who wanted to be captain as well as executive. I was not one of them. I always wished the captain to back me up in what I did as executive, and I always did what I could to make his position strong and stiff, for I sometimes required a pretty stiff hand to back up some of the things I had to do to make the ship what I knew she ought to be. " To have the captain under your thumb " was one of the fool notions that never entered my head.

Porto Grande was the headquarters of our African

squadron, when we had one, and here many officers and men were buried. We were much disgusted to find that the authorities had seen fit to order our cemetery sold, after having levelled the graves and destroyed the tombstones and monuments. One of our vessels had been sent to look into the matter, and, after she had made a proper row, the governor promised to do what he could to protect the graves. We found that he had stuck up some small posts to mark the boundaries, where before we had a stone wall capped by a proper iron fence; and, not considering this much of an effort, we again made a row, and he again promised to do something; but I am sure he never intended to do more than get rid of us. I was anxious to teach him a lesson, but our orders would not permit it. I found that one of the tombstones from the grave of an American officer was being used for a chopping-block in a private house. Without much ceremony I had this removed to its proper place, and reported the whole matter to the Navy Department. We arrived at this place on May 23d, and, having replenished our coal supply, again started south, bound for Harpers, the American settlement on Cape Palmas, intending to call in at Freetown, Monrovia.

On the morning of June 5th we ran in and anchored off the latter place, where I had my first experience with the native Africans. Their antics were only exceeded by those of our coloured countrymen who had sought homes here in their native land, or rather the land of their ancestors. As soon as we anchored, our minister to Liberia came on board, and was received with all the honours due his high position. I found him a well-educated man, much given to self-admiration and the use of high-sounding words. He was very good-looking, of a commanding figure, very black, and named J. Milton Turner. He wore evening dress and a very becoming high hat. The two Harvard graduates, coloured, who accompanied him were apparelled in the same way. After a short visit, during which he talked incessantly of the call I was to make on the President of the republic, he took his departure, and was saluted with seventeen guns. At the first gun he stood up in the stern of his small boat, held his tall hat aloft in one hand, and the American flag in the other. His efforts to balance himself as the boat pitched and tossed about made of him a striking figure.

In an hour or so Mr. Turner was back on board, still in dress clothes, with a message from the President that he would be glad to receive me that afternoon at a stated hour. We had taken on board at Porto Grande twelve Kroomen, trained surfmen, for service on the coast of Africa, to save our men from the effects of the sun. These men were named after the twelve apostles, and were regularly enlisted as a part of the ship's company. They were splendid specimens of the African boatman, and knew their business thoroughly. We also had a very able whaleboat, which I proposed using to land the officers, who, in full dress, were to form my staff in this visit of ceremony. When the boat was manned and ready to leave the ship, Mr. Turner insisted that I should go with him in his small boat, which I finally consented to do, to get rid of his importunities. I sent our whaler in first, and then consigned myself, epaulets and all, to Mr. Turner and his two oarsmen, feeling as I did so that I was taking chances both from drowning and from the vicious-looking tiger-sharks that were present in great numbers.

The bar at the entrance to this harbour was known as one of the worst on the coast, and on this occasion the surf was breaking heavily on it. As we approached it I watched our whaler ahead of us to see how she would behave. The cockswain, a perfect black Hercules, St. Paul by name, handled the steering oar, and at the proper moment sent the boat racing on top of a wave over the bar in the most approved style. Our little cockleshell also went over beautifully, but not without wetting all of us pretty thoroughly. When we landed I asked Mr. Turner why he had insisted on my coming in with him, to which he replied, " You see, sir, if you had not landed with me, these niggers here would have said that you considered yourself too good to come in the same boat with me."

After a walk of five minutes over a bare, sun-baked clay hill, without one sprig of anything green, where the naked negro children were playing, unconscious of their nakedness, we came to the humble home of President Roberts, of the Republic of Liberia. He had been raised a slave near Petersburg, in Virginia, and I found him a person of pleasing manners and assured ability—just the man to preside over the destinies of his fellow-Africans. He had gathered his Cabinet about him, and I was presented to the different members—the Secretary of War, the Secretary of the Navy, the Secretary of the Treasury, and so on through the list. During the conversation that followed I heard the rustling of a silk dress, and instinctively rose to my feet. There before me stood a short, neat, very black woman, and, without waiting for an introduction, I shocked myself by saying, " How do you do, aunty? " to which she replied, with a courtesy, " Very well, thank you, sir." I was instantly aware of my mistake in so addressing the wife of a President, but was relieved of all embarrassment by the hearty laugh of Mr. Roberts, and the query, " What part of the South do you come from, captain? "

Some very warm, sour champagne was served, and after pledging the high consideration of my Government for the Republic of Liberia, I took my departure, followed by the entire Cabinet and half a hundred naked young negroes, ranging from four to eight years of age. Mr. Turner insisted that I should call on each Cabinet minister according to his rank; and, for fear of giving offence, I did so. At each house or hut I was entertained with such food and drink as the owners possessed, and everywhere a hearty welcome. I was told—and it was painfully evident without the telling—that the people were wretchedly poor, and the revenues of the republic barely sufficient to pay the salaries of the Cabinet ministers, and therefore no public improvements could be undertaken. There was not the first sign of an army or navy, or indeed a need for either; yet the two secretaries were on hand and ready at least to draw their pay when the treasury was in condition to pay it.

Capturing a Shark

After visiting the mayor I returned to the ship, this time in my own boat, and was most favourably impressed by the cleverness with which our Kroomen brought us over the wicked-looking bar. The sharks were snapping at the oars most of the way, and if we had capsized nothing could have saved us—at least the white men of the party; the blacks do not seem a favourite article of food with these sea-tigers. Of course I had read, as many others had, very glowing accounts of the missions, churches, and schools of Liberia. I can only say they were conspicuous by their absence at the time of my visit. The word " republic " was never more abused and insulted and misused than by applying it to what I saw in Liberia.

During the time we had been at anchor off Monrovia a particularly large man-eating shark had remained constantly about the ship, swallowing empty meat cans and such other trash as suited him.. As soon as I had time to spare for him I prepared a beautiful bait for his dinner, which he took readily, and it was all twenty good men could do to capture him after he was hooked. We hoisted him up nearly to the main yard, and literally " shot him full of holes." More than a hundred rifle and revolver balls were fired through him, and, thinking he was dead, I had him lowered on the upper deck, and allowed such men as had a spite against him to stick their knives into him, if they could. He was old and had a very thick hide. Finally, one of the men took a battle-axe from a gun carriage and struck him a hard blow on the top of his head, which seemed to wake him up again. He raised himself as quick as a flash and brought his tail down with a crack that made all hands stand clear of him in a hurry. We then killed him " entirely," as the Irishman said, by cutting his tail off, which of course severed his spinal column and put an end to him. After decapitating him I cut out fourteen feet of his backbone and had it cleaned and preserved, with the head, as a sample of what a man-eater is like in size.

The stomach contained a curious lot of things: first I took out a turtle shell, which measured eighteen inches across the back and was as clear and transparent as the most beautiful piece one could see in a shop in Naples. Then I took out the thigh bone of a bullock, and a good large one it was. The last thing I found was a black flint stone weighing twenty pounds, which I suppose he had swallowed, or rather picked up, with the turtle from the bottom. I did not find any gold watches or diamond rings. When the jaws, which had four rows of teeth, had been dried and shellacked, I could pass them over the head and shoulders of the largest man in the ship without their touching his clothing. In other words, he could have swallowed an ordinary man without the trouble of biting him in two. I afterward presented them to the library of the Portsmouth Navy Yard, where they may still be an object of interest to the curious.

From Monrovia we ran to Cape Palmas, which was to be the southern point of our cruise. On arrival we found there was no real trouble with the natives. They had threatened to lunch on some of our missionaries, but had not carried out their threat. A short exercise on shore with a Gatling gun firing at a target, which we left for them to study over, convinced them that they really could get on without eating American missionaries.

The question of coal had now become a most serious one; have it we must, but how to get it was the question. There was none in sight anywhere within our reach. The prospect of beating back under canvas against the trades was not a pleasing one. While on shore one day I made inquiries about the wreck of a large English steamer on the sands, and found that she had been loaded with prepared fuel— coal bricks they were called. On boarding her I found to my great satisfaction that the fuel was still in good condition, and that there was plenty of it. After some trouble I arranged with the owner to purchase as much as we could stow, and then hired enough natives to boat it off to us through the surf, which was always breaking heavily on the beach. We used our own boats for the purpose, but the sun was too hot to risk working our own men, except to stow the fuel after it was delivered on board. For four days we worked away steadily, and succeeded in getting enough on board to carry us back to Sierra Leone.

Most of this time I was at work myself, spending many hours on shore and about the wreck, where I had a good chance of observing the native workmen. They were a muscular lot of savages, and, generally speaking, worked well. The lazy ones were stimulated by the head man with a good stout whip which he carried as a sort of badge of office. They were stripped to the skin, and had enormous pads of matted hair on their heads, which apparently was the growth and accumulation of years. I was interested in seeing them feed. When meal time came each would pull a handful of Chili peppers, which were as hot as anything could be; then from the nearest tree he would secure half a dozen fresh limes, which he split open and salted; these, with hard bread and a small portion of dried fish, formed the ration of as hard-worked a lot of men as I ever saw. Their work was performed under a tropical sun, where white men could not have done anything. On board ship we were practically living on salt rations, because there was nothing on shore to buy, except fruit, which was very good, and black pigs. Even the pigs in this country were black.

We were glad to point the good ship north again, and when we anchored at Sierra Leone the official calls fell to my lot, as the captain was still on the sick list. The following extract from my journal is of interest:

" On this occasion my staff consisted of young Zeilin, of the marines, an excellent fellow. Wasn't it hot! The house of the governor is on a hill about half a mile high, and when we arrived at the door the perspiration was running over the tops of my shoes. The governor gave us some brandy and soda with *ice*, the first we had seen since leaving Madeira, which had a wonderfully cooling effect. When we left, he invited us to dine the following evening, and we were quick to accept the invitation—grub has been awful on the coast of Africa.

" After leaving Government House we had to climb about two miles more over the hills before we reached the barracks, where we had more brandy and soda and plenty of time to cool off. The officers and men, part of a West India regiment, had just returned from Ashantee, and had lots of interesting things to show and plenty to talk about. Among other things, the colonel had a couple of young boa constrictors about four feet long and very gentle, but able to give one a good squeeze if allowed to coil around the body.

" On the way back to the ship I called to see the great character of Sierra Leone, one Sibyl Boyle. He had been taken from a slave ship when about eight years of age, and, having no name of his own, was given that of the ship Sibyl and of her Captain Boyle. He was an industrious lad, and gradually worked his way up, until now he is the richest and most influential man in the place, and has a fine family around him. If some of his neighbours would only follow his example we might hope that some day Africa would be developed by her own race, but as things stand now the white race must eventually own the whole outfit."

One of our officers, Lieutenant J. D. J. Kelly, was condemned by medical survey at Sierra Leone, and sent home *via* England. The doctors thought him in the last stages of heart disease, and doubted if he would live to reach London. I knew nothing about such things, of course, but differed with the medical men on principle; there should always be two sides to every question, and I took the only side left in this case. Kelly seemed much cheered up by my assertion that his heart sounded like a music-box to me, and he left us in fairly good condition. Twenty-five years after this I find him in good health, and writing very vigorous articles for one of the leading newspapers of his country.

Having refilled our coal bunkers at Sierra Leone,

we put to sea and headed for Madeira; but the coal-dealer had done us a dirty trick—the coal would not burn; at least most of it would not, so we had to work up under sail to Porto Grande. On the way up we lost our first man by death since leaving Key West. He was a young chap who had run away from home to go to sea. He showed no concern about dying, and never gave me the slightest clew by which I could find his family, though I used my best efforts to make him do so. We sewed him up in his hammock, backed the maintopsail, hoisted the flag at half-mast, called, " All hands bury the dead! " and launched him overboard with a stand of grape for company on his long trip.

Back once more at Porto Grande, we lost no time in cramming our bunkers full of coal and starting again for Madeira. This time I felt sure that we could not steam directly to our port of destination; I therefore put the ship under sail and stood off into the Atlantic, determined not to get caught again as we were on the coast of Africa. The climate was now suitable, and I resumed the drills, which had been suspended for fear of overworking the men in the tropical sun. The effects of careful training and instruction were beginning to show, and I felt that we should be able to hold our own with the best of them when we finally reached the Mediterranean.

Day by day we gradually gained on the island of Madeira, until I at last felt that I could safely start the engines and do the distance under steam. The sails were snugly furled, the light yards sent down, and the gentlemen of the engine room had us in their hands.

News from Home

We had been a long time in making the last lap of our trip, but on July 16th we ran in and anchored once more off the beautiful town of Funchal, in the island of Madeira. All hands were anxious for news of sweethearts or wives, and as soon as the health officer gave us a clean bill we sent in for our mails, and there came many fat-looking bags. For the first time in five months I had news of my family. In all that time my letters had been accumulating, and not a line had reached me. I had been rattled many times over the thoughts of what might have happened, but now it was all right. Going away to sea is awfully hard at times, but it is no end of fun when you come back again. I opened the latest-dated letter, and found that my people were all well and somewhere up in the north of England. I stowed the others away to be read when I had more time at my disposal.

The captain was much improved since we left Porto Grande, and I was able to get him on shore at once, where I knew he would be comfortable away from the noises of the ship and the smell of the paint I was going to put on her. All hands took hold with a will, and at the end of ten days everything was in fine shape and the ship ready for any service she might be called on to perform, while she was beautiful to look at, and I was not afraid to have any one inspect her. The captain had quite recovered, and was himself again—kind and genial, and a seaman every inch of him. When I had him on board and everything ready, we got under way for Gibraltar, where we arrived safely a few days later.

CHAPTER XVII

IN THE MEDITERRANEAN

At Gibraltar I was granted leave, and was fortunate enough to catch a P. and O. steamer the next day, bound for Liverpool. My fellow-passengers were for the most part officers of the English army invalided home from India, where they had been broken down in the Queen's service. They were a fine lot of patriotic men, anxious only to get well enough to rejoin the colours and die in harness. My room mate was a Major McLean, of the Rifle Brigade, who had come to America with the troops sent over at the time the Trent affair threatened to involve us in war with England. We soon became very good friends, and he gave me much interesting information about his service in different parts of the world. He considered his experience at the time of the Trent affair unique, and it certainly was. When the transport with him and his men reached the mouth of the St. Lawrence, they found the ice so bad that they could not get to Montreal, so they went to a port in the State of Maine, and, by permission of our Government, were sent to their destination to get ready to come back and fight us. He thought it a very dangerous thing for us to have done, but I assured him that one or two brigades of English troops, more or less, would not have made the least difference to us at that time, if we had made up our minds to fight.

I found my family at Carlisle, in the north of England, and from there we journeyed slowly back to London, tarried there a few days, and then on to Paris, and shortly to Italy.

After a delightful drive over the Cornice road, we arrived at Spezzia, where we found comfortable quarters and quite a navy colony at the Croce di Malta, a quiet, well-conducted small hotel, where one could have a charming breakfast in the open air under the shade of the fig trees.

The Congress had in the meantime been docked and cleaned and thoroughly overhauled. I found her lying in the stream, looking smart and ready for work, which the admiral soon gave us with a liberal hand. After a week or ten days we joined the flagship at Marseilles, which was selected as a suitable port for giving liberty to our men, who had been on board steadily since we left Key West. Our three hundred and fifty, added to the eight hundred of the Franklin, kept the police force of the city pretty busy until their money was spent, when they once more settled down to their regular routine life.

Captain English believed in the old custom of giving liberty by watches, and this plan was followed in this case; but it was the last time it was ever done on that ship. It was favoured, I suppose, because the trouble was sooner over. I can't imagine any other reason for it. The idea was that the men would get drunk and raise all sorts of rows whenever they went on shore, and therefore the more we sent at a time the sooner it would be done with. The men certainly justified this opinion at Marseilles.

The captain went to Paris for a week, and so escaped much annoyance; but I had it to face, and it was very bad. I made up my mind that I would do all I could to prevent a recurrence of such scenes as I had witnessed, and, when the captain had had a full description of it all, I prevailed upon him to allow me to arrange the crew in conduct classes. After a reasonable time I found that the men could be relied on to behave themselves decently, and liberty was given them in every port we visited. Of course we had men, and I regret to say some of them the best seamen on board, who got drunk and fought the police every time they went on shore. The only reason we had them was because of this: if they could have controlled their taste for liquor they would have remained on shore. I had a very warm place in my heart for these chaps, and always found them leading when there was hard work to be done, and in the right spot when there was trouble. But they certainly were hard to manage. The great majority of our men were quiet, respectable lads, who went and came when they were off duty and had money to spend.

From Marseilles the admiral took us with him for a long cruise, stopping first at Barcelona, and then running down to Port Mahon in the Balearic Islands, where we landed the battalions of the two ships for shore drills. The officers senior to me were either sick or had some other good excuse, and I was therefore detailed to command, much to my disgust, for

Features of Port Mahon

I have always found soldiering the least desirable part of my profession. We managed to amuse the natives of the island and please the admiral, so the drills were considered a success. The only real good of it all was the physical exercise the men received. In former years, when we maintained a large Mediterranean squadron of sailing ships, Port Mahon was our head-quarters, and the people, when we visited the port, seemed glad to see our ships once more, and treated us with great courtesy.

All my life I had heard of two things that came from Port Mahon and from no other place. One was *sobra sada*, a sausage, made in a peculiar way, or rather from unusual ingredients; and the other date fish, a long shellfish much resembling a razor clam, which is ob-tained from the soft stones of the harbour and vicinity where he makes his home. The stones are broken open, and in the mass is found embedded this peculiar crus-tacean. I tried the qualities of both of them, and at once became a convert to *sobra sada*, which, broiled and served on toast, is one of the best breakfast dishes I have ever eaten.

On the conclusion of our Port Mahon visit we ran off to the southward and cruised for some weeks about the island of Sicily, visiting several ports, and finally anchoring at Messina. Here we remained long enough to receive and send mails and get a taste of fresh food for the men, when we sailed for the Ionian Islands, visiting among other places Zante, which produced practically the supply of currants for the world. Then, after a stop in Suda Bay for target practice, we ran down to the Piræus, and finally to

Naples, where we moored in the inner harbour, prepared for a stay of ten days.

While in Suda Bay I had one day to spare, which I spent on shore with my gun and an officer companion. We found very little in the way of game, but I was much interested in observing the Greek natives, who spend their lives in primitive simplicity. They are herders of sheep, and small farmers, as they think; but their poverty is beyond anything the farmers of the United States could understand. Even the inhabitants of our poorhouses would consider themselves wealthy when compared with these excellent, hard-working, simple people. I stopped at one of their houses in the hills to get a glass of water to drink with my luncheon at noon. The family soon assembled about me, and offered me what they had in the way of food. This consisted of a large wooden bowl of black olives—olives in their natural state allowed to ripen on the tree—black bread almost as hard as a stone, and a cup of goat's milk. They never ate meat, and when I showed them a ham sandwich, which my servant had prepared on board ship, they made me understand that they had never before seen or heard of ham, and the same thing happened when I showed them a piece of cold beef. I wondered at the change that must have come to them since the creation of the Venus of Milo, which had been found in this country.

We were moored near some Italian war vessel at Naples, and soon found friends among the officers, who took great pleasure in arranging short trips for us, frequently going themselves to show us objects of interest. Among these officers I came to know two brothers very well. One morning it was rumoured that a duel had been fought, and one Italian officer instantly killed. Later in the day I learned that these two friends of mine had had a quarrel; that one had drawn a pistol and fired at the other, wounding him, and thinking that he had killed his brother, put the pistol to his head and blew his own brains out. The wounded brother recovered. Not much of a duel about that, certainly.

We had been at Naples but a few days when a gale came on—one of those furious blasts that last only a few hours, but frequently do great damage. The stern chains of the Franklin, secured to the stone breakwater, began to show signs of parting, and the admiral, in order to ease things up, made signal for both ships to send down lower yards and topmasts. The spar drill I had so carefully given our men enabled us to land our lower yards across the rail in twenty minutes, leaving nothing showing above the hull but the bare lower masts, which was fine work, and most gratifying to officers and men. The Franklin was a much heavier-sparred ship than we were, and took nearly two hours to get things snugged down in good shape. The following morning, the gale having blown out, the admiral signalled, "Cross royal yards and loose sails to a bowline," as a colour evolution. The whole foreign fleet had their glasses on us, and we received compliments on the smartness of our drill. We felt sufficiently rewarded for all the hard work we had done when the signal, "Well done, Congress," flew from the flagship.

From Naples we cruised along the coast of Syria,

and then ran on to Nice. Each ship had an allowance of coal for the year, and the greater part of ours had been expended, so that we could not expect any active cruising for several months. In fact, we remained tied up to a buoy for five months. It looked as if we would ground on our beef bones before we got away from it. Our race boat, in which I took a personal interest, that extended to training the men, won from all comers and held the championship. During the winter the Russian admiral came in with a flagship noted for her smart work aloft. We watched her drills carefully for a few days, and, having learned all her tricks, followed her motions and beat her badly in everything she tried. The decks of the Congress were particularly well suited for quick work, and her crew by this time was in excellent condition. Each man felt that the reputation of the ship depended on his personal efforts, and the result was all we could ask.

Nice, only half an hour away, was crowded with visitors from all parts of the world, among them many of our own countrymen. We were invited, of course, to entertainments of every possible kind, which we had to accept and in some way return. This came hard on many of the officers who had only their pay to live on, and no allowance from the Government for entertaining, such as was given to the officers of all other navies—the " table money " of the English admiral was equal to the whole pay of our admiral; but we had it to do, and we did it handsomely. We established Thursday as our reception day, and our dances were attended and enjoyed by guests from every country in Europe, as well as a great many Americans.

At the Gambling Tables

Monaco was only half an hour away by rail, and many of us lost what little money we could spare at this fascinating gambling resort. I always secured a return ticket and reserved a few francs to pay the cab after my humiliating experience, when I had to wake my wife up in the middle of the night to borrow money to pay for driving me home from the station. Everything was done at Monte Carlo to attract people and make them enjoy themselves. The gambling games were fairly conducted, the *cafés* were the finest in Europe, and the music the best that money could furnish. The society was mixed. Most of the people who visited the place went first to the *cafés*, then to the gambling tables, and then listened to the music. Of course, there were some who listened to the music for the love of music, but most of those whom I observed looked as if they wished they had not come. I often felt that way myself. The great interest to me was watching the crowd of gamblers as they lost or won. As a rule, the Americans played the best game, and took their medicine most quietly. Occasionally some foreign chap would lose his fortune, and by way of making up for it blow his brains out; but this was a rare occurrence, as the guards were very clever men, and usually detected such characters in time, and shipped them off by rail to kill themselves somewhere else.

Through the Catholic priest at Ville Franche and my own servants I learned of the great suffering among the poor of the town, and made up my mind to do what I could to relieve them. They were miserably poor, and the suffering was very great. What was left over from feeding our four hundred men and thrown overboard would go a long way toward providing them with meals if the material could be utilized. I had a number of large tin cans made with proper covers, and these at meal time were placed in charge of the police of the ship, who saw to it that all scraps of bread and meat and meat bones were collected and placed therein. All the coffee and tea left over were carefully saved, and the coffee grounds as well. Our men took an active interest in the scheme as soon as they understood what was intended, and we were able to feed four or five hundred people all the winter through. The Catholic institutions on shore received our cans every evening and returned them early the next morning in time for use after breakfast, and from their contents prepared good, rich soup and plenty of coffee and tea—much stronger than the poor peasants had ever known before. When I went on shore I was kept busy returning the salutes of those who had been comforted by our charity. It was a source of great satisfaction to me to feel that I had done some good to these deserving poor people.

When the winter was over and gone, with all its gaieties, we went to cruising again. At Gibraltar we found many friends among the officers of the garrison. Among others I recall very clearly a captain of a Welsh regiment who was most amusing and witty. He came off to represent his regimental mess, and was prevailed upon to remain to dinner and take potluck with us. In a moment of misplaced confidence he told how the officers of the United States storeship Ino had dined with them during the civil war, and how they had all gone under the table one after another. One of them, who wore false teeth, had been put to sleep in a large, comfortable chair in the captain's room, and when the morning came there was no end of fun finding his teeth for him. I saw by the look on the faces of our fellows that the captain had sealed his fate by this story. At midnight they carried him ashore carefully, took him to his quarters, and deposited him in the identical chair where the Ino chap had lost his teeth. We saw him again after three days, when he assured us that we had done him up in proper shape. He really had a keen sense of humour.

A new survey of the harbour of Malaga was wanted, so we ran up there, and Elmer, our navigator, soon had it completed. When we arrived we found a regatta arranged for the following day, in which we were asked to compete. Several twelve- and fourteen-oared Spanish boats were to race, so we entered our twelve-oared racing cutter, much to the satisfaction of the Spanish officers. They had never seen our people pull a race, and when we led their boats to the finish line by quite three minutes they never wanted to see them do it again. During our entire stay we were crowded with visitors, which was rather surprising, in view of the relations then existing between the two countries; but they came by hundreds from all directions, and represented all classes of society, from the general commanding to the common labourer with his gamecock under his arm.

On June 18, 1875, we anchored in Algiers, after a pleasant run from Gibraltar under sail. I enjoyed here seeing a balloon ascension, the most successful one I ever witnessed. The balloon had been used in the siege of Paris, and afterward in the Carlist war in Spain, where it was captured, and the occupants only escaped being shot as spies by the earnest interference of the French minister. On this occasion everything worked perfectly, and the party, after sailing out over the harbour, at a height of about two miles, descended until they struck a current of air setting toward the land, when they rapidly disappeared behind a mountain ten or twelve miles away.

Tunis was our next port, and we anchored there on July 1st. The American consul, Mr. Heap, lived with his charming family about six miles out of town toward the ruins of Carthage; and here, after the official visit had been made, we found a most cordial welcome. Our country was ably represented at this point at least, and I could see the respect in which our consul was held by all classes.

The Bey of Tunis had expressed a desire, after visiting the Congress, to see the effect of the fire of one of our Gatling guns, and requested that we land one and give him an exhibition drill. The captain directed me to take the matter in hand and make the necessary arrangements, which I did on July 3d.

I had a small-arm target anchored at a point six hundred yards from the shore in front of the palace, so that the ladies of the harem could see the firing, and when everything was ready, landed the gun with its detachment and quickly went into action. I fired six hundred shots, and in the smoke, before any one could see us, dismounted the gun and placed it and the crew behind a stone wall. When the smoke cleared away there was neither gun nor man in sight. The firing took one minute, and in order to show the Bey the effect, the target was towed in, and he counted five hundred and thirty hits on it. He was rather stupefied at first, but later on complimented me on the drill of the men and the accuracy of the fire. After I had explained to him fully the working of the gun in all its parts, he directed his secretary to order a battery of six of them, which was done.

The numerous old wells at the ruins of Carthage contained great numbers of bullfrogs of an enormous size, and as I was fond of frogs' legs I started in a boat to try my luck on them. Fortunately, I took for the trip a very able whaleboat, the one we had used on the west coast of Africa. When we were about four miles from the ship we were caught in a sudden furious gale of wind. For two hours we fought hard for our lives, and when we finally reached the ship we were all pretty well used up and of course as wet as rats, and had no frogs to show for our trouble. A great sea was running all about the ship, and it required my best efforts to save the boat and get the men on board without losing some of them. We celebrated the Fourth of July properly at Tunis, and in the evening got under way for Malta.

This key to the Suez Canal had been fortified by the English until one could fairly say that it was impregnable. It was always strongly garrisoned, and the headquarters of the fine Mediterranean squadron. Our arrival was the signal for a round of dinners and luncheons that lasted almost to the hour of our departure. I met, on this occasion, one of the most interesting men I have ever known—Colonel de la Fosse, of the One Hundred and First Regiment, English army. He was a fine, brave old soldier, full of patriotism and love for his Queen. He had been in Cawnpore at the time of the Indian Mutiny, and was one of the half-dozen officers who succeeded in cutting his way out. We spent many hours together, and I listened while he modestly recounted his experiences. We left this celebrated port and hospitable garrison with real regret, hoping that it would be our good fortune to visit them again.

After leaving Malta we called in at Tripoli. We had orders from Washington to collect such articles as might prove of interest to the Centennial Exposition to be opened at Philadelphia in the following year. The frigate Philadelphia had been burned by Decatur in this harbour, after falling into the hands of the Moors, and I knew that a piece of her wreck would be considered of interest. I therefore fitted a launch with proper grapnels and tackle, and after a long search located the wreck and was fortunate enough to secure part of a petrified timber which had been charred through. Many of the iron spikes by which the planking had been secured still remained in the piece, and it was curious to note the effect of heat and their long immersion in salt water. They were much softer than when first driven—in fact, were almost like soft lead. I secured one of them and afterward had a set of jewelry made from it for my wife by a jeweller in Geneva. The trinkets were beautifully finished and perfectly burnished, but no amount of care would prevent them from rusting; the moisture seemed to exude from the inside of the metal. The piece of timber was boxed and sent to the Exposition, where I afterward saw it, and it was regarded as an object of much interest.

Upon our arrival at Corfu we were thrown into a state of considerable excitement by the receipt of news that the American consul at Tripoli had been insulted by the Pasha, or some of his people, and that we were to be sent there to demand and exact proper reparation. We had lately been at that port and, having in view the nature of the defences, wondered how one wooden ship could do much against them. However, the orders came, and we left at once to carry them out. When we arrived off the town we found all hands much excited, and there was great marching and countermarching of troops about the batteries and through the streets. An officer was sent on shore to communicate with the consul, and when his boat approached the landing place the crowd jeered and spat at him. He promptly returned to the ship and reported the affair to the captain, who sent a company of marines and a Gatling gun in to prevent a possibility of trouble. The officer landed without molestation and soon had the consul on board. The Pasha, having heard of the conduct of the mob toward our boat, hurried to make ample apology, which was accepted, and the insult to the consul was then taken up. He had reported the matter to the State Department, and our orders from Washington were positive. We were not to investigate anything, but to demand and exact ample reparation for what had taken place.

The consul insisted that he had been grossly insulted, and his premises invaded by armed Turkish sailors. The Pasha insisted that a thorough investigation showed that there had been no insult to him, but, on the contrary, the consul had attacked or assaulted a Turkish sailor, and it was only out of consideration for our Government that he was not fined and locked up.

Our captain cut the discussion short by stating what his orders were, and that immediate apology on the part of the Pasha would prevent serious trouble; to which the Pasha replied by manning his batteries, and stating that he had done nothing to apologise for, and that the Sultan would cut his head off if he did it. At this stage of the game we cleared for action, swung our ship around so that the broadside would bear on the town, and sent word to his Excellency that if at the end of four hours we had not received his favourable answer we should open fire on the batteries. Within an hour after this ultimatum was delivered the United States steamer Hartford, on her way home from China, came in, anchored near us, and cleared for action. The Pasha, thinking probably that the entire American navy was coming, decided that he would apologize at noon the next day. An officer of rank was detailed to witness the ceremony, which took place at the American consulate. The Pasha, a very dignified gentleman, did the proper thing in every way, said that he ate dirt in the presence of the offended person, and used many other figures of speech. The consul, a gentleman from the far South and not of a forgiving turn of mind, demanded that the dirt should be actually eaten, but our officer put an end to the business, brought the consul and his family on board for safe-keeping, and we sailed for Corfu, the orders of the State Department having been carried out to the letter. Those of us who knew the real facts in the case were not very proud of the whole performance. The consul was living on the seashore, some distance from town, when the Turkish fleet arrived and sent boats in to obtain water. One of the sailors ventured into the kitchen of the residence to obtain a light for his cigarette, where the consul found him, and, having boxed his ears soundly, kicked him out of the inclosure. The other sailors sat on a stone wall and jeered at the consul, who made complaint that the law relating to harems had been violated by this intrusion of the sailor, and hence the deadly insult. This was all there really was to it.

Upon arriving at Corfu again I was granted a short leave, which I spent with my family in Switzerland. When my leave was up I rejoined my ship at Naples, spending one day and night in Rome on my way there. This trip from Geneva to Naples will always remain in my mind as a horror. The weather was very hot, the cars very dirty, and the customs officers, on the various frontiers I crossed, very officious and trying; but Naples was the same fascinating place. We joined the flagship at Villefranche to have our semi-annual inspection, which was somewhat overdue, and also to submit casually to the "bossing" which flagships always have in store for every one except the flagship. We got through our inspection very creditably, and immediately sailed for Leghorn, where we were to have our decks calked and do some trifling repairs. After dropping both our bower anchors in the stream, we warped our stern in and made fast to the breakwater, in order that we might not take up room in swinging, and also as security against the gales, which at times blew with great fury and did no end of damage. The breakwater was of stone, fifty-seven feet high, and most solidly built.

The gale I had been looking for came at a most convenient time; the captain and his family had gone to Rome, and the calkers had nearly completed their work, when, without much warning, it struck us with hurricane force. I naturally thought that, secured as we were behind the breakwater, we were perfectly safe; but such was not the case. One of our chain stern-fasts crushed the iron pipe through which it passed, and in a few seconds ripped a hole in the side of the ship five feet long. This warning was instantly heeded, and in a short time our lower yards and topmasts were on deck, which left only the upper parts of our lower masts above the breakwater to catch the wind. At the same time our two heavy sheet anchors, which stowed well aft in the waist, were let go and the chains hove taut, which prevented the ship from forging ahead quickly and bringing up on her fasts with a jerk. When all this had been done we found ourselves very comfortable, but in a little while a new danger threatened us: the sea, which rose rapidly as the gale increased, began breaking over the top of the breakwater, and tons of water came pounding down on our decks. In face of this I could only batten the hatches down to keep the water from get-

A Lively Octopus

ting below, and grin and bear it until the gale blew out. It was an annoyance rather than a serious danger. If we had broken loose from the breakwater we would certainly have sunk six vessels as we swung to our anchors, not to mention the probable damage to the Congress. The idea of changing our berth was out of the question; we could only hold on to the one we had with all our might.

After the gale had blown itself out, which it did in three days, the fishermen came back in large numbers and began fishing off the sea face of the breakwater, where the loose stone foundation, or riprap, attracted the fish in large numbers. I had given notice that I would pay a small sum for an octopus, the larger the better, as I thought I might be able to keep it alive until I could send it to Philadelphia. A few days after the gale I heard great shouting on the breakwater, and one of the men came to me with the information that my octopus was caught, or rather *he* had caught two fishing boats and half a dozen fishermen. He made things pretty lively for all hands at first, but some one succeeded in getting a rope around his neck, and by choking him nearly to death we eventually captured him and took him on board ship. After a long struggle I got him into a large tub, which he filled to the top, and where he seemed satisfied. When the tub was suddenly flooded he would instantly dye the water as black as ink and so hide himself. I found, to my regret, that the rope about his neck had fatally injured him, and he died after I had observed him for three or four days. His tentacles were as large as a man's arm and ten or twelve feet long. Each one was covered on the lower side with suckers, ranging in size from the body, where they were as large as a silver dollar, to the end of the tentacle, where they were smaller than a ten-cent piece. After he was apparently dead, if I struck my fingers quickly across one of the suckers, it would catch me every time. When he was alive and free to move in the water he could have drowned a man, or indeed several men at the same time, in a very few minutes. I was surprised to find later that the small octopus was largely used for food.

When our repairs had been completed we returned to our winter quarters at Nice. Here we prepared to spend the winter much as we had spent the last one, but the Navy Department had other work for us, and late in November orders came for us to proceed, without delay, to Port Royal, South Carolina, and report our arrival. A few days only were necessary for our preparations and we were off, leaving a forlorn lot of women bravely waving farewells from the docks. Our captain was fortunate enough to be allowed to bring the ladies of his family home with him in the Congress, but the bitter attacks of certain newspapers had had their effect, and the day of the " family ships " was over for all time in our service. The station at Ville Franche was also broken up, and the ships sent cruising in various directions.

As we ran down to Gibraltar for our final coaling the Gulf of Lyons took a last shot at us in the shape of a gale of wind, which blew viciously for two days and then let go. When it was over we drank champagne as well as water out of teacups, for we had rolled pretty much everything loose, and broke all the crockery the mess owned. Two days were spent in coaling at Gibraltar, and I said good-bye to the Mediterranean for some years to come. We left many good friends behind us, and everywhere a record that was a credit to the country we had tried our best to properly represent.

On the run to Madeira the superstitious feelings of our men, and indeed some of the officers, were much excited by a curious incident. We were under sail and the moon shining brightly, when, for some reason, it became necessary to shorten sail. When the topgallant sails were clewed up there stood a man on the fore-topgallant yard clearly outlined against the flapping canvas of the fore royal. The officer of the deck hailed the officer of the forecastle to know what that man was doing aloft, and was assured in reply that the men were all on deck. But there stood the man in plain sight in the moonlight. The officer then hailed him, but could get no answer. Finally he sent a man aloft to tell the chap, whoever he was, to come down at once and report on the quarter-deck. All hands were by this time much excited, and waited anxiously to see what would happen. Just as the man who had been sent from the deck reached the foretop, the figure on the yard disappeared, as if he had fallen overboard. The watch was mustered and all hands were found to be present. After this sleep was out of the question; the men stood about in groups, watching the fore-topgallant yard, waiting to see the figure reappear, many of them too frightened to reason, and all of them expecting some awful disaster to befall the ship. On the following night, when the moon was about in the same relative position to the ship, the sails were again clewed up, and after changing the course slowly a few times, there was the man again standing in the same position on the yard. The mystery was solved: a shadow from some of the canvas on the mainmast was responsible for the ghost.

Another of our ships had had a very curious ghost experience while cruising in the Mediterranean, which is well worth recording. At about midnight, when over a hundred miles from land and while everything was perfectly quiet about the deck, the sound of a tolling bell was distinctly heard. It could be plainly heard by the officer of the deck as well as the men, and it continued for several minutes. To the crew it sounded like a funeral bell, and they decided that some one was going to die. With much difficulty the men were finally sent to their hammocks and ordered to keep silence. The next morning the story was all over the ship, from the forecastle to the officers' messes. When night came again many had forgotten the incident, but at about the same hour the tolling of the bell was again distinctly heard, and the whole crew gathered on deck to listen in superstitious silence. The officers were much puzzled, and many theories were advanced to account for the strange and unusual noise. The third night found captain and all hands, officers and men, on deck, determined if possible to find a solution of the mystery. At the proper time the sound of the bell came clear and distinct, tolling as if for a funeral. The captain and several of the officers then began a careful investigation, which soon cleared the matter up. The galley of the ship, where the cooking was done, was under the topgallant forecastle, about twenty feet from the ship's bell. The fires in the galley were put out at nine o'clock, and it was found that at a certain point in the process of cooling the contracting of the metal in the galley made it give out a cracking noise which accorded with certain tones in the bell and caused it to ring. The very puzzling ghost story was solved, and the men went to their hammocks, many of them still shaking their heads and predicting that there was trouble in store for somebody.

From Madeira we literally rolled our way across the Atlantic. After coaling at St. Thomas, we reached Port Royal, where we found a few old monitors and one or two small vessels, all in ignorance of the reasons for assembling a fleet at that point, the orders for which had been issued. Captain English was to be the senior officer for a time, and it turned out later that we were assembled for the purpose of drilling the men. It was recognised on all hands that our ships were rapidly deteriorating, and Congress did not seem disposed to give us any new ones. It was the beginning of that long period of neglect of the navy by Congress that made officers' hearts ache. All we could do was to keep the men in good shape, which we certainly did, and hope that a change would come to our rulers.

Admiral LeRoy arrived in February, and took command of the squadron, which consisted at that time of ten or twelve ships. We had been drilling steadily all the time, but now the work was vastly increased. Owing to the length of time we had been in commission and the careful training the men had received, we easily led all the ships except the Brooklyn. She had been flagship of the Brazil squadron, and showed the effect of careful, painstaking work. It required our best efforts to keep even with her. There was much talk of a racing cutter she carried that had beaten everything in the South, and when she challenged us for a five-mile race our chances of winning were considered very poor. Our crew was in excellent shape, but our boat was not as good as the Brooklyn's, which did not prevent our men from betting all the money they had on the result. When the stakeboat was reached, our boat was just two lengths behind, a part of which they made up on the turn; and in the pull in, two miles and a half against a strong tide and stiff wind, they passed the Brooklyn's boat and won at the finish by forty-nine seconds. It was one of the hardest races I ever saw pulled, and condition told, as it always will, in such a contest.

CHAPTER XVIII

THE CENTENNIAL AND TRAINING-SHIP DUTY

As the result of an inspection held at Port Royal by one of the bureau chiefs of the Navy Department, the Congress was selected to represent the navy at Philadelphia during the Centennial, and we found ourselves moored off the foot of Arch Street early in May.

The part played by the Congress in the Centennial of 1876 was most creditable to the navy, and very expensive, though gratifying, to her officers. She represented the navy, and was seen and admired by thousands of Americans from all parts of the country. The opening day I landed in command of the crew, who, with a detachment of marines, were the only United States forces in the parade, and therefore held the right of the line. After marching fifteen miles, much of the way in mud halfway to our knees, we were placed in position to receive the President and his party when they had formally opened the Exposition. I waited in the broiling sun nearly two hours after the time set, when I was informed that the crowd had walked over the militia and surrounded the President, so that it was not possible to move him. I marched my men through the crowd, extricated the Boston cadets from a very unpleasant position, where they had been placed to do police duty—to which they should never have been assigned since they were visitors—and soon had things moving again. After one of the hardest days I ever knew we returned to the ship, and without a single man straggling or showing the effect of drink, and all because they had pride in their ship and their service.

We remained at Philadelphia until late in July, when we were ordered to Portsmouth, New Hampshire, to pay off and go out of commission. Before sailing, however, the Board of Inspection put us through our paces, and the following letter shows how well we performed. It was written to Admiral Porter, and signed by Commodore John Guest, senior officer of the board:

"PHILADELPHIA, *July 8, 1876.*

" SIR: The board has inspected the U. S. S. Congress this day.

" It is not enough to say that she is in good order in all her departments and an efficient man-of-war. The whole organization and condition is as near perfection as our system will admit. She is admirable.

" To Captain Earl English and his executive officer, Lieutenant-Commander R. D. Evans, great praise is due for the handsome and creditable specimen of the American navy which they have exhibited here at this Centennial period. The board has taken great pride and pleasure in observing the condition of this ship."

This letter was in addition to the regular inspection report, which did not contain a single unsatisfactory answer in the long list of questions. I mention this as a tribute to the officers and men who made up the splendid crew of the Congress.

When we reached Portsmouth and were ready to haul down the flag over what had been such a happy home to us all, I was shocked at the number of boarding-house sharks that flocked about the ship, ready to relieve the men of all their belongings. I made up my mind to " do " those same sharks, if I could; and I did. I arranged for a special train to run through to New York and Philadelphia, which backed into the navy yard, and when the pennant came down the whole crew, with their bags and hammocks, marched into it instead of the boats which were waiting to land them in the rum mills. I went through on the train myself, and when I saw the men land clean and sober near their homes it gave me a very lasting thrill of pleasure.

After the Congress I enjoyed two months' leave, getting acquainted with my family again. I was then ordered to signal duty in the Navy Department in Washington, where, with the able assistance of Lieutenant Maxwell Wood, I developed and patented a signal lamp for long-distance signalling, which performed its functions very satisfactorily. When winter came, however, I found myself looking about for a ship, and, owing to the good reports about the Congress, I was ordered to command the training-ship Saratoga, one of the old sailing sloops of war. She had been lying in reserve as a gunnery ship at Annapolis, and required a complete overhauling and refitting, which we gave her at the Washington yard.

A Sailor's Log

In the spring I sailed in her, and for four years commanded her, doing the pleasantest duty that has fallen to me in peace times during my naval career.

My duty was to enlist American-born boys between the ages of fifteen and eighteen years, and drill and educate them for the naval service—not to serve as officers, but as enlisted men, to man the ships and fight the guns. The first crew I enlisted came from the section of country about Washington and Baltimore, and a fine, hardy lot they were. The pleasure of watching them grow up and develop into strong, self-supporting men was very great. One unforeseen trouble met me from the start. I could not hold the boys back. They would learn more than was required of the ordinary deck hand, and during the first year of my command I placed quite a dozen of them on merchant vessels as mates. I finally concluded that I had gone too high in the social scale for the material to start with, and, though I was doing a splendid work, I was not getting the men we wanted. Then I tried what is called the "gutter snipe," and there I found just what I was looking for. When caught at the right age, and then properly educated and treated, the boy of this class made his home in the navy, and was willing to spend his life there.

During my four years in command of the Saratoga I had many interesting experiences. I enlisted boys from all parts of the country, and necessarily saw the conditions surrounding the lives of the poorer classes in many different cities. After one trip to Boston, where I enlisted several hundred boys, I was satisfied that education, or rather over-education, was doing great harm in New England. Book schools were not doing what industrial schools would have accomplished. Because a tailor or a shoemaker had been President, every tailor's and shoemaker's son was being educated to fill that high office, and the result was bad—in many cases very bad. Over-training of any kind is not good, and I found mental over-training the worst of all. My experience—and I had plenty of it—was the same over and over again. Each morning when I went to my office at the navy-yard gate I found a long line of fairly well-dressed boys with very shabbily dressed parents. In every case the boy had spent his life at school, winding up in many instances in the high school, and after that finding nothing to do. The parents were striving hard and stinting themselves that the boys might appear well and dress like gentlemen, while the lads were growing more and more ashamed of their surroundings and their honest fathers and mothers, who had been and are to-day the bone and sinew of this great republic. To save them from pool rooms and worse, they begged me to enlist them as apprentices in the navy and begin anew their educations. I almost had it in my heart to wish that every high school in Boston would burn to the ground, and that every boy and every girl should be taught to work with their hands and make a living, as their honest parents had done before them.

While commanding the Saratoga I crossed the Atlantic four times in her, each time with a crew composed in most part of boys. On one trip I ran a line of soundings from Cape Hatteras to Horta, in the island of Fayal, and thence over some supposed shoals to the southward of that island, and then to the coast of Africa. This duty was wonderfully interesting, particularly when, after two hours' hard work, I was rewarded by holding in my hand a specimen of the bottom, which had been hauled up in some cases through over two miles of water. The microscope showed beautiful lacelike shells, which I afterward found extended in a belt from Petersburg, Virginia, to the vicinity of the Western Islands, where they became covered with volcanic ooze. On this trip I had with me Mr. F. B. McGuire, of Washington, who acted as agent of the Smithsonian Institution, and made a large and very valuable collection of fishes, which was highly valued by Professor Baird and his associates. Upon my return I was able to make a good report of work done, not only in the way of training boys, but upon deep-sea soundings and the food fishes of the Western Islands.

I had expected to have many accidents among the green boys, from the constant drills aloft with spars and sails; but when my time was up a careful examination showed that I had no fatal accident, and only a very few serious ones. The rivalry among the boys was very great, and once I had the whole crew betting as to which one of two boys could beat the other over the royal yard. To decide the question I started them aloft one evening just before sundown, as we were fanning along under full sail before a light breeze on the edge of the Gulf Stream. They were both as active as cats, and went aloft very rapidly, but one, in passing the maintop, unfortunately lost his grip on the rigging and pitched over backward. I was stand-

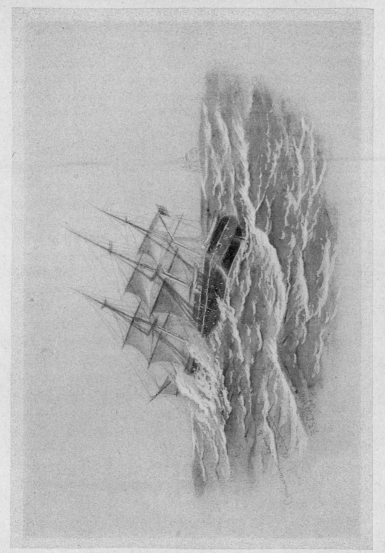

The Saratoga.

ing on the deck watching them, and as the lad fell, I distinctly heard his head strike the projecting muzzle of a gun, and I supposed he was instantly killed. One of the officers whipped off his coat, and was in the act of jumping overboard to his rescue when the boy called out that he was all right. In a few minutes he came up over the stern, having caught one of the trailing life lines, and was apparently none the worse for his ducking; but the moment he saw the blood which was streaming from a wound in his head he fainted dead away. His scalp was pretty well torn from one side of his head, but in a few days he was running aloft again as smartly as ever.

On one of my trips I ran up the Mediterranean as far as Naples, and on my way back fell in with the English fleet, commanded by Admiral Sir Beauchamp Seymour, who afterward bombarded Alexandria. We were all anchored together for ten days at Ville Franche, and my sailing ship was closely watched by the captains of the splendid ironclads. The work of my boys pleased them greatly, and the admiral paid us many compliments on the smartness of our drills. Captain George Tryon commanded the Monarch, and he and I had so much in common over our shooting and fishing yarns that we formed a friendship which continued until he found his grave in the unfortunate Victoria. I always regarded him as one of the best of our cloth, and a great credit to the British navy. In the same fleet was a jolly young lieutenant, Hedwith Lambton, who afterward performed such gallant service in South Africa. I knew him again in Chili when I commanded the Yorktown and he the Warspite. Our acquaintance ripened into a warm friendship, which I value very highly. Among other commanding officers of Admiral Seymour's fleet I was glad to meet Captain Freemantle, of the Invincible, who had recently performed an act that did him great credit. He was on the bridge of his ship when one of his men fell from aloft and struck the water with such force that he was disabled and rapidly sinking. Without a moment's hesitation, and with all his clothing on, the captain sprang into the sea, made a long dive, brought the disabled man to the surface, and saved his life.

My pleasure was much enhanced during my last cruise in the Saratoga by having on board, as my guests, three officers of our army, Colonel Warner and Majors Randolph and Taylor, of the artillery. They saw much to interest them in the various ports we visited, and were lavishly entertained at the different garrisoned towns. The following extract from my journal will give an idea of what our life was in port:

"Of course, beating a sailing ship through the straits is no fun, and even dangerous at night, owing to the number of steamers running through, and the danger of collision; but we had a fair night, and of course I had to be on deck all the time. As I had not had my clothes off since four o'clock Monday morning, I required numerous cups of coffee to keep my eyes open.

"Mr. Sprague, the consul, came on board at ten o'clock, and at noon we all started in full feather to call on the officials. We found Lord Napier of Magdala most polite and agreeable and thoroughly in-

terested in America, and a great Grant man. After
our call on him, we paid our respects to the naval authorities and the officers of one of the regiments, and
when we came home found an invitation from the consul to dine with him; also a notice that an English
officer would show us through all the galleries at 10
A. M. to-morrow. While we were at dinner two cards
came from Lord and Lady Napier of Magdala, one
for an ' At Home ' for to-day, the other a formal invitation for dinner on Thursday. We also had an invitation from the mess of the Forty-sixth Regiment
for Friday, all of which we have accepted. We have
our hands full.

" *Gibraltar, 12th June.*—Wednesday we had a delightful dinner with the consul, after having visited
all the galleries and the signal station on the top of
the rock.

" Thursday we dined with Lord and Lady Napier.
No end of style. The ladies were all charming, after
the fashion of English women. The gentlemen left
the table with the ladies, and did not return to their
wine, which is a new fashion brought here by Lord
Napier from India. It has many good points, I think,
but the English do not fancy it much.

" Yesterday we went through the town, made some
purchases, and in the evening dined with the Forty-
sixth Regiment—and a most delightful dinner we had—
returning to the ship at midnight. I like the way these
English regiments hold on to their traditions. The
Forty-sixth during our War for Independence were in
America, and on account of some bad conduct of their
men our general issued an order that no quarter

should be shown them; that any one of them caught should be at once executed. The colonel of the Forty-sixth thereupon had a red pompon placed in the hats of his officers and men as a part of their uniform, and sent word to our man that they were the only people in the British service who wore the red pompon, and he could with safety execute any one found with it on. The pompon can be seen in the crest of the regiment, and they are having just now a bitter fight about it. When the Forty-sixth came here, Lord Napier noticed the red on their hats and could find no order permitting it, so he directed its removal; but the colonel and officers have petitioned the Queen to allow them to use it. After dinner they showed us the Bible on which General Washington was made a Mason. One of our army officers offered a thousand guineas for it, but the colonel replied that they had already refused forty thousand dollars for it. It was once captured by our people and returned to the regiment; and the French got it twice, but each time sent it back.

"*Sunday*, P. M.—We have been up to our eyes in Englishmen. Yesterday morning we were engaged to breakfast with the Forty-sixth. Our breakfast was an entire success, and when we went to the range our friends of the Forty-sixth met with a most crushing defeat. After we had beat them with our own gun we took theirs—the Martini-Henry—and beat their best score. About four in the afternoon Colonel Bennett turned out his regiment and gave us a drill which was beautiful to see. We got back at seven and dressed for a dinner at the engineers' mess, for which we had accepted an invitation. We had a beautiful dinner, and got on board at midnight. I had intended going to sea to-day, but when we got on board found a note from Lord Napier, saying that he had ordered a target put out, and would have the thirty-eight-ton gun fired for us Monday afternoon. As each shot costs fifty guineas (!), of course we had to stay, and so shall not get away until Tuesday. I was shocked on our arrival here to get a telegram saying that Zeilin had been killed. Poor Billy! He must have been thrown from his horse. Before we left home he had been riding in a very desperate sort of way, and his friends had predicted that he would come to grief. Now I must get to bed and try to make up the lost sleep of the last three nights.

" *At Sea. Off Cape de Gatte, 18th June.*—We managed to get away from Gibraltar Tuesday morning, and I flatter myself we did it handsomely—much better than our New York affair, of which so much was said. The night before we left we had an awful 'ranky' dinner with the artillery, which was very enjoyable. We had much scientific talk, but managed to pull through.

" Tuesday afternoon Lord and Lady Napier and all the swells turned out to see the thirty-eight-ton gun fired, and it was evident from the first that we were to be immensely impressed. After the gun had been cast loose and run into battery, we were shown how easily it would work, and with what perfect accuracy it could be controlled. Just as the colonel in charge was telling me this, the monster got away from them, and out it went with a bang that almost upset the carriage! Of course, all hands caught the mischief, though it was simply due to a lack of knowledge of the complicated machinery. It took over ten minutes to load the gun, and when it was fired at a target, about a mile away, the shot struck seventy yards short and bounded heavenward. When it was loaded the second time and all ready, the order was given to fire, but the primer failed, and they continued to fail for four or five minutes, when, by pouring powder into the vent, they managed to get it off. This shot struck fifty yards over. The third and last shot stuck in the gun, so that it took some fifteen minutes to load it, and when it was fired the projectile went one hundred and twenty yards wide of the target. Lord Napier was awfully disgusted, as well he might be, and we were not in the least bit impressed or frightened."

We made a new record for sailing vessels from Gibraltar to Naples, and I was much gratified at the comments of the Italian officers when we entered the latter port. We ran in under all sail and picked up our buoy without lowering a boat, and then furled everything very smartly, which, in that day of mastless ironclads, attracted much attention.

After several weeks of interesting cruising I reached Villefranche, where I found that I had not been forgotten. The following from my journal shows that my kindness to the poor, when executive officer of the Congress, had made a lasting impression:

" *Villefranche Sur Mer*, *17th July*.—Night before last I was, as I had expected to be, up all night. In the morning at daylight we were in the mouth of the harbour, but not a breath of air; so we hoisted out the boats and towed her in. The place looked as natural as possible, but I missed the face of the old pilot, who used always to get thirty francs when one of our ships came in. The same old one-gun battery returned our salute, taking about half an hour to do it. As soon as we were anchored I sent for the mail, and before long my old friends began to pour in. First came the bumboat people, and then the washerwomen. I could not remember the name of one of them, and was really ashamed when they all knew me and were so glad to see me, and asked after my children. I suppose a dozen or more of them had interviewed me, when Carolina (my former cook) came and wanted to cry at sight of me, but I talked too fast for her. The poor soul has had great trouble, and her husband has deserted her, leaving her with three children to support. I sent for my steward, and gave orders that she should have plenty for them all to eat while we remain here. Carolina had not gone, when Antionetta Allari came rushing at me past the orderly, who had by this time made up his mind that it was no use trying to stop them. Antionetta is fat and lovely, and was disposed to kiss me, and with tears in her eyes asked after my wife and children. Then came Angelica in the same way, and I don't know how many more, all asking after my family."

On one of my trips to Tangier my old friend Colonel Mathews arranged a wild-boar hunt for me, which I enjoyed very much when it was over. After riding on horseback about fifteen miles over a very rough country we came to the jungle where the first drive was to be made. A tribe of Moors, under their venerable old chief, were to do the driving, and I was to do the shooting. The chief inspected my gun, a Hotchkiss magazine service rifle, and suggested that I take a double-barrelled shotgun and load it with balls; but I preferred to work with the tool I had selected, with which I was familiar. He explained to me that the cover was very thick where I was going to shoot, and that the pig would be close to me before I saw him; and that I would only have time for two quick shots before he charged and was on top of me. I was not over well pleased with this description of what I had to face, but decided that I would kill with my magazine rifle or let the pig go. I had not the least intention that he should get me.

When we had penetrated the jungle half a mile or more we found a well-beaten pig-track, and, selecting a favourable point, I took my station. The chief explained that I would first hear the dogs, of which they had a large number, give tongue; then I would hear the men shouting as they drove the pig in my direction; and, finally, when sure that he was coming to me, they would fire blank cartridges in their guns to keep him moving. The old man took his departure and left me alone with my gun. I looked about me for a convenient tree up which I might climb in case of necessity, and having found one a few yards from my station, felt decidedly more comfortable. Then I waited while the flies buzzed about my head and the mosquitoes stung me wherever my skin was exposed. I was almost on the point of giving up the job when I heard the far-away barking of a dog, and then a dozen or more joined in, and the sound came rapidly my way. I examined the gun to make sure that it was ready, and while doing so found that my hands were shaking just the least bit. However, I was out for pigs, and it sounded as if a whole drove were coming my way, and I must have one at least. The baying of the dogs was now mixed with the shouting of the Moors, and in a few seconds I heard the guns begin. About thirty yards from where I was standing, and in the direction of the dogs, there was a slight rise in the ground, and while I was intently watching for the pig I saw his head come above the weeds and grass on this rise. He stopped for a moment, and, with his head partly turned from me, was apparently trying to judge the direction in which the beaters were coming. I considered him quite close enough for comfort, and, throwing the gun to my shoulder, fired at a point about where I supposed the point of his shoulder-blade to be. Then I stepped nearer my tree and, with the second cartridge ready to fire, waited to see what would happen. Everything was quiet where the pig had been for a few minutes, then the dogs and men were upon us.

When I found there were no pigs coming, I walked out and met the chief, and showed him about where one had been when I fired at him. On approaching the spot, there he was, sure enough, and as dead as a herring. He was a vicious-looking beast, with tusks seven inches long, and weighed over five hundred pounds. At close quarters he would have used a man up in very short order. A second drive was decided on, and this time I fired at something I saw moving in the bushes and killed a jackal, which pleased the Moors better than the killing of the pig, as this animal destroyed many of their sheep. Before I left Tangiers I secured a young wild pig, which became a great pet on board ship. She finally came to an untimely end from eating too many live-oak acorns at Fortress Monroe. Like all pigs on board ship, male or female, she was named "Dennis," and soon learned to chew tobacco and drink strong hot coffee.

On the way home I stopped at Madeira, and then, taking the trades, ran to Fortress Monroe in twenty-six days. After transferring my crew of boys to ships in service, I proceeded to Baltimore, moored to the dock, and prepared to ship another crew of green lads and be ready to take them to sea in the spring. My time was up, however, and I could not object to my detachment, which came in the early winter. I had been in command four years, and had thoroughly enjoyed the work, which was of vast importance to the country and the service, and to me personally most attractive and interesting. Most of the boys who came under my care have advanced to warrant or petty officers. Those who left the service have good positions on shore; scarcely a week passes that I do not meet some of them, and they are always glad to speak to me and say a good word for the old ship. When war comes, they all flock back to us and do most excellent service. It would be a good thing for the country if we had twenty Saratogas always in commission, making better men of those who sail in them, whether they follow the sea or find their places on the land.

CHAPTER XIX

METALLURGY AND LIGHTHOUSES

FROM the Saratoga I was transferred at once to the position of equipment officer of the Washington Navy Yard, where in a few weeks I found myself deeply interested in the manufacture of chain cables for the navy and gun forgings for the ordnance. Seamanship, with all its pleasures, had to be set aside for the time, and hard thought and work given to metallurgy. The change was very sudden, but only what every officer has to be prepared for, and the effect was undoubtedly good. We were on the edge of the experimental period, during which the navy was to shake off the mould that had been accumulating since the period of the civil war and once more occupy the proud position it had held in former years.

While I was busily engaged in making experiments on steel cables and anchors, and trying to find, with a new fuel (vaporized petroleum), a satisfactory means of welding steel, Secretary Hunt organized the first Advisory Board for the rebuilding of the navy. The board was composed of able officers of the line, engineer and construction corps, and was presided over by Admiral John Rodgers, who was probably the best-equipped officer in the service for the position. I was fortunate enough to be ordered as a member of the board. We sat during the entire summer of 1882, and our report was submitted to the Secretary, who recommended action by Congress. This was the first step taken toward rebuilding the navy, but it was many years before actual work was begun.

A short time after the board was organized I submitted a resolution, to the effect that all vessels recommended by the board should be built of steel. This precipitated a discussion which lasted many months and caused much comment both in and out of the service. I state the fact of having offered the resolution only because I wish to assume the responsibility that necessarily attached to it. The line officers, as a body, stood with me, as did several of the engineer officers, but the officers of the construction corps were solidly against the proposition, on the ground that we could not make the material, and that American ship builders could not build steel ships. The issue was clearly drawn, and the discussion, which covered a wide field, became at times heated. Finally, the Naval Committees of the two Houses of Congress were asked to meet the board in the office of the Secretary of the Navy to hear the finish of this important matter. The meeting was held, and those favouring steel as the material for all naval constructions won the day. It was this action of naval officers that opened the way to the steel industry of the United States, to outstrip all its foreign competitors, as it has undoubtedly done.

At the time this action was taken, it was true, as claimed by the constructors, that we could not manufacture steel plates in this country; but it was only because there had been no demand for them. Once having the demand, the supply followed promptly, and it was of the best quality. We were buying steel gun-forgings and shafting abroad only because we demanded them in such small quantities. When we wanted enough of them to make their manufacture a paying venture, our own people produced them in any desired quantity and of any specified quality. I shall always feel proud of the work, small though it was, that I did in connection with the Advisory Board of 1882.

When I had served less than two years as equipment officer of the Washington yard I was detached and ordered as inspector of the Fifth Lighthouse District, with headquarters at Baltimore, Maryland. The change from metallurgy to a disbursing officer under the Secretary of the Treasury and the care of buoys and lighthouses was radical, but it was a part of my profession and therefore to be done. Being a disbursing officer without bond frightened me somewhat at first, but I soon found that it was easy work, requiring only care and honesty. The duty was pleasant and congenial, and kept me very much in the open air, with fine opportunities for shooting and fishing, which I did not neglect. My district extended from Havre de Grace, Maryland, to Beaufort, North Carolina, and included all the buoys and lighthouses in the navigable waters within those limits.

The condition of the lighthouse service at that time was far from satisfactory. The appointment of the keepers was in political hands, and though the inspector had the examination of the men, it was practically impossible to prevent the appointment of those who rendered political service. An attempt to do this was the cause of serious trouble to me long before my tour of duty was completed. I found that the light-keepers were being assessed a portion of their pay for political purposes, which was clearly illegal, and when I directed them to refuse to pay such assessments I became *persona non grata* to a certain class of men having political power but nothing else to commend them. They were quite honest with me, however, and served notice on me that unless I changed my ways I would come to grief, which I eventually did.

A certain fellow, who had been elected a delegate to a political convention, was nominated to be light-keeper as a reward, but was found so disreputable on examination that I refused to pass him. I would not submit to dictation in my duties by a set of men quite as disreputable as the suggested keeper, and on this issue I was detached and placed on waiting orders. Report was made to the Secretary of the Navy that I was interfering with political conditions in the Fifth District, and, without asking a word of explanation from me, I was punished by being relieved and placed on reduced pay. It was, of course, a gross injustice, and caused no end of comment in the newspapers; but I took it as quietly as possible, and have always felt contented that I was not personally known to the man who could so far degrade the high office he held. The navy had in some ways degenerated into a job lot, at least in the eyes of those who used it for their own purposes, and was sometimes let to a very low bidder.

Finding myself on the beach, as it were, because I would not take a hand in politics, rather than because I had done so, and knowing that I would not have employment again during the time of the Administration then in power, I asked for leave for a year, with permission to leave the United States. In the absence of the Secretary of the Navy the request was granted, and I was busy making preparations to enjoy it, when a telegram came from the Secretary revoking my leave and again placing me on waiting orders. I was really of more importance than I had considered myself, and I must be made to feel my punishment. However, I had felt the sting of insects before in my life, and did not consider them of much importance.

The Baltimore and Ohio Railroad Company was about to build a large steel bridge over the Susquehanna River at Havre de Grace, and Colonel Henry T. Douglas, the able chief engineer of the company, offered me a position as inspector of material, which I was glad to accept. In a few days I was installed in my office at Pittsburg, and had charge of the inspection of all bridge material for the Baltimore and Ohio road. It proved most congenial work to me, and thoroughly occupied all my time, giving me an insight into the manufacture of various kinds of steel and the working of the mills that was to prove of great benefit to me personally as well as to the Government. The bridge in question was the first one in this country constructed of Bessemer steel, and caused much trouble before it was finally completed. The Carnegie firm had the contract, and its familiarity with steel rails led its members into the error of supposing that a bridge could be built of the same sort of stuff. The process of convincing them that this was not the case caused serious delay and much friction, but in the end Mr. Andrew Carnegie showed his admirable qualities, and carried out his contract to the satisfaction of all concerned. The bridge was completed, and proved to be all that Colonel Douglas claimed for it. In the meantime I had learned, from hard experience, many things about the manufacture of steels that I could not have learned in any other way. It was on my suggestion that Mr. Carnegie first seriously considered the question of starting a plate mill for the manufacture of ship plates. Aside from what I had actually learned, the acquaintance I had made among men engaged in the steel industry was to be of vast importance to me in the years to come.

When the Administration had changed, and Mr. W. C. Whitney, the prince of secretaries, had taken his place as Secretary of the Navy, there was a sense of relief among us all. His business methods soon began to show excellent results, and his fair treatment of those under him made officers and men alike feel that he was their friend. After he had been in office but a few weeks he sent for me, and, telling me frankly what the reports against me as inspector of the Fifth District had been, heard what I had to say in reply. I was immediately ordered to resume my duties in Baltimore; but, in view of the large amount of work I had on hand in Pittsburg, I was allowed to delay one month in order that I might complete it.

Once more in the lighthouse service, and this time with the assurance that my side of any controversy would be heard, I felt that I could do many things to the benefit of the service. The change of Administration brought with it a desire on the part of the smaller politicians for a complete change in the keepers of all lighthouses, as well as in other Government places. The Secretary of the Treasury and the Lighthouse Board decided that political opinion was not a sufficient cause for removal. If a keeper was found neglecting his duty he was to be removed at once; but in all cases where charges were preferred against them keepers were to have a fair investigation, and justice was to be done them. Charges were written against nearly every keeper in the district, and many of these documents were worthy of Thomas Jefferson or Henry Clay. I carefully investigated every case, and, after hearing all the evidence, sent in my report. Out of over four hundred keepers I found it necessary to recommend the removal of one, and one only, for neglecting his duties to do political work.

One case on investigation amused me very much; it is a fair sample case. The keeper of a light on the western shore of Chesapeake Bay was charged with offences enough to have hanged a dozen men. The language of the report against him was, as I have stated before, worthy of Thomas Jefferson. I notified all the witnesses to be at the station on a certain day to give testimony in the case. After a long hearing the lawyer who represented the side of the com-

plainants admitted that he had failed to show cause
for removal; but the charge of drunkenness still had
to be heard. The witness to this charge was a fisherman who had been playing cards with the accused
keeper, and upon being sworn testified that he, the
keeper, was undoubtedly drunk—very drunk. I asked
what the indications of drunkenness were. "Well,
sir, the accused was playing ' seven up ' with me, and
had only two to go when I dealt him the Jack and
deuce, and he begged; now, you can't convince any
man in Matthews County, Virginia, that a man who
would do that wasn't drunk; certainly he was drunk,
sir, and ought to be turned out." I sent to the Treasury Department many cases where the evidence wasn't
even as incriminating as the above.

I found most of the keepers of lighthouses in Virginia waters were coloured men put in office by General Mahone and his followers. Many of them had to
be removed, generally because they would go to sleep
and neglect their lights. One of them I had to remove for a very curious offence, or rather he removed
himself when he found I was going to do it. I visited
the station where he was on watch, and was inspect-
ing, when I noticed that he followed me about, spitting frequently when he thought I was not observing
him. I learned from the principal keeper, a coloured
Methodist minister, that the fellow was chewing herbs
and spitting around me as a hoodoo to prevent me
from reporting the various irregularities I discovered.
When he found that I had reported them all, and
asked his removal as well, he jumped overboard and
was not seen again.

New Ships

When Congress had appropriated money for new ships, Mr. Whitney detached me from lighthouse duty and ordered me as chief steel inspector, with an office in the Navy Department. The rebuilding of the navy had begun in earnest, and the work could not have been in the hands of a man who understood better how to handle it. In addition to being an able business man of broad gauge, Mr. Whitney knew how to select his subordinates and get the best work out of them.

I went to work at once on the specifications for the material for the new ships, and it was at this time that I felt most the advantages my Pittsburg experiences gave me. I was confident of what the steel men could do, and I therefore made the specifications harder than those of the British admiralty, which had, up to this time, been considered quite difficult to fill. When I had secured the services of a sufficient number of line officers to look after the inspection of the material, I went with them to the different mills and showed them just how the work was to be done. In a wonderfully short space of time everything was working smoothly, and the shipyards were being supplied as rapidly as they could use the material. This was not accomplished, however, without much complaint from certain steel mills. They thought the specifications too severe, and declared that they could not fill them; but I knew better, and was able to convince the Secretary that it would be bad policy to change. I knew, of course, that pot metal was cheaper than steel, and that our people would go on making pot metal until we forced them to do something better. Men were not in the business for their health, and if they could get steel prices for pot metal, so much the better. Many of the leading firms saw the advantage of working to a high standard, and they admitted afterward that our specifications and inspection had been the very best thing for them in the end. It was marvellous to see with what rapid strides our people went ahead, until in a few years we could make better stuff than any of the celebrated foreign concerns. Eventually the United States became a dangerous rival in the steel markets of the world. It is a pleasure to know that I lived to see it, even if I had so little to do with accomplishing the result.

When everything was running smoothly and the steel being supplied satisfactorily, the Department found a new job for me. I was ordered as naval secretary of the Lighthouse Board, and at last I was in position to do many things I had long hoped to accomplish. Mr. Fairchild, the Secretary of the Treasury, was a most progressive and able business man, and saw the good to come from many of the things I proposed. With the approval and assistance of the board, I succeeded in having the lighthouse keepers put into a proper uniform, and their appointment entirely removed from any chance of political interference.

I had long felt the necessity of some system of lights by which large vessels, particularly the ocean liners, could enter the harbour of New York during the night instead of lying outside and waiting for daylight. Captain Fred Rodgers, the able inspector of the Third District, and Lieutenant-Commander Mackenzie, his assistant, gave me their cordial assistance, and by united effort we worked out and installed the system of electrically lighted buoys now in use. I supplied the money and they the brains, and between us we scored a great success. New York was the first place in the world to be supplied with such buoys, and from the day they were put down vessels came in at night as readily as in daytime.

In my efforts to aid the seafaring people, knowing well their necessities, I sometimes encountered very curious opposition. A whistling buoy was placed in the entrance to Newport Harbour, where the dense fogs made navigation very dangerous for the thousands of passengers who entered and left Narragansett Bay. The captains and officers of vessels on that part of the coast were very grateful, but in a few weeks one of the leading landed proprietors on Bateman's Point, a man of wide scientific reputation, complained of the buoy as a nuisance, and brought every possible influence to bear on the Lighthouse Board to have it removed, regardless of the interests of commerce. He finally asserted that the noise made by the buoy was so dreadful that it turned the milk sour in his fine herd of Jersey cows. When we had secured a proper site and built a lighthouse and fog signal to protect the dangerous point the whistler was removed, and the professor again had sweet milk for his breakfast.

After getting my work in the Lighthouse Board in good shape, I was given a job in shipbuilding in addition to my other duties. Congress had made an appropriation for building two armoured cruisers in Government dockyards, and one of them was to be constructed at the New York yard. For some reason there was great delay in starting the work, which did not meet with the business views of Mr. Whitney. He sent for me and, after discussing the case somewhat, said to me: "We have everything that the Cramps have—engineers, constructors, draughtsmen—everything except Cramp; yet we can't get the ship started. I want you to be Cramp, and get things moving." So I went to New York, and in my very limited way tried to play the part of the great shipbuilder Cramp, who has no peer in his line of work. The keel of the Maine was promptly laid and the material rapidly procured, but, owing to the lack of proper machinery and the vast amount of red tape encountered under the monstrous bureau organization of the Navy Department, progress was very slow. I well remember striking a small water pipe while placing the foundations for a plate-bending machine, and the month and more of anxious work to find out which bureau owned it, and then to get it moved a few feet. I generally left Washington on Monday, spent Tuesday and Wednesday with my able assistants in the New York yard, and on Wednesday night returned to my work in the Lighthouse Board. I had always held that it was better for an officer to wear out rather than rust out. About this time I was confident that I was not in danger of rust.

When the Harrison Administration came in I felt the need of rest, and at once applied for a year's leave, which was granted. I intended to take service with the newly organized Nicaragua Canal Company, but finding that undesirable, was employed by a New York syndicate, which was to engage in the manufacture of wood fibre under a new process. This opened to me a new field of study, and I was busily engaged looking over the various water powers in Maine and examining the supply of spruce wood, when suddenly, without warning, I was ordered to command the United States steamer Ossipee, at Norfolk, Virginia. I was to sail as soon as possible, and take Mr. Frederick Douglass, our minister to Hayti, and his family to Port-au-Prince. The ship was reported by the yard officials as unfit for sea on account of the condition of her boilers. Certain newspapers assumed that I did not fancy the job, and had therefore, in some mysterious way, disabled the ship, to avoid obeying my orders. As the ship had plenty of canvas, I was confident that I could sail her to Hayti, and I was very sure she would drift back with the Gulf Stream when I had landed the minister; so I wired the Secretary that, notwithstanding the report about the boilers, I was prepared to carry out the orders he had given me. At the same time I assured him that I had no feeling as to the cargo he might order carried in a Government vessel, be it ammunition, ministers, dynamite, or mules. I had known Mr. Douglass all my life, and entertained the highest respect for him. Another vessel was ordered to convey him to his station, and the Ossipee, on closer inspection, was found too rotten even to permit of repairs. After being in command two weeks, I was again granted leave and allowed to go on with my outside work.

When I had fairly mastered my subject I was directed to erect a sulphite-fibre mill at Appleton, Wisconsin, which I did, and in nine months had it completed and turning out first-class sheets of wood fibre. During the winter I was engaged on this work the thermometer frequently went as low as 30° below zero, and once touched 39° below; but the air was very dry, and I enjoyed every hour of the time. My water power was at last harnessed, and when all the water wheels were running and the vast mass of machinery doing its work, I felt well repaid for my labour. The knowledge I gained was of great benefit to me afterward when I found myself in command of a ship with her seventy-odd engines of various kinds.

CHAPTER XX

THE YORKTOWN'S CRUISE TO CHILE

In August, 1891, I was ordered to command the gunboat Yorktown, then in the North Atlantic Squadron, known as the " White Squadron," from the fact that the ships were all painted white. I joined her in New York, relieving Commander F. E. Chadwick, who had commanded her since she was first placed in commission. She had the reputation of being a strong, well-built ship, very fast in smooth water, but a little tender in a heavy sea. Her officers were able men, and her crew very smart and well up in their drills and exercises. Ten days after I assumed command the squadron, under command of Admiral Walker, got under way and passed up through Hell Gate, the flagship Chicago leading. We visited a number of New England ports where fairs and shows of various kinds were being held, and where the presence of a number of war ships would add to the attractions of such gatherings. It was not very exciting work, and was in many ways unpleasant duty, but the ships belonged to the people, and we were only too glad to show them how their money was being used. In return for what little courtesy we could show them the people were kind and generous in their treatment of us, and entertained us with true New England hospitality.

At the end of September I was ordered to New York to prepare at once for foreign service. A few days later orders came for us to proceed without delay to Valparaiso, Chile, and report to the admiral commanding the Pacific station for duty. The Chileans had for a year past been fighting among themselves, and unfortunately much bad feeling had been shown toward us, particularly toward our navy, by the revolutionary party in this war. The friction between the two countries had become acute, and the prospect of active service, possibly war, gave great interest to our cruise. We worked incessantly night and day, and on October 8th I hauled out from the navy yard and that evening put to sea. As we passed Sandy Hook the storm signals were flying, and everything indicated a northeast gale; but for the time being the wind was fresh from northwest, and we ran for Hatteras with all sails set and a fair wind. The long northeast swell that was felt all the next day warned me not to lose any time in getting across the Gulf Stream if I wanted to avoid trouble. Owing to the reputation the ship had of being tender under canvas, I did not drive her hard for the first day or two, but gradually, as we learned her tricks, we gave her all she could stand, and I found to my surprise that she was as stiff as a church, and could easily carry all her canvas.

We ran just ahead of the northeaster until we reached the latitude of Bermuda, where we found beautiful weather, which we held until we arrived at St.

A Heavy Sea

Thomas. We made the land in the afternoon just before dark, and were fortunate enough to get in in time to avoid a hurricane which passed to the south of us during the night. We coaled in eight hours, and by noon of the following day were off again, bound for Bahia, in Brazil, which was to be our second coaling port. As we passed through the beautiful West India Islands the marks of the recent hurricane were all about us in the shape of trees and *débris* blown off from the land. These Windward Islands are certainly as grand in scenery as any in the world. I did not wonder at the enthusiasm of Columbus and 'his rascally crew of thieves as they sailed about there in search of the yellow metal and slaves. For the first few days out of St. Thomas the Yorktown raised Cain, because she had a heavy following sea which made her roll very badly. I had my chair lashed, and so managed to hold on, but I was about the only thing in the cabin that did. One minute she was down on her beam ends apparently, the next second she was down on the other side, and in the interval she had done more different kinds of things than any ship I was ever in before; but she did them all very easily and with comfort to her crew. Writing in the cabin was impossible, and there was not much sleep to be had, owing to the constant throbbing of the screws. The weather grew hotter as we ran south, and the fire-room force suffered severely before they became seasoned to the heat. We crossed the line in fine weather for Neptune, who came on board for a visit. We gave the afternoon to him and his antics.

During the night of October 28th the wind suddenly whipped around to the south and blew a hard gale from that quarter. We drove head into it all night, and at daylight had the land in sight ahead and on both bows, but nothing that we could recognise. My cabin had been flooded during the night, and I had spent my time on the bridge, so was well pleased when the navigator found something he could swear by. We had been set out of our course eighteen miles during the night, but now we had the entrance buoys in sight, and in a short time were anchored in the harbour, eleven and a half days from St. Thomas—not a bad run for the little ship. It was my first visit to Bahia, and I found the city, as viewed from the water, very pleasing. The health officer, a much-begilded dago, paid his visit and assured me that there was no fever on shore, the health of the place in his opinion being perfect. I took this with many grains of salt, and gave the necessary orders to guard against infection if possible.

The coal men, bumboat men, and various other sharks were soon on board. Coal was twelve dollars a ton, but have it I must, no matter what the cost, and arrangements were made to fill my bunkers at the earliest possible moment. The American consul soon came on board, and from him I learned that the Chileans had killed several of the crew of the Baltimore and wounded many others in the streets of Valparaiso; that the Boston and Atlanta had been ordered out, and that other vessels were soon to follow. Of course, we were much excited over the news, and most anxious to hurry on our way. We drove the coal men to their limit day and night.

From a copyrighted photograph by Enrique Muller.

Gunboat Yorktown.

A Pig Lost

I had lost so much sleep during the last days of the run from St. Thomas that I found myself quite done up; but a few hours' sleep, a fine fresh lettuce salad, a pineapple, and many glasses of iced water quite put me on edge again, and I was ready for whatever might come my way. In the late afternoon a German steamer from Santos, Brazil, came in and anchored a short distance astern of us. The health officer visited her and then came to inform me that she had six cases of yellow fever on board, and had lost her chief engineer and four men of the crew from the same disease on her way up the coast. It was only after I had used some very strong language that this brass-bound individual returned and shifted the steamer's berth to the quarantine ground. He had assured me that there was no yellow fever on shore, but I did not believe a word he said, and never went on shore myself nor allowed any one else, except those having important business, to go. On October 30th I received a telegram from the Secretary of the Navy to proceed to Montevideo and there await further instructions. This, of course, might mean anything— change of orders, or to await the arrival of more ships before proceeding. One thing I was sure of, however, and that was that I was to lose no time in getting to the point indicated; and I did not. As soon as the coaling was completed and mess stores taken in I put to sea. The caterer of the wardroom mess complained of the difficulty of getting necessary articles, and the loss of one very important one in the shape of a black pig. The pig had been brought on board, but disappeared in a very mysterious way—it was supposed that he had gone overboard through one of the ports.

When once more outside and heading for Montevideo, we found the sea very heavy, caused by a strong southwest breeze. About six o'clock in the evening of the third day out the clouds began to bank up a little in the southwest, and occasional flashes of lightning could be seen, which gradually increased, until by half past eight it was one vibration of light. The effect was most alarming, but at the same time grand and beautiful. The brain was stunned and the eyes blinded by it. As yet not a sound of thunder could be heard, though the storm was evidently approaching us with great rapidity.

I stood on the deck aft watching it, and when, at about 9.30, it struck us, I was blown down as if by some heavy weight. Our sails, though furled, were snatched off the ship in a second, and went whirling through the air like great birds straight up over the mastheads. At the same moment the thunder broke over us like forty batteries of artillery, and the electric fluid running down our conductors was sufficient to make the whole deck as bright as noonday. It was the most awful, grand, and beautiful sight I ever saw. Of course, I realized that a whirlwind had struck us. Nothing could be done to save our sails—they were gone; but I could do something to ease the little frigate and help her out of the scrape. I rang full speed ahead, and pointed her up to the wind so that I passed through the blessed whirlwind in the shortest possible time. Just ten minutes after it struck us it was gone, and so were all our sails and much of our rigging; but I was satisfied to get off as well as we did.' It was the beginning of a nasty, hard, southwest gale which blew all day, and, in fact, at intervals in various directions for several days afterward.

All day Wednesday we had to head her up to the sea and slow her to six knots, as she was taking in too much water over the bows; but with it all she proved herself a perfect beauty, and one of the best sea boats I was ever in. I was on the deck constantly, of course, watching everything, increasing speed whenever practicable, and so managed to plug along, and on the morning of November 7th, at three o'clock, made Maldonado Light, and anchored at Montevideo in the forenoon. What a difference—October 8th in New York, November 8th in Montevideo! We certainly had made a good run, doing the distance, including stops, in thirty days, which, I believe, was the best ever done by a vessel of war.

The usual calls were made on me at once, and in returning them I got a good wetting, as there was a heavy sea running, and the place was totally unprotected by anything like a breakwater. The whole South Atlantic came tumbling in when the wind was in the right direction, and made it very nasty. Captain Lang, of the Cleopatra (English), came on board in a driving rainstorm to call. He had been in command of the Chinese navy at one time, and I found him a most interesting man to talk to. Soon after he left me the rain turned into a southeast gale, and by night it was howling at a great rate, the ship pitching as if she were at sea. This was not promising for taking the coal, which I had ordered to be alongside at daylight in the morning. However, I went to sleep, hoping that it would pass off as suddenly as it came. I knew that everything in that part of the world, from the form of government to the rise of the tide, changed with great rapidity. In this, however, I was mistaken; the weather grew worse rather than better, and the ship began walking away with her anchor. A second anchor brought her up, and she rode it out, pitching bows under in the heavy seas which were breaking clear over the Cleopatra.

As soon as I arrived I wired the Navy Department the fact, stating that I would leave in five days, that time being necessary to complete the new sails which had been ordered, and some of the canvas cut in two hours after my anchor was down. The following day I had a cable from the Secretary of the Navy directing me to proceed to Valparaiso, which was very satisfactory. I got under way at once from the outer anchorage and took the ship inside, where I ran her on to the mud so that we might coal. She was soon a mass of coal dust from stem to stern.

On the way down from Bahia, and when five days out from that place, I had a curious experience with the pig the wardroom mess had lost. At two o'clock in the morning I was aroused by my orderly, who announced, " Sir, Dennis is found." " Who the devil is Dennis," I replied, " and why do you disturb me? " He explained that Dennis was the lost pig, that he had been found in a coal bunker, was very weak and ill, and they wanted the captain to come out and see if anything could be done for him. So out I went, and found the ship's cook with the pig in his arms feeding him condensed milk out of a teaspoon. One of the coal passers, an Irish lad, had gone into the coal bunker to pass out coal for the furnaces. After a few shovelfuls had been taken out he felt something move about his feet, and in a moment heard a faint squeal, which in the black darkness of the place was too much for his nerves. Dropping his shovel, he made at top speed for the fire room, thinking the devil was close at his heels! Upon investigation, Dennis was found, so thin that one could almost read a newspaper through him. He had fallen into one of the coal chutes while coal was being taken in, and, becoming packed in with the coal, had remained in that position without food or water for five days, until released by the coal heaver as I have related. He recovered entirely, became the pet of the ship, and cruised with us clear up into the ice of the arctic regions.

When the coaling was fairly under way I went on shore to call on our minister and stretch my legs. Afterward I took a cab and drove about three and a half miles to call on a Mr. Evans, who had sent me his card, and was well repaid for my trouble and time. On the way to his *quinta* (country place) I passed through the main portion of the city, which was clean and comfortable and well paved. Mr. Evans had quite a history. He had gone to Montevideo forty-eight years before, a boy from Pennsylvania, as a sailor on a brig, and, being steady and of a practical turn of mind, thought he would try his hand at supplying ships. From the first he made a success of it, and when the civil war broke out he had amassed a considerable fortune, which he had well invested. The time soon

came when our credit was down and our vessels could
get neither money nor credit, and at this moment Mr.
Evans stepped in and put his entire fortune and all he
could borrow at the disposal of our people, saying
that he would back the United States for all he was
worth. After the war was over he received his money
back with a good interest, and he at once invested in
real estate, which went up with a boom, and he was
immensely wealthy. Then he bought two blocks of
land in the edge of the city and proceeded to make his
home, which was like fairyland. Not having a wife, he
sent home for a widowed cousin, who came out to him
and had always been his housekeeper and mainstay.
When I was there she was very ill, not expected to
live, which threw a gloom over the fascinating place.
She must have been a wonderful woman, for the house
was full of her work—such embroidery as I never
dreamed of, pictures by the dozen so finely done that
I was persuaded they were oil paintings, and such a
collection of bric-a-brac!

But what pleased me most were the flowers—thousands of such roses as we see in the rose catalogues,
American Beauties, as large as a dinner plate, and
Maréchal Niels so perfect that I just stopped and stood
lost in admiration. I don't exaggerate when I say that
one could have filled a freight car with the most perfect
flowers I had ever seen without making perceptible
impression on the mass. When I went back to the
ship I had two large baskets of the beautiful things,
and one of lemons which I had helped to pull, and both
hands full of choice buds; the cabin was beautiful as a
result. When Mr. Evans first started in business he

had had built in Baltimore a very able boat, which was brought out on the deck of a vessel, and with her his fortune was begun. She was now hauled up in his yard, painted and gilded and surrounded with flowers, and as they would not allow him to fly the American flag here, he had it painted on her mast, wrapped round and round from one end to the other. He had known every naval officer in these waters for forty years, and many of his stories were most interesting.

During my stay at Montevideo I had many cables from the Department regarding the new Chilean cruiser Errazuriz, which for some reason was causing them much anxiety. I found that she was undergoing repairs at Buenos Ayres, and promptly sent an officer in plain clothes to have a look at her. He succeeded in getting on board, and remained more than an hour before he was suspected and invited to leave. During that time he had found out all I wanted to know, and after he had made his report I wired the Secretary her condition, and that he need not worry about her, as I could do her up with the Yorktown in thirty minutes if it became necessary. The news from Valparaiso at this time was alarming. The tension between the two Governments was great, and war might come at any moment.

The instant our new sails were on board I again put to sea. I find in my journal the following:

" *Friday Night, November 20th.*—We are at anchor inside Cape Virgin in the Straits of Magellan, the most desolate spot God ever made; but glad to be here, for it is a frightful night at sea—blowing a howler from northwest, and so bitterly cold! . . .

A Sailor's Log

" The day before we left Montevideo the Philco-mayo, a Chilean gunboat, came into port and anchored near us for the purpose, no doubt, of advising the Errazuriz at Buenos Ayres of our movements, and the latter may make an effort to beat us to Valparaiso; but she will have to ' dust ' if she does it, for we have averaged twelve knots since leaving the river, and won't let any grass grow on our ship's bottom until I report to the admiral. I wish we could have a scrap with the Errazuriz, for I feel confident that we could take her into camp in forty-five minutes by the watch, notwithstanding all her new French rapid-fire guns; but no such chance will offer, I fear.

" Within a mile of us, on the point of Cape Virgin, lies a magnificent great iron ship smashed to pieces and turned upon her beam ends. It was a painful sight as we came by; some poor fellow, no doubt, running in a gale and thick weather, and two hundred yards more could have taken him clear."

At early daylight I was again under way, standing for Sandy Point, where I anchored at 4 P. M., thoroughly worn out and nearly frozen to death by a gale from such awful snow-clad mountains that I was nearly congealed, and unfit for work. I could see the great glaciers forty miles away glinting in the sun. Our recent run through the tropics had unfitted us for this sort of weather, and our suffering was very considerable. I remained at Sandy Point only from sundown one day until 3 A. M. of the next, when it was light enough to see, when I again drove ahead at thirteen knots speed, fearing that the Errazuriz might be trying to get ahead of me.

In Smythe's Channel

The scenery was grand beyond anything I have ever seen, but it was so fearfully cold and blowing such a howling gale that I could not enjoy it as I would if I had not been compelled to face it all the time. That first night we found an anchorage in a snug little hole in Smythe's Channel, and had a comfortable night surrounded by such mountains of snow and ice as Switzerland never dreamed of. Directly east of us was a magnificent mountain, as large as all Switzerland, and a pure clear white to the very top, where the outline was as sharp as broken glass; and in the very front, facing us, a glacier thirty miles long. As the sun set, the light on the blue crystal ice was a sight to be remembered, and the silence most delicious—one could have cut it with a knife, it was so dense. In the early morning, 2 A. M., daylight, we were under way and again driving north through Smythe's Channel, which was much more beautiful than the Magellan Strait. There was hardly a moment when we were out of sight of a glacier as we twisted and turned through this tortuous channel, but always the same biting, bitter cold.

Our second and last night in this inland sea we found a most beautiful spot for the night about sixty miles south of the English Narrows, which are the terror of all navigators. When our anchor was down we could just swing clear of the rocks, which rose sixteen hundred to three thousand feet straight up and down all around us, with a magnificent waterfall almost on our stern. It was as if we had been dropped into a well—only our surroundings were perfect. At each of our stopping places the men landed and put up our

head-board bearing the name of the ship, date, etc.
This is a custom which has always prevailed, and some
of the anchorages in the Straits of Magellan looked
like graveyards. We found the Trenton's mark at
one place. I wish I could have had some photographs
of the scenery, for no one can ever comprehend the
utter wildness and magnificence of it from mere description.

From this last anchorage we got under way at
2 A. M., and before seven were approaching the Narrows. As we came up it seemed impossible that a ship
could get through; indeed, there seemed no opening,
the turns were so short. But she went through, running thirteen and a half knots, and it was a beautiful
sight to see her do it—at least the officers told me it
was; I did not see much of it myself, for I had taken
charge, and my blood was rushing so that I was warm
for a few minutes anyhow. I remembered afterward
that every face—all the men were on deck—was turned
to me. We were in the Narrows scarcely six minutes,
and yet in that short time we had made nearly two
complete turns. After we had passed the Narrows
it was all plain sailing, and by four in the afternoon
we were out into the Gulf of Peñas and the nasty
Pacific was about us. And such a gale, and the most
terrific sea I have ever met! It was running from
the southwest and the gale blowing from the northwest, which was our course up the coast, and the little
Yorktown was like an eggshell in the whirl of waters.
We had to run slowly all night, but in the morning I
gradually increased her speed and for two days did
very well, notwithstanding the gale continued; but

then the chief engineer reported that by some mis-
count we were forty tons of coal short, and I was
counting on that forty tons to bring us to Valparaiso.

I put her under half power at once, and on Saturday night at midnight ran in and anchored at Lota,
two hundred and sixty-five miles south of Valparaiso.
Early Sunday we took in seventy-five tons of coal, and
Monday we anchored at Valparaiso at 5 P. M., fifty-
one days from New York. Every one said we had
made a wonderful passage, but I did not think so. If
we had not lost our sails on the coast of Brazil and
thus met with delay at Montevideo, and if we had had
the coal I had counted upon, we should have made a
good passage, but as it was I was not any too well
pleased.

CHAPTER XXI

CHILEAN HOSTILITY

WE found the Baltimore looking warlike and ready for business. The harbour was full of war vessels, and we anchored nearly two miles from the landing; but at that season it made no difference. All the inshore port was filled with the Chilean navy, and a sorry-looking lot they were. The story of the killing of the two men of the Baltimore and the wounding of eighteen others showed it to have been about the most cowardly and brutal thing I ever heard of. The men, to the number of say one hundred, went on shore on liberty at 2 P. M., and at six or half past a mob of two thousand, assisted by the police to the number of fifty, armed with carbines and bayonets, attacked three of our men in a street car, pulled them out and stabbed them in the back; one of them, Reagan, while being supported in the arms of a shipmate, was shot and instantly killed by a policeman. I don't think the shot was meant for him, however, but for the man who was holding him. Reagan was already, to all appearances, stabbed to death, and they meant to kill the other man; but the ball passed through his shirt and neckerchief and through Reagan's neck, killing him instantly. Whenever half a dozen of our men

258

got together they would fight their way through the cowardly mob, but as they were completely unarmed, of course they had no show, and so were gradually cut down, one after another, and dragged off, in some cases by horses, to the prisons. Of all the wounded men of the Baltimore not one was cut or marked in front of his body; all wounds were in the back, which tells its own tale.

When I had called on Captain Schley, commanding the Baltimore, and reported for duty, I paid my visits of ceremony to the authorities on shore and the senior Chilean naval officers afloat. They were all scrupulously polite to me, but everywhere there was intense hatred for the Baltimore and her crew. At this time I think the feeling was confined to them, and did not extend to us as a nation; but later on it changed and involved everything North American. Captain Schley informed me that he was going north in a few days, probably as soon as the Boston arrived, which I regretted, as I thought he should remain until the trouble about his men had been settled. He was in the midst of a correspondence with the intendente, conducted in the most perfect Castilian, to show, or prove, that his men were all perfectly sober when they were assaulted on shore. I did not agree with him in this, for in the first place I doubted the fact, and in the second it was not an issue worth discussing. His men were probably drunk on shore, properly drunk; they went ashore, many of them, for the purpose of getting drunk, which they did on Chilean rum paid for with good United States money. When in this condition they were more entitled to protection than if they had been sober. This was my view of it, at least, and the one I always held about men whom I commanded. Instead of protecting them, the Chileans foully murdered these men, and we believed with the connivance and assistance of armed policemen. That was the issue—not the question of whether they were drunk or sober. I find the following notes from my journal, made at that time, of interest:

" *Valparaiso, December 4, 1891.*—My time has been about all taken up with official calls without end. . . . I found here, when we came, three German ships, with an admiral, three Frenchmen, and the whole Chilean navy; and in addition to calls on each of them, I had to call on our consul, and the intendente of Valparaiso, and the senior naval officer on shore. All hands have been exceedingly polite to me. They all hate the crew of the Baltimore as a whole, but against us, as a nation, I don't think they have any feeling. It is not my business to make trouble here, and I don't intend to give offence to any one until I have orders from home, and then I shall do it with my guns and not with my tongue. I am giving all the time I can to get at the bottom facts about the trouble on hand. As far as I can now see, the mob that set upon the Baltimore's men and brutally murdered them was made up of the worst element of the city, and included discharged sailors from the Chilean fleet and probably soldiers; but it is plain that some of the Chilean sailors helped our unfortunate men in every way they could, and it is known that one officer, a lieutenant of artillery, cut down and generally knocked out seven or eight leaders of a crowd who were trying to get at some of our men in a restaurant. In fact, he drew his sword and defended the door until our men had escaped.

" My position is that even if our men were all drunk that does not justify the police in shooting their heads off. If such be the law, we must either make them change it or stay away from a country where drunkenness is so severely punished. The Government of the United States must have ample apology for this affair, and the families of the men hurt must be paid, or we had better pull out every American from Chilean soil, for their lives won't be worth having. Strongly as I feel on the subject, I can not see any good reason why I should not be perfectly civil and polite to them, even if I have to shoot them to-morrow.

" As soon as my anchor was down the senior officers sent at once and made proper calls, and I, of course, returned them; and then, being the last comer, I called on them all in succession—first the Cochran, then the Esmeralda, then the Huascar, then the Lynch, and then the Condell. On each I was most pleasantly greeted, and the officers were cordial; the men, on the contrary, scowled at me, and looked as if they would be glad of a chance to cut my throat.

" *Saturday, December 5th.*—To-day we have papers up to October 31st. . . . It is curious to sit in this quiet place and read in the home papers of the excitement over Chilean affairs. . . . One paper has it that the Newark and Philadelphia are to come with the Atlanta, and that Gherardi will command; while another, of the same date, says that he goes at once to the West Indies for the winter. There is a telegram published here this afternoon that Walker is ordered to Brazil with the Chicago, Atlanta, and Bennington; and so it goes. One thing, however, I am certain of, and that is that the Yorktown is here without any question, and ready for any sort of business.

"*December 6th.*— . . . At a dinner the other day we had much talk about the recent war in this country, and afterward went out to look at some of the places where the fighting was done. The idea prevails in the United States that the Chileans, and particularly their navy, fought with great bravery; but I find on investigation that such is not the case, at least not according to our standard. Balmaceda's men all seem to have been a miserable lot of traitors, and when the time came to fight they all either ran away or went over to the enemy. To-day I have been on board the Cochran to a dance. The captain invited us. The people were very cordial to us, and we stayed about twenty minutes and then went on shore for a walk.

"*Monday Night, December 7th.*—We are all anxious to-night to know what Congress has done, and what President Harrison has advised about Chile. I do hope it has been so strong and plain that there may be no mistake about it. The feeling on shore is very uneasy, and I could see to-day when walking through the main street with Schley many anxious faces. The mob is all for war with the United States, or any one else as far as that goes; but the sensible men know it would be suicide and nothing else. The Baltimore and Yorktown would give their navy a drubbing in two hours, and when the Boston comes we could shell the town into ruins and never be hurt. Everything to-day looks bad for Chile. The discontent of the army over the preference shown the navy has gone so far that there is great alarm and fear of another revolution, and all the soldiers have been taken out of the forts around the harbour and men from the fleet put in. News from Santiago is also alarming. Fifteen hundred rifles and two thousand revolvers were yesterday stolen from the Government arsenal at that point, and are now supposed to be in the hands of the Balmacedists. Several of the Chilean naval officers have intimated to me very plainly that they would not stand any nonsense, and I don't hesitate to say that I would not be surprised to see another revolution in a month. Recently some officers of the army, who had been promised promotion, received commissions which did not suit them, so they tore them up, put the pieces in a bag, and sent it to the Secretary of War. How is that for military discipline?

" *Tuesday Night.*—No news yet of the President's message nor what Congress thinks of affairs in Chile. The Baltimore received orders to-day to proceed to Mare Island, and in a few days I shall be here alone to face the music until Wiltse comes in the Boston.

" *December 11th.*—The Baltimore sailed away for Mare Island at 9 A. M. to-day, cheered by all the foreign ships except the Chileans. First we gave them three times three, then the French cheered them, and the Germans followed suit; both nations had up the signal, ' Wish you pleasant trip,' to which Schley answered, ' Thank you.' The senior Chilean ship, the Cochran, hoisted a signal, but we could not

make out the flags, and the Baltimore did not answer,
so I suppose they could not read it. The signal was
kept flying until the Baltimore was out of sight, when
they hauled it down. I suppose we will now be told
that Captain Schley did this as an insult to the Chilean
flag. For all official purposes I shall assume that the
signal was not read, and could not have been, because
the officer of the Cochran waited too long before
hoisting it. . . .

"I have followed strictly the regulations and customs for intercourse with foreign ships of nations with
whom we are at peace, and the result is that the
Chilean officers have been most careful in observing
toward me the greatest courtesy; they were smart
enough to see that while I had no 'chip on my shoulder,' yet I would yank up the first man who ventured
to neglect the least point of etiquette. People on
shore are very generally saying that the presence of
the Yorktown has done much to produce a proper
and friendly feeling, and at the same time some of
the long heads are saying: 'Commander Evans is
smart; he is learning all about the Chilean ships.'
which is a fact; and none of them know just how much
I have found, nor will they ever, unless we have war
with them, when they will find my shells searching out
their most vital points. I am quite prepared to have
some people say that I am leaning too far toward a
friendly solution of the trouble between the two countries. They little know how hard I have to hold
myself. One of the Chileans came on board to-day
and sat in my cabin fully an hour, giving me an account of his exploits during the war. He was most

Chilean Insolence

entertaining with his bad French, and I got from him some very valuable professional information, and he went away much impressed with the friendly way in which I had received him. All I did was to give him a glass of champagne and let him talk. We have news that the Boston left Montevideo to-day, and Walker and his ships sailed from Hampton Roads yesterday for Brazil.

"*Saturday Night.*—The President's message, at least the portion of it about Chile, is published here to-day, having been wired through, and Mr. Matta, the Chilean Secretary of State, has sent a most insulting message to their minister in Washington to be delivered to the State Department. He says, in so many words, that Egan and Schley have lied all the way through, and that President Harrison has knowingly used false information in his message to Congress. And all this is given to the press here before it reaches Washington. I don't see how Mr. Harrison can help sending a fleet down here to teach these people manners. Among other things Mr. Matta says, in relation to the Baltimore matter, that Chile is prepared to administer justice without the advice or interference of the United States. No doubt there will be great excitement when this is all published, which it probably is in the New York papers to-day, as it was all wired through this morning. I certainly would like to hear what Mr. Blaine has to say in reply.

"*Sunday, December 13th.*—I have been on board the Chilean flagship to-day to attend a dance, and was struck with the cordial way in which all their officers came forward to greet me and my officers. Many ladies asked for introductions, and I was assured that the Yorktown was becoming most popular on shore, and that people thought very highly of me. I took it all in very quietly until I was introduced to a young woman who proclaimed that she was a Yankee. She proceeded to tell me what a splendid man I was, and so different from Captain Schley; she hated him and all the officers of the Baltimore. Her cheek and insolence were so massive that she staggered me for a moment, but only for a moment. Then I said to her, very slowly: 'We are all the same in our service; the officers of the Yorktown and the Baltimore are as much alike as eggs in a basket, and you must not say disagreeable things about any of us.' She replied that she was ashamed to be known as an American, to which I answered that I did not think she would ever be recognised as one, and immediately returned her to the captain of the ship, who had introduced her to me at her request, and then I left her. It is easy to imagine how angry she made me. . . . The feeling to-day is very unsettled, owing to Matta's foolish and insolent letter published yesterday, and no one can tell what the result may be.

"*Monday, December 14th.*—The press of Valparaiso has to-day begun publishing the correspondence about the Baltimore row, and editorially they demand satisfaction. They say we owe them a large sum for stopping the Itata and thus prolonging their war; that our ships and men acted as spies for Balmaceda; that our sailors landed and raised a riot in their streets, that the United States must apologize and pay a heavy sum as indemnity, and that Egan must be at once recalled. They also published to-day a story wired from Montevideo that the Boston's men landed there, fought and killed some of the police, and in fact held the town. I don't of course, know how much truth there may be in all this, but these people are using it for all it is worth. The trouble seems further from a settlement to-day than at any previous time.

" *Wednesday, December 16th.*—There is no change in the situation on shore—still very bitter and haughty. We are coaling ship, to be ready for anything that may come. *Later.*—I am somewhat worried to-night as to what I shall do in a matter, small in itself, but possibly annoying in its results. There is a correspondent of a New York paper here for whom I do not much care. Last Thursday he went to Santiago de Chile to interview President Montt, and when he returned came to me with the story that Montt wanted to see me, and asked that I would come to Santiago for the purpose. Of course, I do not believe this, nor that Montt ever sent any such message, but I am not certain of it. Such an invitation ought to come through the United States minister. This was before the publication of Matta's insolent letter to the Secretary of State, which, with other things that have occurred, has determined me not to have any intercourse of an official character with any of them unless I am ordered or forced to do so.

" Well, to-day Mr. Egan telephoned down from Santiago to say that he wanted to ' chat ' with me over the telephone, and as I was not on shore he asked the naval *attaché* to come aboard and ask me if I did not think that I ought, in view of the turn things had taken, to telegraph Schley at Callao to come back here with the Baltimore, and would I come to Santiago to consult with him (Egan). My answer was that Secretary Tracy was at one end of the wire and Schley at the other, and I had no doubt the Secretary would send the Baltimore back here if he considered her presence necessary; also that I saw no good reason why I should leave my ship to consult with him about matters over which I had no control and could take no action. I am quite determined to attend to my own business and not get mixed up with the political part of this muddle. If I should go to Santiago, and if Montt did send me that message, he would be offended if I declined to call on him except in company with our minister—which I undoubtedly should do—so the best thing is to stay where I am. But it worries me, and I may have to give in and go.

"The papers here grow more and more insolent, and I don't see how Mr. Harrison can avoid sending an ultimatum at a very early day. In the meantime the Chileans are working like beavers to get their ships ready, and in two weeks from now the whole fleet will be ready for service. My relations with them all are in accordance with the strictest etiquette, and will remain so until the shooting begins—and even after.

"*Thursday, December 17th.*—I had to go on shore to-day, *nolens volens*, as Mr. Egan *must* talk with me through the 'phone. He did about all the talking, and I listened. Yesterday he discovered that they had fifteen men—ten soldiers, disguised as policemen, and five spies—around his house; and he also thinks he has discovered a plot to burn his house, by setting fire to the house next to his, and thus get possession of the refugees now under his protection. Five persons were arrested as they left the Spanish legation in the evening, and one of them, ex-President of Ecuador, was detained several hours in the common jail. Egan is much excited, evidently expects trouble, and, I think, rather hopes to see it, but I can't join him in that.

" The afternoon papers publish a telegram from San Francisco, saying that the San Francisco has sailed with sealed orders, probably for Chile. I shall be glad when the admiral arrives, as I am not in the least pleased with the present outlook here.

" After I had done talking with Mr. Egan I went for a walk, and was scowled at by no end of cutthroat-looking chaps."

On Friday, December 18th, came a long cipher cable from the Department, which required four hours for its translation. The contents were not of the most peaceful nature. My reply gave the information wanted in something like two hundred words. It took me all night to put it into cipher.

CHAPTER XXII

STRAINED RELATIONS

On the following morning the Valparaiso papers said the trouble between the two countries was about settled; that there would be no war, and that we had found out that Chile was in the right all the time. If the editors had seen the message I had received and my reply I think they would have changed their minds somewhat. Press reports from the United States published the same morning indicated great activity in the Navy Department. One of the papers had, in large headlines, " What we may expect when the Boston arrives." The article then went on to state that she had landed ninety-five men on liberty in Montevideo, and ninety of them were arrested. I felt sure that the Boston's men were not in any such condition as this indicated, and I was confident at the same time that the article and many more like it were meant to influence public opinion against us and prepare them for more riots and bloodshed.

Monday, December 21st, brought me a telegram to keep my ship filled up with coal, which led me to wonder if they regarded me at the Department as some kind of an idiot. Of course I was full of coal and everything else I should need when the time for action came.

A Curious Christmas

All my plans were made down to the smallest detail, and my mind made up as to what I would do under certain conditions. The head of the house of Grace & Company must have had some serious telegram from New York on this day, as he said to me in the afternoon that things looked bad for a settlement. Mr. Egan 'phoned me in the evening that his son had been arrested at Santiago the previous day as he came out of the legation, and later two other persons had been arrested in the same way and held for two hours or more. The situation was becoming very critical, and the conduct of the authorities seemed like madness to me—almost as if they intended to force us into war. I was quite ready for it if they said the word.

I was determined to meet the Chileans halfway in any proposition they had to make, and therefore, when I received an invitation for a Christmas tree, I accepted it and presented myself at the proper hour. It was pleasant to see some fifty-odd children enjoy themselves, but the grown people were as nasty a lot as I ever met. I was introduced to them all and tried to talk to them, but one after another had something disagreeable to say about the United States. One and all of them hated the officers of our navy who had been there before us, and they did not hesitate to tell me so. My visit was cut very short, and I returned to my ship feeling as no Christian ought to feel on Christmas eve.

Our surroundings naturally drew all of us closer together, and I gladly accepted the invitation of the wardroom officers to take my Christmas dinner with them. They had also, as their guests, the consul and

several of our countrymen from shore. We had a
charming dinner over " sweethearts and wives," and
forgot for the moment the troubles threatening us.
The following from my journal gives an accurate account of incidents at this time:

" Events crowd on rapidly now, and our troubles
here must soon be settled one way or another. The
Boston came in yesterday, and I was glad to see her,
but to-day she is ordered north, leaving me alone
again to face the music here. It is a great surprise to
every one. Wiltse signalled me this afternoon at five
to repair on board, which I at once did, and found him
up to his eyes in a cipher telegram which was too
much for him. We soon unravelled it, however, and it
was, ' Proceed north immediately with the Boston,'
etc. He will be off to-morrow, and the Yorktown
will again hold the fort, which shows a gratifying confidence in me on the part of the Secretary. I feel the
weight of responsibility which rests on my shoulders.
The Boston will be off to-morrow, and in the meantime I have information that a riot is threatened here,
and that two regiments of artillery came here to-day
from Santiago. Of course, they would not have sent
them unless they feared another row, and if it comes my
duty will be a hard one. There will be only two ships
here, one French and one American—except, of course,
the vessels of the Chilean fleet, which can not be
counted on at such a time. If trouble comes, the English and Germans here will call on us for protection,
and I shall have them on my hands as well as our own
people. So I am not yachting in the real sense of the
word.

Sensational Journalism

"*Saturday Night, December 26th.*—The Boston has gone, and we are once more the only Yankee here. Wiltse called on most of the officials, and the newspapers give him a good send off. One paper says that his politeness, following so soon on the courteous conduct of 'Señor' Evans, commanding the Yorktown, had gone far toward removing the bad impression made by the Baltimore. Another paper copies a long article from the London Times, showing how easily the Chilean navy could clean us up, capture San Francisco, and do no end of awful things. Still another says that the Chicago, Concord, and Wilmington will soon be here, and when they have gone north the people of Valparaiso will have had two thirds of the Yankee navy passed in review. Such insolence!

"Mr. Egan 'phoned me to-day that he had not attended the inauguration of President Montt. I suppose the press will make all sorts of a row over that. I am sure that if he had gone he would have been insulted, and it is likely that some attempt on his legation would have been made in his absence. His position and that of the United States is much strengthened by an incident which occurred day before yesterday, the arrest of General Velasquez. He was Secretary of War under Balmaceda, and about two months before the collapse of that government was thrown from his horse and had his leg broken. He had been arrested by the Junta government and bailed for ten thousand dollars, but day before yesterday was again arrested, on the ground that he was organizing a revolution, because arms were found in his house. A

273

mob gathered and demanded his blood, but enough of a guard was on hand to drag him away and place him in confinement on board the Magallanes, one of their receiving ships. I am told to-day that he was shot to death on board that vessel at midnight last night, and the authorities do not deny it, but say that if he has not been killed he will be, and that his friends will never know how or when. Now this is a fine prospect for the gentlemen who are refugeed in the legation at Santiago! If they are given up, every one will undoubtedly be killed, and the nations of the earth will justly hold us responsible. While I do not believe in the right of asylum, and would not permit our legations to be used for that purpose, still, having once received these men, we must stand by them even if it leads to war. Just at this point I was called on deck by some quick volleys fired on shore near us, followed by a few straggling shots. One of these fine nights they will send some of their bullets over us, and then they will have a surprise party.

" *Sunday Night.*—I found out this afternoon in a curious way about the firing last night. It was continued at intervals all night. This morning early the Esmeralda came in with colours at half mast, having on board the fragments of patriots killed at Iquiqui and Caldera Bay. She was draped in black, and looked as if she had not been scrubbed for a year—quite the most grief-stricken craft I ever saw. Just at four o'clock a boat came to us from the senior officer afloat to ask us to participate in the ceremonies afloat to-morrow, when they are going to bury the remains of some naval patriots. So little could be made out of what the young officer was trying to tell us that I took my boat and went on board the Cochran to get things straight. Captain Vial, who commands her, . . . when I assured him that we should be glad to join in honouring their dead, did not know where to put me. He told me he was much gratified by my acceptance, but had feared that I would decline because these officers had been killed during the war. In other words, we were on the Balmaceda side, and would not even go to the funeral of the other party. I was not to be caught by such stupid trash. I told him that in my country we knew no difference among Chileans, alive or dead; that we never in any case carried our feelings beyond the moment of dissolution, etc. When I asked him what the firing was about last night, he said the men in the naval battery on shore thought some smuggling was going on and fired, and some soldiers in adjoining works, to give the idea that they were ready, took it up, and hence the row. While he was telling me this plausible yarn I was observing his decks and wondering if the smuggling racket would account for all the ammunition I saw piled ready for use. The truth is, they expected an attack, and no doubt shot some of the suspects just to keep their hands in. I shall go to their wake tomorrow, as I told Captain Vial, on the water; but, as I also told him, I will not allow one of my men to land.

" No news from Santiago to-day, except that Montt was inaugurated and that the Chambers could not agree on a Cabinet, which is unfortunate, as the present lot will have to hold over, and they will continue to menace our legation and thus make matters worse. As to Egan, he has done only what he was instructed to do from Washington, and he has done it capitally well. The Chilean Secretary of State has found himself outclassed every time he has tackled the little Irishman, who really writes clearly, forcibly, and beautifully, and so far they have not scored one point against him.

"The whole diplomatic question in dispute is a simple one: 1. 'The right of asylum in foreign legations.' 2. '*Salvo conducto,* for such refugees, to a neutral territory.' In 1866, during a revolution in Peru, the Chilean Government directed its minister in that country to insist on both principles, and they were enforced, and *salvo conducto* furnished to neutral territory. In 1888, at a Congress of the South American Republics, the Chilean representative presented and had embodied in a treaty, which was afterward ratified by all, a clause that refugees should be protected when sheltered in foreign legations, and charged only with political offences; and that *salvo conducto* should be demanded and furnished all such refugees, reserving to the Government in whose territory the legation is located the right to demand the speedy removal of the parties from its territory. Thus this practice became international law as far as the parties to the treaty are concerned, but the Junta government, through Mr. Matta, now says the Government of Chile has changed. Mr. Egan replies that local changes and edicts of Chile can not change international law and practice. The Chileans are knocked out and refuse to continue the discussion. Having admitted his right to give them asylum, their present attitude is absurd, and only makes a permanent prison of the legation; the men would undoubtedly be killed the moment they were turned out.

"*Monday*, P. M.—We helped to bury the patriots to-day, or rather we escorted them to the shore from the Esmeralda, and then returned to the ship. Of course, I would not go on shore for the funeral, but I did go later to call on the senior officer in command of the naval station, to get what news I could out of him, and was moderately successful. He let it out that they would send four of their vessels to Iquiqui, some time in January, at the suggestion of President Montt. Of course, their idea is to defend that place against us and rely on the rest of the fleet and the forts to hold Valparaiso. He had no idea of the value of the information he was giving me, or he would not have talked so freely. Afterward he said many things which lead me to believe that they expect an attack every night, and I should not be surprised to see it any hour.

"When I left him I met the head of the house of Grace and Company, and he showed me a long telegram from W. R. Grace, dated in Washington yesterday, of the most alarming character. Grace has been in Washington for the past ten days trying to convince Secretary Blaine that we must not have war. He wires that Harrison is for war, that the Navy Department is making every preparation for war, and that Blaine, while in favour of war under certain conditions only, can not stem the tide, and that unless Chile makes ample apology at once nothing can prevent war. The message is to Grace's business house, and therefore can be relied on as giving his best information; and he is a warm personal friend of Mr. Blaine. Taking all this into consideration, the crew of the Yorktown will sleep at the loaded guns to-night, and every night until I get some better news. While I can not deny to myself that things are on the ' ragged edge,' so to speak, yet I can not conceive of the Chileans being stupid enough to allow it to come to blows—it seems incredible folly. And yet it may come. News from Santiago to-day is to the effect that President Montt is still unable to form a Cabinet. If this condition continues much longer, it alone will bring revolution.

" *Tuesday*, P. M.—After the alarming telegram I saw yesterday I went on shore again to-day and found that the English minister had long messages from his Government, which he had shown to Mr. Egan, and here again I was much surprised. The despatches say, in plain language, that the English Government considers that war between the United States and Chile is inevitable; and yet I have not one word from the Department to put me on my guard. I certainly do not understand it in the least.

" *Valparaiso, Chile, December 30th.*—The steamer has just gone out. Every one that goes I hope may be the last until we go. While I was ashore, walking up the street with Fred May, three *rotas*, the most villainous-looking scoundrels I ever saw, crossed over and followed us some distance, muttering about ' damned Yankees.' I saw Fred get a fresh grip on his stick, and I did the same, and, keeping one eye over my shoulder, just as they were close behind us we suddenly turned and walked through them, as it were, before they had time to do anything. We were in the main street of the town, otherwise I have no doubt they would have attacked us, and if they had we surely would have pounded the life out of two of them at least.

"There is a rumour to-day on the street that Chile has offered thirty thousand dollars as a settlement of the Baltimore affair, but I can not learn that it is true.

"*December 31st, Night.*—There is to be a row at midnight and I have been asked to join in it, but declined. The Chileans are going to fire twenty-one guns and burn fireworks to usher in the new year, which seems an odd thing to do, but these are odd people. The war feeling is about the same to-day, and the papers publish a telegram in which Admiral Brown is made to say that there will be no war with Chile, and that he is not coming back with the San Francisco; and, further, that the affair of the Baltimore will be submitted to arbitration, which seems too silly to notice. When the United States is willing to submit the question of the murder of her sailors in uniform to arbitration, I must look for other employment—the navy won't any longer suit me. They can arbitrate 'till the cows come home' about the people in the legation at Santiago, but if they ever hint at such a thing about the Baltimore's men, then I think the voice of the American people will be heard in no uncertain tones.

"*January 1, 1892.*—Just before midnight last night we ordered champagne, and each one stood with his full glass until the bell struck, when we all drank to our friends at home a 'happy New Year.' Then we went on deck, whence we could hear and see the Chileans making their row. The whole city of Valparaiso was red and green with lights, presenting one of the most beautiful sights imaginable.

" The Chilean vessels added to the effect by flashing their electric lights in every direction, and everything that could make a noise was doing its best, but not a sound came from the Yorktown except the low murmurs of the men as they stood around the guns. It was an impressive sight."

As the Cochran fired the first gun of her salute she sent off a flight of rockets; one of them, a war rocket, just missed the Yorktown. We were in plain view on account of the beams of the numerous search lights from the Chilean war vessels, and it seemed that the rocket must have been purposely aimed at us; but there was room for doubt, and as it had not struck us I assumed that it was an accident. I at once hoisted a large American flag and turned both my search lights on it, so that if any one really wanted to hit me he could know just where I was. I was determined, if trouble came, there should be no ground for saying we had been accidentally struck in the dark. When the search lights, a few moments later, again lighted us up, they showed the crew of the Yorktown standing at their quarters and the guns all ready for business. The second war rocket from the Cochran went through the rigging of a German steamer some distance away from us, but no more came our way. I again quote from my journal:

" *January 1, 1892.*—The telegrams in the morning papers from Washington are most warlike. Before I was through with my breakfast a long cipher message came from the Secretary, directing me to keep him posted on all movements of Chilean warships; and one from the President, to proceed to Santiago and confer with our minister, ascertain present situation, and especially the sentiment of Chile toward the United States. It is extraordinary to send a naval officer to find out the sentiment of the country, and I have a job on my hands. The responsibility of the position almost frightens me. I could wire back a message to-morrow that would cause a declaration of war in twenty-four hours. I shall leave for Santiago in the morning and spend two days there, getting such information as I can, and looking at the actual condition of things, that I may give the President such an answer as will enable him to lay the matter before Congress. Of course, I shall be uncomfortable and much worried all the time I am away, but that is what I am paid for.

"*Later.*—This afternoon the most important part of the finding in the Baltimore case is published. The judge finds that two Chileans are implicated; that the row was begun by the Baltimore's men, who were drunk, and that their testimony was of no value; that Reagan was killed by a revolver shot from some party unknown. He does not seem to see the absurdity of two Chileans having stabbed over a dozen men in a fight which went on at the same time in half a dozen different places covering a space of more than half a mile. I am curious to know what Mr. Blaine will say when he gets the news.

"*Monday, January 4th.*—Glad to get to the little ship once more last night at midnight. I have been making out a cipher message of one hundred and seventy-eight words to the Secretary, and it consumed

the entire day, so that I have not been on shore; but
the message has gone, and by now the Secretary and
probably the President knows just what I think of
the situation at Santiago. My message gave the de-
cision in the Baltimore case and some news of the
Chilean navy, and then I said substantially that the
United States legation at Santiago, containing many
refugees, was virtually a prison watched by uniformed
police and spies in plain clothes—the latter removed
during my visit. General sentiment of Santiago and
Valparaiso brutally hostile to the United States. New
Chilean Secretary of State expresses friendship, and
hopes matters will be promptly arranged. . . . I was
too anxious and full of business to enjoy the trip. . . .

" Santiago is a large, straggling city in a great dust-
covered plain surrounded by brown mountains topped
with snow. The minister met me at the station, and
we drove a mile or so through very rough streets to
a very dirty hotel. I started with Mr. Egan and the
three officers who were with me, to walk to the legation, a distance of about ten blocks, and I was amused
at the scowls the party received from the people on
the way. When we came in sight of the legation I
counted eight uniformed police and five of the worst-
looking devils of *rotas* in plain clothes that I have ever
gazed on, all guarding the place. I walked around,
counted these brutes, and looked them over, and they
were very uncomfortable under the scrutiny. In the
afternoon the spies were withdrawn, leaving only the
police in uniform.

" After I had paid my respects to Mrs. Egan I was
introduced to the party of refugees, and was really

impressed with the scene. Our minister, an Irish agitator representing a great Government, and under his protection many of the finest men of Chile, blue-blooded and aristocratic, treating Mrs. Egan like a queen, and looking to the self-made, brave little Irishman for their lives. The whole thing was impressive and curious. I managed to say a few words to each of them, but with General Gana, formerly Secretary of War, I had a long conversation; his French was awful, but perhaps he thought the same of mine. He is seventy years old, and was an intimate friend of Admiral Dahlgren, for whose memory he entertains a high regard. In fact, he considers all Americans superior people. He was for many years general of the army, and gave his whole life to the service of his country; and yet they would tear him to pieces were it not that the American flag protects him.

" I also had some talk with Señor McKenna, who was President of the Balmaceda Senate, a most thoroughbred, delicate-looking gentleman. He is enormously wealthy. His position and surroundings are most irksome, and the confinement is telling on his health. It was pathetic when he told me that if his countrymen did not kill him he would make his home in North America, where he could rear his children with the advantages of civilization."

The sacking of Santiago by the rebels after its surrender probably has no parallel in history for wanton waste and destruction. The houses to be sacked were all placed on a list, which was given to a regiment of half-breeds from the mining districts, and they were ordered to do the job. I can certify from personal observation that they did their work very thoroughly. I stood in front of what had been the beautiful home of Mr. John McKenna, and wondered how human beings could be found to do such work. Every article of value had been stolen or destroyed, and the floors and woodwork, even to the window casings, torn up and broken to pieces or carried away. It was a fearful picture of what civil war might mean at its worst. I again quote from my journal:

" On Sunday Mr. Egan gave me a breakfast at Santa Lucia, a rock which rises some hundreds of feet in the heart of the city, and on top of which is a fair restaurant, and whence the view is fine. The party was mixed, which for my purpose suited very well, and I got much valuable information from them, especially from a Chilean army officer, who had been a junior officer in the British army. He resigned, to find employment about Iquiqui, where he was when the war came, when, believing the rebels to be right, he joined them, fought well, and after the fall of Balmaceda was promoted and is now on duty at Santiago. I got a lot of information from him. When the Baltimore row took place he was sent down to Valparaiso to investigate the matter privately and report to the authorities in Santiago. He was soon satisfied that the police shot Reagan, but in order to decide the point fully he demanded such orders as would compel the authorities here to give him the witnesses he wanted. He went to Santiago and reported his conviction that the police had done the killing, for which the authorities jumped on him and ' gave him the devil,' and would not let him return here. Now he has given them notice that if they have any trouble with the United States he will leave their service. The day we left Santiago the minister saw me off, and we had the same salute of scowls from the people. On my way to Santiago I am sure I was guarded by two very nice-looking officers in uniform, who observed my every movement. and on my way down I had a similar escort, probably sent by the authorities to see that no harm was done me.

"*January 5th.*—To-day I have been on shore for an hour and saw the consul's son, who has come out as secretary of legation. He left Washington on December 10th, and tells me that the war talk there was very strong—that Harrison was wild over the Baltimore matter, and it was all Blaine could do to hold him back. I don't wonder. To-night I have been reading up the papers, and find the tone of our Administration very dignified, though savage. I don't see how war can now be avoided. Sorry to see that Jack Philip was detached from the Atlanta if she is to come here; but he will have a beautiful command in the New York, and do the service credit anywhere.

"*January 6th.*—This afternoon I went for a few minutes to a grand ball on board the Cochran, and when I came back found awaiting me a half-tipsy chap who had come to tell me, confidentially, that my ship was to be attacked to-night or to-morrow night by the Chileans, and he warned me to make every preparation, as they were in earnest, and would begin the war with the United States by sinking or capturing the Yorktown. Nice information for a fellow to sleep on! The chap said he had been well treated by the

Americans and would stand by them. Of course, I don't place much confidence in the story, but I am on my guard all the same, and to-night we have steam up and the men sleeping at the guns among the ammunition.

"The captain of the Cochran has just sent an officer on board to say that he will fire a salute of twenty-one guns at one o'clock in the morning, as that will be the anniversary of their revolt. Such idiots! I don't think I shall sleep much *este noche*.

"*January 8th.*—The Chileans certainly did celebrate night before last, to the annoyance of all quietly disposed persons. The harbour was ablaze and salutes were fired until midnight, and I was not certain that they would not take a shy at us, so I watched them closely, and am thankful that nothing unpleasant happened. I am equally sorry that something very unpleasant did happen to-day—nothing less than the stoning of my gig while she was lying off the landing-place, waiting to bring me off. When I landed I noticed that the people scowled at me rather more than usual, but it passed out of my mind until a party of young fellows on a street car made themselves offensive.

"After I had attended to my business I came down and called my boat in, and while waiting for her to get alongside I became aware that there was a crowd of rather larger proportions than usual on the mole, and they seemed excited by something. Just as I stepped into my boat one of them advanced quickly toward me, and the cockswain said, ' Look out for that fellow, sir! ' I said, ' He won't trouble me,' stepped into the boat, and shoved off, and then discovered that the crew were all fighting mad. On inquiry I learned that a lot of toughs had amused themselves by throwing stones at the boat and daring the men to come on shore. I was hot all over, and without going to my own ship I pulled straight for the Cochran, whose captain, Vial, is senior officer in command of the city as well as the fleet. I could hardly hold myself down while I told him of it; but I did, and then read him the riot act. I demanded of him immediate and efficient protection by the police, and served notice on him, then and there, that a repetition of the offence would be sufficient evidence that they could not control their people, and that I should arm my boats and shoot any and every man who insulted me or my men or my flag in any way. Vial was greatly shocked, or pretended to be, turned as white as a sheet—my manner was not very mild, I fancy—swore and damned the discharged soldiers, and said they were doing all they could to involve the country in war with the United States, while he and the navy were determined that it should not be; and then, in his excitement, he gave away something I am sure he was very sorry for: he said, ' We have just discovered to-day a plot to attack the American legation at Santiago, and we have the men under arrest.' What a set of savages we have to deal with! After a few moments Captain Vial hastened on shore to jump the police, assuring me that I should have an ample apology to-morrow, and assurances of protection. Of course, I shall wire the affair to the Department after I have settled it, but in the mildest way I can. I don't want to be sensational, and I hope the papers won't get hold of it.

A Sailor's Log

"If they bother us again I shall consider that the time has come to shoot. The anxiety of the position here is very great; it interferes with my sleep, and is telling on my temper.

"*Valparaiso, January 9th.*—Lots of things have happened since last night. Just at midnight I heard a sharp hail, 'Boat ahoy!' and the answer, 'American consul.' I was out in a minute, and there the consul was, as large as life, and evidently with something important on his mind. When we reached the cabin he said Mr. Egan had just telephoned to ask me to have my steam launch at a certain point about five miles from the ship at six sharp this morning, as he was coming unexpectedly to pay me a visit. Of course, I knew what that meant, and everything was made ready, and at about 2 A. M., after providing the consul with a shakedown, I went to bed. We were up at four, had some coffee and eggs, and the executive officer shoved off in charge, with the consul to show him where to go, and half a dozen revolvers, with cartridges, etc.

"At 7.30 I saw the boat returning, and was much relieved when she came alongside.

"The first man out was Mr. Egan; then came Mr. McKenna, formerly Minister of Foreign Affairs, then President of the Chilean Senate, and lately a refugee in the American legation. After him came his cousin, William McKenna, late Governor of Santiago under Balmaceda; and then their wives and servants. My heart sank into my boots when I saw the women, but fortunately they went on shore afterward; and their husbands, who would be torn to pieces if they were caught, are now sleeping as calmly as two children, within twelve feet of me. The American flag is a wonderful thing when all is said and done. Here are these two men with no claim on us beyond our sentiment of right and humanity, whose lives have not been worth a nickel for months, now resting quiet and secure in the midst of the Chilean fleet, and under the guns of ten heavy forts; and all because a small gunboat flying the American flag has them in charge.

"Other important things have happened: Captain Vial has been on board to apologize for the stoning of the gig yesterday and to assure me of protection, and the English admiral has arrived in the Warspite.

"*January 10th, 11* P. M.—Just back from a conference with the English admiral on board the Warspite, and more tired than last night, but must write a few lines, because if I do not set down things as they happen I shall forget them.

"Admiral Hotham, R. N., is disposed to be very nice. Mr. Egan, who went back to Santiago last night, wires me to-day that he has a long message from Mr. Blaine, directing him to *ask* the Chilean Government: (1) 'If they will give *salvo conducto* to those who still remain in the legation at Santiago'; and (2) 'Do they want to withdraw the letter of Mr. Matta, Secretary of Foreign Affairs, which was so insulting to our Government?' This looks to me very much as if it were going to rain in a few days in Chile.

"To comprehend the situation we must consider that Mr. Egan brought the men, now on board, without written *salvo conducto*, but with the tacit permission of the authorities. They refused to give a written permit, thus hoping to dodge the question, but Mr. Blaine is nailing the matter, and will make them settle the *salvo conducto* question at once. Egan will not now allow any more refugees to leave the legation without written permits. This is the beginning of the end of the Chilean trouble.

" *Monday Afternoon, January 11th.* — Yesterday evening came more cablegrams, and to-day I have news from Egan that the Chilean Government pledges safe conduct to the refugees now in the legation out of the country, and to-morrow night they will be down on me to the number of six or eight—not only those in the legation, but others. There is no Spanish vessel of war in the harbour, and at the request of the Spanish and American ministers I have consented to take on board the refugees now in the Spanish legation. I wish they were all clear of the country and we with them.

" This ship is constantly overrun with the wives, daughters, and cousins of the men now on board, and I suppose, when the others come, things will be much worse. A large party has just gone away, among them a beautiful daughter of Mr. McKenna, who said to me as she left, ' I love zis plaice '—and much they may love it!

" Mr. Egan also tells me that the police have been removed from around the legation, but the Chilean Government is not prepared to withdraw the offensive note of Mr. Matta. It is willing to say that no offence was meant, but will not withdraw the note. Egan replies that ours are a thinking people, and, given the language of the note, they can decide for themselves as to its offensiveness. After it is withdrawn we will settle the Baltimore affair. All the refugees once out of danger, we shall then be in a position to say what we propose to do, and then go ahead and do it; but up to this time we have been heavily handicapped by our wards, who would undoubtedly have been killed at the first warlike demonstration.

"*Tuesday, January 12th.*—Last evening I dined with Admiral Hotham on board the Warspite, and had a good dinner and friendly treatment. To-day I am notified by Mr. Egan that he will be down to-morrow with more refugees—all that are left in Santiago, it seems. They will be escorted by the Spanish and Italian ministers, who are all coming on board the Yorktown, and will probably spend the day with us. I have no idea what I shall do with so many people, but one thing I am sure of, and that is that I shall salute all these ministers; and when I have fired my forty-five guns the people of Valparaiso will know that the question of *salvo conducto* is settled, for the present at least. Egan has come out of the whole business with flying colours, and were it not for what might be said I would wear a green ribbon in my buttonhole to-morrow simply to show my respect for the sandy little Irishman. The consul is on board for the night, and will go with my boats to-morrow morning to show them just where to find Egan and his party, and after they come the cabin will be more crowded than it is now.

"I shall do all in my power to send the refugees away in the first steamer that leaves here.

"*January 17th.*—It is some days since I last wrote,

but the cabin is so crowded that I can only write late at night. Four days ago, early in the morning, I sent in two boats, met the train, and brought off the whole lot of refugees from the United States and Spanish legations, accompanied by the United States, the Spanish, and Italian ministers. I made them as comfortable as I could, being assured not only that they came by permission of the Government, but that they would leave on Saturday (yesterday) in the steamer John Elder, of the P. S. N. Co., for Europe. Tickets were bought and everything made ready. In the meantime, when the ministers were about to leave the ship, the one from Italy asked that I would not fire him a salute, and I did not. The Spaniard, Count Brunetti, had requested me to take two refugees from his legation, which I did, and therefore (if for no other reason) saluted him when he left. On Friday Mr. Egan wired me that the Santiago authorities had changed base, and would not give safe conduct to the refugees, and that they would arrest them when the John Elder touched at a Chilean port—all because we had saluted the Spanish minister, and thus called attention to the fact that they had permitted the refugees to leave.

" I promptly requested Mr. Egan to say to the Minister of Foreign Affairs that I was responsible to my own Government and not that of Chile for my conduct, and that I considered his remarks about my salute to the Spanish minister offensive and would not submit to them; also that I should cable the matter to my Government, which I did, and, as they have not said a word about it, I assume that they approve of my action.

" Of course, the refugees could not go on the John

An Embarrassment of Refugees

Elder, and we now have them quartered on board. The bother and discomfort are very great, but the expense is the more serious matter to me. The John Elder put to sea at 2 P. M., and at four this afternoon we had news of her total loss on the rocks at four this morning —all hands saved. What an escape the refugees had! If they had gone in her they would all have been shot by this time.

" The English cruiser Melpomene has gone to the scene of the wreck. Of course, I have wired the Secretary very fully, and he and the President know the whole situation. I have wired for permission to land my passengers at Callao, twelve hundred miles away, but fear he will not permit it. A Chilean squadron will leave here to-morrow, bound south, and I have information that they will attempt to stop Walker in the Straits of Magellan. I have wired it to Washington."

From the time I received the refugees on board I was in constant anticipation of trouble. The morning they came I had my ship cleared for action, and fully expected to have to use my guns before the affair was concluded. Threats had been openly made that if I took the refugees on board, the Chilean ships would take them out again. The excitement was very general, and feeling ran high. While Mr. Blaine had not insisted on written *salvo conductos*, he had exacted verbal ones; and the Chilean Government was not aware of what was going on, but anxious to get the parties out of the country. But Santiago could not control Valparaiso, and in the latter port, with its turbulent population, lay the danger.

During the first few hours after their arrival I no-

ticed that none of the refugees would show themselves
above the rail of the ship, notwithstanding I had chairs
on the poop deck for them. Senor Ibaños, formerly
minister to the United States, was among the last lot
that had arrived, and when I asked him what the
trouble was he showed me a letter from a friend on
shore warning him and his friends that if they raised
their heads above the rail they would be shot, and that
boats were lurking about my ship for the purpose of
shooting them. Up to this time I had allowed the
fishing boats to fish close alongside the Yorktown, but
I now gave orders to keep them away and to double
our sentries. The orders the sentries had would have
made it serious work for any boatman to show anything
that looked like a gun anywhere near us.

I had my boat manned, and with the letter spoken
of, and several others of the same tenor, called on Captain Vial, of the Cochran, and gave him tersely my
views of the situation. I pointed out to him that I did
not command a prison ship, but that his countrymen,
who had taken refuge on board of me, were the guests
of the United States, and that they were there with the
knowledge and consent of the Chilean Government. I
assured him that I would protect them to the last ex-
tremity, and warned him to keep all boats away from
the immediate vicinity, or they might come to grief.
At the same time I notified him that I would only allow
boats from men of war showing the Chilean flag to
come alongside the Yorktown, so that in case anything
unpleasant happened I should know whom to hold responsible. After this there was no more trouble, but I
was constantly on the lookout and prepared for it.

CHAPTER XXIII

A WELCOME DEPARTURE

ABOUT January 20th I received telegraphic orders permitting me to land my passengers at Callao, Peru, at my discretion. I at once notified the Chilean authorities that I would leave Valparaiso in six hours. I also visited the English admiral and gave him the same information. He called my attention to the fact that four of the Chilean ships had steam up, and to the further fact that it had been announced in the Valparaiso papers that when I went to sea their ships would go after me to see that I did not land the refugees and get up another revolution. I told the admiral very plainly that if any ship or number of ships followed me to sea and undertook to follow my motions I would regard it as an act of gross discourtesy and insult to my flag, and would resent it on the spot. I never learned whether he communicated with the Chileans on the subject or not, but when I got under way at the time I had fixed and steamed out, nobody pursued me, or attempted to do so. The condition in Valparaiso had become almost unbearable, and it was with a sense of great relief that I found myself at sea.

During the early part of the first night out, while

running at very high speed, a suspicious noise was heard in the high-pressure cylinder of one of the engines. When the cylinder head was taken off I found two hardened steel wedges, which had been placed in the valve chest, no doubt, when we first arrived at Valparaiso by some evilly disposed person, with the intention of sending us all to the bottom. It could easily have been done when we first arrived, and before we knew what kind of people we had to deal with. It was simply a miracle that I escaped a serious disaster, for if the cylinder head had been knocked out with the pressure of steam I was carrying, the side of the ship would have gone with it. As I stood watching the group of machinists and firemen working about the engines I could see the blood come into their faces until the whites of their eyes were bloodshot. I knew pretty well what they were thinking, and was very careful that all parts of the ship were thoroughly guarded until my refugees were landed in Peru, safe and happy.

One of the performances that had most tried my patience and temper at Valparaiso was the way they ran their torpedo boats about my ship, using her apparently as a target. At first I considered it only as an exhibition of bad manners, but, in view of the various warnings I had had, I concluded that there might be something more serious in it. It was plain to all hands that an effort was being made to impress the officers of the foreign ships in port, who watched closely with their glasses. I was unwilling to play the part which had apparently been assigned me. When they ran at me the second time one of the boats missed my stern by less than six feet. I went to quarters at once and

gave orders, if one of them even scratched the paint
on the Yorktown, to blow the boat out of the water
and kill every man in her, so that there could be no
question of an accidental collision. I then saw the
officer in charge of the drills, and told him that he certainly had great confidence in the steering gear of his
torpedo boats; that if anything should jam so that one
of them struck me I would blow her bottom out. He
replied that the water in the harbour belonged to his
Government, and that he proposed to use it for the
purpose of drilling his boats. I answered that I was
fully aware of the ownership he had stated, but that
the Yorktown and the paint on her belonged to the
United States, and that neither must be defaced by his
torpedo boats. After this incident they did not run at
us so much, though the newspapers encouraged them
to do so.

Before the refugees were well clear of me at Callao
I had coal lighters alongside, and in a few hours I was
ready to start back to Valparaiso to see the trouble
out. In answer to my telegram saying that I was ready
to sail, I was directed to await further orders at Callao.
The following from my journal is of interest, as showing
my feelings at the time:

"*Saturday Night, February 6th.*—A mail is in, and
I have nice letters from friends commending my course
at Valparaiso; very satisfactory, but I wish the newspapers would let me alone. Why should they call me
'Fighting Bob'? Some of them say they must take
my statements with 'very large grains of salt.' But
generally they seem to commend me, which, if one must
figure in them, is the best way; but as I see my duty

I shall do it, hoping for the approval of the Government. When they send me orders I shall try to follow them. Some of the letters say, 'We are waiting for you to stir up the war,' and the writers will never know how near I came to doing it. Looking back at it now, I am glad I did just what I did, and in the way I did it. I would not change it if I could. Of course, I could have 'stirred up the war,' and it may be that people would have justified me, but I could not justify myself. In the discharge of my duty I gave the Chileans a fine chance to fight if they wanted to, and the odds were enough in their favour—nine ships to one. But they backed water every time, and I maintained a dignified and resolute position.

" Of course, if they had provoked it I should have engaged their nine ships without hesitation, and the chances would not have favoured my getting the Yorktown out of their harbour. I am glad also that I got away from Valparaiso just when I did, for I am sure that if we had been there when the President's ultimatum came I should have had to open on them, the feeling was so intense. They would have insulted me again, and I should have attacked them. If the Government is going to demand a salute to our flag, and will send a lot of ships, I should like to be in command of one of them. But it is useless to send a single ship; it would only be insulted, as the Chileans respect nothing but force."

The excitement and worry of Valparaiso had told severely on the officers of the Yorktown, especially on me. I was therefore much pleased when the railroad officials at Lima tendered us a trip over the Andes on

Harbour of Valparaiso, Chile.

the Arroyo road, which was a real pleasure and recreation. They were good enough to give me a special car and engine for the use of the party, which consisted of sixteen officers of the Boston and Yorktown. The car was just large enough to hold us, and the engine was in proportion, so that the train looked like a toy concern; but the speed was sufficient for my taste. I had, of course, heard of the splendid work Meigs and his fellow-Americans had done on this road, but I had no conception of its wonderful details, nor do I believe any one can have until he sees them. It dwarfed all the railroad work I had ever seen; indeed, all the work of any kind. The road was completed to a point thirteen thousand two hundred feet above sea level, which left only about two thousand feet more to climb before crossing the divide, after which it was intended to descend the eastern slope of the mountains to the head waters of the Amazon.

The wild flowers along the roadside were beautiful. Up to an elevation of ten thousand feet the sides of the track were covered with wild heliotrope. All the way to the top of the mountain daisies of several varieties were in abundance. The scenery was grand beyond description. In many places the engineers making the surveys had been suspended over the face of the cliffs thousands of feet from anywhere. The location of such a road seemed to me more wonderful than the construction which followed, though the latter was certainly a monument to American genius and pluck.

When we reached the station at the highest point of the road, I got out and walked a short distance to test the theory that the heart's action is much weakened at such an elevation. I was quickly satisfied; the distress was immediate, and I was ready to sit down again when I had walked a hundred feet or less. I found the men in charge and the drivers of the llama trains there were strong and hearty, but it had required many months to accustom them to breathing the rarefied air. These llama trains deserve a mention. The curious, long-necked, delicate-looking animals were used to transport silver ore from the mines in the mountains to the railroad on its way to the smelters. The ore was placed on their backs in bags, and so long as you put one hundred pounds or less on each one they would climb the mountain trails in a wonderful way; but if you put more than a hundred pounds on them, they would lie down quietly and stay there until you removed the extra weight.

On the run down from Chicla, steam was cut off and all brakes put on; but even then we tore around curves and through tunnels in a way to make one's hair stand on end. At Lima I dined with our minister and retired early to my hotel, hoping for a restful night, but I was sadly disappointed. Fleas and mosquitoes bit me, foul smells attacked my nostrils, and cats and dogs, which seemed to abound, squalled and barked all night. About five in the morning I heard the most extraordinary noise, something between the squeal of a pig and the cackle of a hen, and, on looking for the cause from my window, found a little, dried-up, old she-devil of a Peruvian woman, who seemed to be in charge of all the servants, and was berating them for everything she could lay her tongue to. She never drew breath until eight o'clock or after.

The English flagship Warspite arrived at Callao about this time from Valparaiso, and her crew, to show their good feeling for us, invited forty men from the Yorktown and one hundred from the Boston to dine on board with them, and afterward gave them a minstrel performance. The admiral at the same time entertained six American officers, and had to meet them five of his own, which, with himself at the head of the table, made a jovial party of twelve. The Warspite was off in the early morning, so that we could do nothing to show our appreciation of their courtesy.

During our stay at Callao the weather was very damp, with constant fogs, and the effect on a steel ship was enough to break an executive officer's heart. The plates wept rust from every joint and rivet, and with constant care and attention it was almost impossible to keep the ship looking her best. Injury was unavoidable from the rust in places where neither scraper nor paint brush could reach. We had a fair sample of what all seafaring men know as a " Callao painter," which turned all our beautiful paint work black as a pot, hence its name. It also offended our nostrils and affected our stomachs unpleasantly. The vile odours which arise from the water during the " Painters " have been attributed to various causes, but on this occasion they were immediately followed by a very severe earthquake, which led me to think that possibly the gases escaping from the earth had caused the phenomenon. Many people believed that the accumulated sewage of centuries in the bottom of the harbour had something to do with it. Whatever the cause might be, I was constantly dreading an epidemic of typhoid. I fortunately escaped with one case only.

The mail on February 28th brought home newspapers as late as February 10th. I find in my journal the following:

" The correspondence between Blaine and Montt is published, and certainly the Chilean ought to go home after the skinning Blaine has given him. It amuses me to see that Montt objects to my cablegram of January 18th. The cable was addressed to the Secretary of the Navy, and he and the President evidently did not consider it objectionable, or they would not have given it out for publication. Or if they did disapprove, they have never said so to me.

" *February 29th.*—The good ship Boston got off on time Saturday, crowing over the poor little Yorktown for having been left ' in the soup,' as it were; but I am sure the Secretary will look after us and not let us suffer. To-day our repairs are finished, and I have wired the Secretary that we are ready for sea, and I hope for orders soon. The weather here is very trying, not only to officers and men, but also to the ship.

" Some of the home papers seem rabid on the subject of Mr. Egan; but his course has been dignified and just, and certainly his letters show great ability. His appointment was the most extraordinary thing in diplomatic history, but his conduct at Santiago has justified it. Harrison's message is splendid, and if it does not make him the next President I shall be surprised.

" *March 2d.*—Our orders have come—to 'Frisco in

my own time and way. The men are cheering like mad
all over the ship. We shall sail on the morning of the
4th, and be in 'Frisco April 2d or 3d. Needless to
say, I am delighted with my orders."

After leaving Callao one of my officers developed
typhoid fever, and in order to insure his recovery I
ran into Acapulco and bought a goat, so that he might
have the advantage of fresh milk. Here I again met
Admiral Hotham in the Warspite, and the moment he
learned that I had a case of serious illness he sent his
boat to me with the only piece of ice in the harbour.
His courtesy and kindness to me were unfailing whenever we met. I wired the Department from Acapulco,
and went to sea at once. I was in the port less than
two hours.

When off the Galapagos Islands the water was
covered with turtles. I counted five hundred in sight
at one time. Many of them were asleep, and as I had
to swing ship for compass deviations, I took occasion
at the same time to supply the crew with plenty of
fresh meat. Two whale boats were lowered and
manned for the purpose. They pulled up quietly to
the turtles one after another, and before they were
fairly awake the men had yanked them into the boats
by their flippers. In less than an hour both boats had
been filled and were alongside, when the catch was distributed among the different messes and the boats
hoisted in their places.

North of the Galapagos Islands I had a curious
experience. I had for days noticed a large number of
what I supposed to be fish breaking the water at some
distance from the ship. I took them to be skip-jacks,

a species of the mackerel family, as their motions much resembled those of this fish, which I had often caught in the Atlantic. I broke out my trolling lines, and with the most seductive baits fished zealously for several days, but entirely without success. Not a scale could I capture. It was only after many months in the arctic later on that I discovered that I had been fishing for young fur seals.

I felt sure that the Yorktown could steam from Callao to San Francisco without recoaling, a distance of about forty-five hundred miles, and meant to give her the reputation of having done it; but when off San Diego we struck a streak of bad coal, and as I only had fifty tons remaining on board I deemed it prudent to run in there and replenish my supply, which I did. I only remained overnight and then hurried on my way, arriving in San Francisco March 26, 1892. On the way up from San Diego after passing Santa Barbara we had a succession of gales with biting cold weather, which caused us much suffering, fresh as we were from the heat of the tropics. My typhoid fever patient was a plucky youngster, and fought hard for his life, but I could see that he was growing weaker day by day, owing to the unavoidable discomforts of the pitching, rolling ship. However, I landed him the moment we arrived, and sent him to the Mare Island Hospital, where he rapidly recovered.

CHAPTER XXIV

FROM CHILE TO BERING SEA

THE people of San Francisco gave me and the crew of the Yorktown a very hearty welcome. They made it plain to us that they considered the treatment of the Baltimore men an outrage which they were quite ready to fight about. The general feeling seemed to be that if I had brought on a war they would have considered that I was right, and would have backed me up for doing so. As soon as I landed I was recognised, though in plain clothes, and the outspoken commendation of the people was most embarrassing to me. I consoled myself, however, with the thought that their condemnation would have been impossible to bear.

After one day at San Francisco I docked the York-town at Mare Island, and, being anxious to get ready for service at the first possible moment, put my men to work scraping the outside of the ship as the dock was pumped out. When the last water had disappeared we were ready for the paint, and in forty-eight hours again ready to go to sea. This action led to a bitter attack being made on me by some of the local labour unions, who claimed that I was taking the bread out of the mouths of the poor workmen when I ordered my crew to scrape the bottom of the ship. I contended that it was as much my duty to clean the bottom of the ship as it was the top, and that they had no more right to paint the outside of her than they had the inside. In any case I had done what I considered my duty, and the ship was ready for sea in a very short space of time.

"*Mare Island, California, April 8, 1892.*—We have been two weeks waiting to know what we were to do, but no word came. The men were working hard all the time, hoping for liberty, money, etc., when the work was done, but no money was sent for them, and the yard people would not do the few repairs necessary, nor would they put stores and coal on board. To-day came telegraphic orders, and every man and boy is up to his eyes in coal dust; and at the same time we are taking in provisions and stores of all kinds, and I shall go to sea on Monday most uncomfortable. This sort of thing is anything but good for the navy. My men had every right to expect leave here, as they have not put foot ashore in the United States since we left New York, and while of course they do their work, they do it without heart. Our orders are to proceed to Port Townsend, Washington, and there await instructions.

"*April 10th.*—Another telegram came yesterday to delay departure until a general court-martial could try three of the Yorktown's men, which will delay us probably a week. The court is ordered for next Monday, April 18th, and we shall probably sail for Port Townsend on Thursday or Friday, where we shall arrive four or five days after sailing. The present programme is for us to wait there until time to stop the sealers and then go to Bering Sea, where we shall spend most of the summer. It will be interesting to see that part of the world; but having fried us in the tropics for months, they are now going to cool us off near the Arctic Circle.

"*Mare Island, April 14th.*—I am informed, unofficially, to-day that I am to be senior officer in Bering Sea, and have five ships to do the work. Of course it is a compliment, and it is good to be so well thought of by the Secretary, but it will give me no end of work and care. If one is to serve, it is best so. To-morrow I go to 'Frisco again to complete my sea outfit for arctic weather, and at the same time make arrangements to have fresh provisions sent north each month for the crew; it seems that we can get nothing of that kind up there.

"*Mare Island, April 18th.*—The people out here are awfully good to me; I never knew anything like the feeling they show. They are now talking about the marvellous way in which I brought the Yorktown up to the yard and took my buoy. There's nothing in it; we only came fast and made a nice turn in a narrow space. If they had seen us come through the English Narrows they would probably have had a fit. I have been in command of the Yorktown nine months to-day. This summer will be anxious work for me, but at the same time interesting.

"*Mare Island, April 23d.*—I was in the commandant's office day before yesterday when the second terrible earthquake came, and I was never so frightened in my life. The first movement was light, but then came the dreadful twisting, and the building creaked and groaned as if it must surely come down, and I don't see now why it did not. The general court-martial, sitting in the next room, promptly adjourned, and, as I heard all hands making for the open, I asked the admiral to excuse me, and it was surprising to see how my old game leg got down the stairs. After it was over I examined the building, and found every arch broken through and the plaster ready to fall in every room. The poor women and children all over the island spent most of the day afterward on the sidewalks—some of them were made ill from it; and I learn from the newspapers that the northern part of the State suffered great damage and loss. At seven in the evening another shock came, but not so severe. Of course, it is only a question of time, if this sort of thing goes on, when the buildings will fall and cause great loss of life.

"A telegram came from the Department yesterday, asking when I could be ready for sea. I requested the admiral to reply that I had been ready ever since I arrived, but I don't believe he did it. I have the idea that a vessel of war should always be ready to do service.

"*Mare Island, April 25th.*—The latest telegram to the admiral about us reads, ' Have the Yorktown ready for sea at the earliest possible moment, but do not allow her to leave without further instructions.' I wonder if the Department is afraid I will run away with the little frigate and turn pirate. Young Jackson was walking about yesterday, and will be well of his typhoid fever in a month or two.

"*Mare Island, April 26th.*—At last the orders have come, and I am directed to proceed to Port Townsend, collect all the information I can about the sealing fleet, and carry out the instructions which will reach me there. Of course, that means that I am to spend the summer chasing sealers.

"*Port Townsend, April 30th.*—We certainly do have bad luck sometimes, and this is one of the times. We left Mare Island on Wednesday at noon, and have made steamer time up here, but with such a nasty gale behind us that the little ship has rolled more than at any time since we left New York. Thursday I was on deck all day and most of the night, and the strain on my wounded foot was so bad that it gave way, and I am now on my back. Rheumatism followed the strain, and I have suffered very much, but am now ' on the mend.' It is plain that I am to have a pretty hard summer with the fogs, gales, sealers, and other ' varmints.' I am now in command of five ships, but without orders from the Department, and hence at a loss to know what they expect me to do. My instructions will, no doubt, come at the last moment, and give no end of trouble. This morning the shore people have been off to welcome me, and the newspapers are most complimentary. Too much ' Fighting Bob ' business.

"*Port Townsend, May 3d.*—My orders have come, and they seem endless, and the telegrams are dropping in by the dozen. The people block up the decks, they are so thick; and, in addition to it all, my cabin table and chairs are piled up with printed documents and charts until I am distracted. My orders are confidential: I am to prepare the fleet, which I am ordered to command, for a six months' cruise in the North Pacific and Bering Sea—the second largest fleet in commission, and the most active and important work of our navy at present. The Yorktown, Mohican, Adams, Ranger, and Rush compose the fleet, and if I can do half what my orders call for I shall consider that I have done well. The orders are certainly ironclad, and make me complete boss in the North Pacific and Bering Sea. I shall make a stab at it, and only hope that I succeed and make no blunders. Commanding a fleet without clerks or a staff of any kind is hard work.

"My old bones are better, and if the clear, bracing weather continues I shall pull up to my average in a few days. The view from the ship is finer than anything I ever saw in Italy. Snow-clad mountains, one hundred and thirty miles away, standing out clear as crystal against the most perfect sky and looking as if one could walk to them in two hours, and air that feels as brittle as spun glass as I breathe it.

" *Port Townsend, May 5th.*—The grind still goes on, and playing admiral with no staff is not an easy thing. However, I shall make out somehow, and have the fleet ready for sea next Tuesday or Wednesday, and then wait the word from Washington to sail. I have a serious work ahead of me and appreciate that much depends on the way it is done. It has been much delayed here by the crowds and jams of people, who flock to the ship until we can scarcely move for them. But I know they mean to be kind; they say they admire and like me, and it would be ungracious not to see them. Even more—they would be offended and could not understand if they were told that my official duties were so pressing that I could not see them; so I work along as best I can. Of course, I can only do a very small part of what is expected of me socially. Some of these people came on board with a band to welcome us; it made me feel like a fool. Last night was the first occasion of my appearance in the ' social whirl ' here. I attended a reception where I was placed in a parlour, and then each person was formally presented to me— all kind and friendly, some charming. To-morrow I am to go to two receptions of the Governor and Mrs. Ferry.

" *Port Townsend, May 7th.*—Yesterday and to-day have been great days for this place, and very hard on me because of all the work I have had in addition to the functions in connection with the centennial of the discovery of Puget Sound by Captain Vancouver. For days the committees have been running after me constantly to help them out with all sorts of details, which I have done, and yesterday active work began on the arrival of his Excellency the Governor. I went, with all the other officers, in full dress, to pay our respects at a reception given by the President of the First National Bank.

" As there are some revenue marine vessels in my command, their officers came as well, and we made a good show, in a long line of carriages, much observed by the people. At the residence of Colonel Landes a company of State troops was drawn up who gave me a salute as I marched by them. I was escorted to the parlour where were the Governor and Mrs. Ferry surrounded by the wealth and fashion of Port Townsend. Colonel Landes introduced me with a most kind speech, which concluded by saying that ' the American people were proud of ' me. Then Governor Ferry said many more flattering things, and then they introduced me to every one in the room, and each one said something kind and cordial. To-day we have fired three salutes, twenty-one guns each, dressed ships with flags, and otherwise disported ourselves, to the great gratification of the Port Townsendites. Early in the day I was caught and put as the chief support of the Governor, and something happened to me which really touched me. I was standing on the sidewalk near the grand stand when quite a crowd of plain-looking people— men, women, and children—came up, and one said, 'Governor Ferry, we want to speak to the captain of the Yorktown and introduce our wives.' Of course, I spoke to them all, and every one had a kind word for me. Then a lot of miners, hard-looking chaps, came and sized me up, and each one said, 'Cap, shake,' and I shook till my hand was almost disabled. After the review we drove to the beach to a mammoth clambake, and there the ladies embarrassed me with their kindness—saying and doing things to me that they might have done to Admiral Farragut.

"*Port Townsend, May 10th.*—Eastern papers have come, some saying that Mr. Blaine admits that my telegram from Valparaiso was 'improper.' Mr. Tracy, my superior and commanding officer, has not said to me that he approved of my course in Chile, but he gives me the most important command in the navy, and I shall go on just the same, and do as I did in Chile, what I feel to be my duty to my country. They are heaping the work on me now. Yesterday I took the Rush and went over to Esquimault to spend the day with Admiral Hotham, and get from him and his officers their plans for the summer. My visit was most successful and delightful, and I am glad I went. The admiral kept me to luncheon and dinner; we had a most satisfactory time, and made all arrangements for co-operation during the summer. They will send the Melpomene and Daphne, and their commanding officers will be practically under my orders, so I am really to have a big command.

"I left here at seven in the morning, and returned at 2 A. M. to-day, but could not get to bed until 3.30, as my desk was full of letters and telegrams, the answers to which had to go at seven. I was up again at eight, and have scarcely had the pen out of my hand since, except for an official interview with the commanding officers of the Mohican and Adams, and I see no chance for a let-up until we go to sea. I have wired to-day that four vessels of the fleet are ready to sail, and that I am anxious to get away. The other four vessels can join us later at Unalaska. I now have eight under my command—quite a showing for a commander. But Chilean refugees and arctic outfits have hardly left me money to pay my bills.

"*Port Townsend, May 11th.*—The final orders have come, and we are off day after to-morrow (13th) early in the morning with the Yorktown, Adams, Mohican, and Rush, leaving orders for the Ranger, Corwin, Bear, and Albatross to join me at Unalaska. I have written, with my own hands, detailed instructions for each of them, besides many letters of all kinds. Surely I shall have no end of work this trip. We sail under sealed orders, not to be opened until we are outside the straits. It seems a curious thing to do in time of profound peace, and I wonder what it can mean. Until some letters came to-day I had not realized what an amount of talk the papers had made about my work in Chile. I was not aware that my cables to the Department had been published. It is bearable to have the papers call me ' Fighting Bob ' when I see that my friends approve of me and are pleased and proud of the notoriety."

CHAPTER XXV

THE NAVY AMONG THE SEALERS

THE preparation of the fleet for service had been hard work, but the prospect of doing something braced all hands up wonderfully. At first it looked as if we would surely have a collision with the British navy over the seal question, and I knew, of course, that that meant a bitter and destructive war. The long struggle over the *modus vivendi* was not concluded when my instructions were sent me, and I knew the moment I read them that if I carried them out we would have war on our hands within a week. Hence I was much relieved when the terms of that instrument had been agreed upon, and the whole contents wired me for my guidance. My first orders contemplated the seizure of all sealing vessels found within certain limits, and the orders of the British admiral were to protect the Canadian sealers in the same limits. It is easy to see what any action on my part would have led to. Fortunately, wise counsels prevailed, and united action between the two navies was decided upon.

While these sea preparations were being made I used my best endeavours to find out where the sealing fleet would rendezvous, in order that I might be on hand to seize the supply steamer, which would much simplify my work during the summer. With the assistance of detectives, sent us from Washington, I interviewed the men most likely to give the secret away; but I found that they were absolutely in the dark, as all the vessels of the fleet were to go to sea with sealed orders, which were to be delivered to them only on the eve of their departure.

To make the situation clearer, it may be well to give here, in a few words, the course pursued by these sealers, of whom so much has been written. The fleet was composed entirely of schooners, large and small, and numbered about one hundred and ten. They were not owned, as many people supposed, entirely by British subjects. Many of them had American owners, but sailed under the English flag. Many others sailed under the American flag. All were controlled by the Sealers' Association. Each vessel had its regular crew for working her, and in addition from ten to forty men, according to her size, who were known as hunters, and who did the killing. They were armed with double-barrelled No. 10 shotguns for the seals, and a good outfit of Winchester rifles for revenue officers or others who interfered with them. Each schooner carried a number of dories or small boats to be used in sneaking on the sleeping seals; and each of these boats had one or two long gaff-hooks, or poles with several hooks on the sides, for the purpose of catching, if possible, the bodies which sank rapidly after being shot.

When the seal herd appeared off San Francisco, usually early in February, from its winter quarters in the south, the fleet joined it, and remained with it until it entered the Bering Sea through one of the passes.

Seal Poachers

During all this long trip of the herd around and across the North Pacific the work of destruction went on. The great majority of the seals were females with young, hurrying on to the Pribilof Islands to their breeding ground, and therefore each one killed represented two lives—mother and pup. In almost any kind of weather, the schooner would heave to in the morning and hoist out her boats, and, drifting away, leave them to their deadly work until a full boat or darkness compelled them to stop. Many boats were lost in the fog, and their crews lost their lives either from drowning or starvation. Yet the profits were so large that men willingly took these chances. Less than half the seals killed in this way were recovered, as their bodies sank very quickly. It is easily seen what was to be the fate of a herd of animals where the females, bearing only one offspring at a time, were being thus destroyed. As the herd approached the Aleutian Islands, and the time for giving birth to the young drew near, the females moved through the water with great rapidity, hurrying on to their breeding grounds, and very few of them, comparatively speaking, were killed. The slaughter in the North Pacific proper was fearful.

Before leaving Port Townsend I had been supplied with printed notices warning sealers not to enter Bering Sea, and these the Department expected me to serve on every vessel in the fleet, no matter of what nationality. The number of vessels was one hundred and ten, and as a matter of fact I found at the end of the season that the force under my command had boarded and served notice on one hundred and seven of them. Some of them had been boarded so often

A Sailor's Log

that their log books were veritable collections of autographs of American commanders. It had leaked out before sailing that the Canadian vessels would refuse to obey a warning served by an American officer, and, as I did not wish to make trouble when it could be avoided, I took a sufficient number of notices to Admiral Hotham, who indorsed them in his official capacity, which effectually spiked the guns of these would-be sea lawyers.

When finally ready I sent all but two vessels to the North Pacific to follow and serve notice on the sealers. With the Yorktown and one revenue cutter I ran direct to Unalaska, where I arrived after a very rough passage, with much fog to contend with about the passes. As soon as coaled I ran north and skirted the ice all the way around the Pribilof Islands, to make sure that no sealers were lurking about the sea. Then, with the assistance of the cutter, I guarded the passes to prevent any one from entering, while the rest of my force continued its work to the north. My men suffered from exposure and the lack of fresh provisions, but we were always able to give them all the fresh fish they wanted. We had only to stop the engines and get the lines overboard, and in a few hours catch three or four hundred pounds of beautiful codfish. Sometimes I gave them salmon, but I soon found that they could not eat this many days in succession—it was too rich. Codfish was our mainstay. The following from my journal may be of interest:

"*At Sea, June 4, 1892.*—Had a good breakfast today—broiled king salmon, potatoes, cold reindeer roast, onion salad, and a slice of cold English ham—

318

Delmonico could hardly beat it. But yesterday I tried
to eat a piece of bear-meat—well, a Chinese baby dead
of the smallpox, or a mangy dog that had lived on fish
and the little bugs we sometimes find on berries, might
be something like it. A kind skipper gave me the meat
before I left Unalaska, and my steward let his skill out
on it. I afterward let out almost my eternal soul on
account of it. Such is life in the arctic, and I am not
enjoying it. But as I write this I am surrounded by
such beauty and grandeur and calmness as one sees
rarely in a lifetime. We are anchored in the open Bering Sea, five miles from the chain of the Aleutian
Islands, and from the deck one can count over a dozen
of the most graceful, beautiful snow-covered peaks in
the world, all dazzling, blinding white. Then I can
see two active volcanoes, puffing out smoke and steam
as the devil snorts and roars inside the crust, and three
extinct ones—all strange to look at but most beautiful and curious. The rim of the crater of one of them
is surmounted by what looks, from this distance—
sixty miles—like a huge frill of lace, the snow on
the contorted lava giving the effect. Add to this
that the day has been the first clear one we have
had, and warm, and one would think I might be content, and so I am after a fashion. There is nothing
for me but duty, and, contrary to much ' guff ' given
me in my youth on that subject, it does not fill the bill
entirely.

"We came down here yesterday—or rather we
started yesterday—from Unalaska, to see if we could
catch some sealers who have for several years made
this vicinity a sort of headquarters for their work. We

passed the fishing fleet on the way down, hard at work packing codfish, but nothing in the shape of a sealer. Indeed, I can not see what they would come here for, as I have not laid eyes on a single seal or even a pup. I wonder why seals were made, anyhow. And if I had my way with the curious old idiots who went about the world discovering places—Straits of Magellan, North Pacific Ocean, Bering Sea, etc., etc.—I would feed them on bear-meat and then chuck them down one of these lovely volcanoes. We are here to-day owing to these idiots, and as I wished for a quiet Sunday, I found a place to anchor; and here we are, where I shall stay until day after to-morrow, when I hope to do some target-firing—using a sealer for a target if I can find one—and then clear out for the western end of the islands and so back to the beautiful Unalaska.

"*Sunday, June 5th.*—The little blow of last night was the breaking out of a southeast gale, and now the weather is as nasty as usual in these waters—blowing a gale, cold as charity, thick as mud, and raining in torrents. We are snug, however, and shall hold on until to-morrow, and then run to the west. Every day that passes is so much gain for us on our way somewhere —it may be 'Frisco, it may be China, or it may be some Atlantic port. One can imagine how low we have fallen when we look upon Unalaska as quite a metropolis.

" The men to-day have caught more than two thousand pounds of codfish from the vessel in less than three hours' fishing. It is blowing a gale, and in spite of it and the pouring rain they would fish all the

time if I would permit it; but if they were ordered
to do so they would consider it a great hardship,
and growl accordingly. The life here is more monotonous and isolated than I could have thought
possible.

" *Iliuliuk, Unalaska, June 8th.*—Here we are, back
again, but no target practice and no sealers so far.
Yesterday morning the weather was so bad that we got
under way and came back here. At midnight I put the
ship's head off shore until the fog lifted, and we saw
land for a moment, which was all I wanted, and at
6 A. M. we were anchored in this snug little hole. An
hour later the Corwin was in, and we had our first mail
since leaving Port Townsend. I have a peck of letters,
of course, and the newspapers seem to have begun on
me again.

" My work here is really beginning to crowd now,
and I have a matter of vital importance on hand, in
which I hope to succeed; but the chances are dreadfully
against me. Every year the British sealing fleet has
chartered a large steamer to meet it at some out-of-
the-way place in the Aleutian Islands, where all the
skins are transferred and so sent back to Victoria,
British Columbia, and a fresh supply of provisions laid
in. Such action in American waters is, of course,
illegal, and I am straining every nerve to find their
place of rendezvous for this year. The steamer is supposed by the Navy Department to be the Danube, and
if I can find her I shall seize her and her cargo and
all the schooners that have transferred to her, and take
them to Sitka—I hope between the 15th and 25th of
June. Last year thirty-eight sealers transferred to the

steamer in one day twenty-five thousand skins, and received from her a large supply of provisions. Our patrol fleet was then very small and composed of slow vessels. I hope to convince them that we are not up here this year for our health."

CHAPTER XXVI

STRIKING AT THE SOURCE OF SUPPLIES

THE problem of how to catch the supply steamer was a very interesting one, and many people have asked me how I did it. The Navy Department had been misled by information purposely sent them from Victoria, and they in turn tried unintentionally to deceive me by sending me this false information, saying that it came from a reliable source. The rendezvous, as given by them, was over eighteen hundred miles from where I caught her. The case I had to deal with was similar to that of an enemy's cruiser on your coast in time of war. What was her objective? I knew that her intention was to take skins from the fleet and give it provisions, and therefore if I kept touch with the fleet I should eventually find the steamer; and I did. Several vessels were detailed to watch the schooners and see which way they were heading, and as soon as I had this information I felt sure that in that direction somewhere I would find the steamer I was looking for.

It is sometimes an officer's duty to do a thing that his Government must afterward disavow and punish him for having done. Such a case was the capture of the Confederate cruiser Florida in Bahia, Brazil, by the United States steamer Wachusett during the civil

war. I felt that I might have to do the same sort of
thing and face the music. If I found the steamer I
was after in one of our ports, having violated our revenue laws, it would be all plain sailing; but suppose
I found her at sea? What then? I read plainly between the lines of my orders that the Washington authorities considered it of vital importance that she
should be captured, and I made up my mind to get
her legally if I could, illegally if I must. If I took
her at sea, the Department could disavow my act and
punish me; but in the meantime my mission in the
North would be accomplished and sealing broken up,
at least for that year. The schooners would have to
go back to Victoria for provisions, and it would then
be too late for them to return to Bering Sea and do
any real harm. I again quote from my journal:

" *Iluiluik, June 11, 1892.*—We are off to-morrow,
and I am sending the Albatross to Port Townsend on
Tuesday. Yesterday I spent in bed with neuralgia in
the muscles of my wounded leg—very painful, but I am
up to-day.

" The two British ships, Melpomene and Daphne,
are in, and their captains are fine chaps and seem ready
to help me to knock these sealers out in every way. Of
course, they don't know that I intend to seize the
Danube, if I can find her, but I think they suspect me.

" *Karluk, Kodiak Island, June 15th.*—On Sunday we
left Iluiluik in a dense fog, and worked our way up
here, six hundred miles, where we are suddenly in a
mess. We have caught two American schooners violating the law, and may have to seize them both, which
will greatly embarrass me in my efforts to catch the

Big Fishing

English chaps. Johnson, in the Mohican, has seized five, and I hear his ship is damaged by grounding. We are off as soon as we can get our anchor up.

"This afternoon I saw a wonderful thing in the fishing way—a haul of the seine in which they caught fifteen thousand salmon. It was a beautiful sight, and they gave me all the king salmon my gig could carry. Afterward our men borrowed the seine and caught over two thousand, which they are now salting down. The Kodiak is the greatest salmon river in the world, supporting seven canneries, each of which puts up over six hundred thousand fish per year. The water is absolutely alive with them; my cockswain caught one with a boathook while we were waiting at the beach.

"*Alitak, Kodiak Island, June 16th.*—Just before leaving Karluk we caught a fool of a schooner captain who had been violating the law; he thought I did not know it, and gave us some trouble. He started to get under way in the afternoon before I had settled his case, but I sent a boat with orders for him to anchor his schooner and come on board. Before he got to our gangway he took his hat off and came over the side with it in his hand and shaking as if he were going to have a fit. I never saw a man so scared in my life. After getting some information from him he was allowed to go on his way.

"The people up here seem to think I am some kind of a military governor, or something, and come to me with the most absurd complaints. I don't mind any of them until it comes to the missionary-school teachers. They nauseate me. The conditions up here, as I see them, are about as bad as they could be, and the whole

22

business is a disgrace to our Government; but I am a policeman this trip for sealers only.

"The northeast gale is still raging, but we have found the sealers' snug harbour, I think, and are as comfortable as possible, anchored in a sort of lagoon which can not be seen from the outside. Six sealers have run in out of the gale, and we have them anchored under our guns, where they will stay until I am through with them. As we came up the coast this forenoon we made out three schooners, and, as it was blowing half a gale, they tried to get away from us; but it was no use. I let this little frigate out a link or two and just drove the schooners as one would drive geese.

"We found the Corwin in here, and as I am satisfied the transfer of skins will be made in Prince William Sound, I have sent her there to catch the gang, if possible.

"*Friday, June 17th.*—Still the northeaster howls, and the little Yorktown tugs and quivers at her anchors; but the land keeps the sea off, and we are snug and cosy. Three more sealers ran in last night in the blow, and were much surprised to find themselves in my clutches. One of them gave away the place of rendezvous of the English fleet—Port Etches, Prince William Sound, where I have two vessels waiting for them; but I shall run up there myself to-morrow afternoon, I think. It is only three hundred miles, and I want to make sure of that capture if I can.

"*Port Etches, Prince William Sound, 1 A. M., June 21st.*—There is no night here at this season. We left Alitak Sunday morning, after the gale had blown out, and I have been on my feet almost ever since. There are practically no charts of this region, and running full speed, as we do most of the time, is anything but funny. We got here at midnight, just after sunset, and now, at 1 A. M., it is almost sunrise.

" We found the Mohican here, she having captured three American schooners and sent them to Sitka, and having been herself on the rocks and knocked about somewhat. But she will do for service in the Bering Sea this summer. The steamer to receive the skins is expected to-morrow or the day after, and I still hope to capture her."

I had made all plans for the capture of the steamer, and was confident of success. The vessels of the force were gathering for the final move when, on June 21st, I ran into Port Etches, and to my dismay found that the United States steamer Mohican had been lying there for five days, doing just the thing I had cautioned her commanding officer not to do—alarming the sealers so that they would neither transfer skins nor provisions, but seek another port for that purpose. I jumped the Mohican out in short order, and then arranged with the commanding officer of the Corwin to make the seizure. I directed him to run off to the south for a certain distance, and then change his course so as to bring up behind the end of Montague Island, about twelve miles from Port Etches, haul his vessel close inshore, send down his topmasts and cover his lower masts with bushes, so that he would be well hidden from inquisitive eyes. He was to remain in that position twenty-four hours, and then run over to Port Etches and see what he would find. The captain was an able, fearless man, and I knew he would carry out my orders.

He said to me that the twenty-seven schooners then in port were well armed and would fight to a finish when the time came. I replied that he had several guns of his own, and that he might rely on the Yorktown to be somewhere near when the shooting began.

After the Corwin and Mohican had gone I visited what seemed to be the flagship of the sailing fleet, a handsome Burgess schooner of one hundred and fifty tons, having on board a number of gentlemen who were cruising during the summer as a matter of recreation. I told them that I was bound south to look after matters at Unalaska, and asked that they would warn all arrivals to keep out of the Bering Sea during the summer, as I should certainly capture them if they went in. Then I cleared out at top speed, perfectly satisfied that a few days would settle the fate of the chap who had caused me so much thought and trouble. The Corwin waited a few hours, when the fog shut in as thick as pea soup. The captain, fearing that the steamer might get away in the fog, decided after twelve hours that the time had come to act, and proceeded cautiously to carry out my orders. He found the British steamer Coquitlan in Port Etches, and seized her. She had received about thirty thousand skins, and at the time of the seizure, in a dense fog, had her hatches open and was transplanting cargo in violation of law. The case against her was so plain that there was no room for resistance, and she was towed to Sitka as a prize, where she was bonded for six hundred thousand dollars, which all went into the United States Treasury, and, I suspect, paid most of the expenses of our summer's work.

Warning the Sealers

I again quote from my journal:

"*Unalaska, June 25th.*—Back again to this metropolis. On the way out and down the coast from Port Etches the sealers were thick, all standing for Port Etches. We were kept busy, day and night, boarding them, and the work was severe on officers and men, as it blew hard most of the time and the sea was nasty. It was funny to see them try to get away from us—in which none succeeded—and several had to be shot at to bring them to. Yesterday morning at daylight we were in Uniak Pass, on our way here, and as the fog lifted we made out a schooner in Bering Sea and went for her at full speed. She made sail and tried to get away; but three shots from one of the rapid-fire guns stopped her, the third one striking within a few feet of her. We took her in tow and brought her here, but after a careful search let her go, as she was a whaler bound for the arctic. If the people we sometimes hear of who think the navy has nothing to do could come up among these islands and see the work the navy is doing here and hear the things that are said of it, they would change their minds—if they possess such a thing.

"We have warned nearly every one of the one hundred vessels at sea when we left Port Townsend less than six weeks ago, and the navy is respected hereabouts as it has never been before; all hands have a very wholesome regard for us. I don't know what the Department and Secretary Tracy will think of the work we have done; but there can be but one opinion among people who know of it.

"*Bering Sea, July 5th.*—We have had the fog so

thick for two days that it seemed as if one could make a hole in it with the finger, and the finger would pop, like a cork out of a bottle, when it came out. But we must go, all the same, sleep or no sleep.

" We left Unalaska on the 3d, after a week of very hard work coaling, cleaning engines, etc., after our driving trip to the north. I bundled the Adams off on the 1st, the Rush on the 2d, and we followed on the 3d. Captain Parr, of the Melpomene, says he thinks I am interested in the coal contract, as I seem disposed to burn up all there is in Bering Sea. He does not propose to trouble himself over Canadian sealers, and will take things easy, which I can't do; it isn't my way. Unalaska was at its best when we left—plenty of fish and flowers; the mountains covered with snow, and long arms of it running down into the valleys and right into the grass and flowers. No one would credit a picture of it. In five days after the snow has melted the grass is knee-high, and the ground covered with violets, lupines, anemones, and beautiful orchids, but no perfume to any of them. The Alaskan lily is also abundant, a very beautiful, almost black flower. Salmon and trout and salmon-trout in profusion, and such line-fishing as I never heard of before; but I had no time for an hour of it—too busy to think of it. All the returns for the quarter, not only for my own ship, but for all the vessels of the fleet, must pass through my hands and receive my approval, with no one to help me but an officer who has a watch to stand. I have very little time to amuse myself.

" On the afternoon of the 3d we passed close to the island of Bogosloff, an arctic volcano which came

up in 1874 and has not yet cooled off, to judge from
the clouds of smoke constantly rising from its surface—
not from one particular spot, like Vesuvius or Etna,
but from the entire surface of the island, making a cone
of steam, wafted by the wind this way or that, and
reaching many hundreds of feet into the air. We saw
it from a distance of forty miles, and soon after we
passed it the fog shut down on us and here we are—a
sorry sight to see. The coal sent us is cheap, dirty
stuff from Nanaimo, British Columbia, and makes a
dense black smoke which unites with the fog and spat-
ters the little ship until she looks like a chimney-sweep.
Officers and men are constantly black and clothes
ruined.

"*July 6th.*—A gray day, or rather night; everything is gray—sky slate-gray, water blue-gray, air
smoke-gray—all most depressing. We are working a
traverse up to St. Paul's Island and covering as much
ground as possible, but as yet no sign of sealers. It
is very like old blockade days—every one on the lookout, lights screened, and no fog whistle. Very unlike
the White Squadron picnic.

"The papers say that Congress is going to give
admiral's full pay to two officers who have been commanding squadrons. I wonder if they will give me
any additional pay? I command more vessels than
both these captains together, and do more work in
a month than they do in a year. No commander ever
had such a command before, either in our service or
any other that I know of, but I hear of no more pay
for me."

CHAPTER XXVII

THE HOME OF THE SEALS

" *St. Paul Island, July 8th.*—I spent last night on deck in a dense fog looking for this blessed island and listening to the seals jump and play around us. As soon as we came within seventy-five miles of the land we found them thick, and I don't wonder the sealers want to get in here, for they could fill a schooner in a short time. The fog was too much for us all night, but this morning early we made the land and anchored at ten. As soon as I had had my breakfast I went on shore with most of the officers and visited one of the ' rookeries.' We lay down flat in the grass, and, peering over the edge of the bluff, found ourselves within twenty feet of thousands of the beautiful and much-protected animals. The bulls were savage, and from their constant fights much scarred and cut up, and hence not so handsome as earlier in the season, but still very impressive and dignified. Each had his harem of thirty or forty females, and woe unto the male who ventured near! If any wife tried to escape she was viciously torn and hauled back to her place. The two-year-olds, male and female, are not permitted on the breeding ground, and it was most amusing to watch them form into parties of eight or ten and try to slip

332

past the old bulls. As soon as one discovered them, the old chap nearest to them would rise on his hind legs, bellow viciously, and make a start toward them, when the whole gang would tumble over the rocks into the sea and go frolicking away like a lot of children. The young ones—I saw one born while watching them —were thick all over and among the rocks, and it was most curious to watch the mother, as she came from the water, pick out and suckle her own pup. There were thousands of them, all bleating like lambs, and making enough noise to deafen one; yet the mother always recognised the voice of her own pup, and dragged herself through the lot until she got to it. The pups did not know the mother, and many would try to get to her, but she snapped and bit until she got the right one. It was certainly one of the most interesting sights of my rather varied experience.

" We walked back to the killing grounds over a carpet of such beautiful wild flowers as I have never before seen; my cabin is full of them, but all odourless.

" At the killing grounds the natives had just driven out and killed five hundred seals, and as a three-year-old was being skinned a spear head was found completely inclosed and healed up in his flesh. It is the kind used by the Alaska Indians, and must have been in the seal two years.

" When I had returned on board and had my dinner, the officer of the deck reported a schooner in sight at sea. The boats were down, lower booms out, and fires banked; but just ten minutes after I gave the order we were under way and humming out after her. It was most gratifying to see how quickly and quietly everything was done. As we neared the schooner I was surprised to see her lower her mainsail and heave to, but it was explained when we passed under her stern and found she was our old friend Jane Gray, which we had seized, towed into Unalaska, and afterward released. Her captain said he did not want any more of our rapid-fire practice at him.

"*Saturday Night.*—More fog and a nasty blow from the southeast which gives us all the comforts of a sea life while at anchor. I have, however, managed to get the whole crew ashore to have a look at the seal rookeries, and they are back on board with a message from the agent that they have behaved so well that he would not object to any number of the same kind coming whenever they please. I am glad the boys were good.

"*Sunday, July 10th.*—It cleared for just two hours to-day, and during that time the Melpomene came in, rolling and wallowing like a tub, and anchored near us. I begin now to understand why the seals selected these islands for their home: they felt that nothing but a seal could stand such a climate.

"*Unalaska, July 15th.*—I am perfectly swamped with work. The letters are piled up until I can see no end to them, and I feel dead beat. We came in late on the 12th, and when I saw the boat-load of mail-bags come off I knew what was ahead of me, and have struggled with pen and ink ever since, and yet do not see the end of it. I have seized the British steamer Coquitlan and sent her to Sitka. I have no doubt the newspapers will make all sorts of a row about it, but that won't save her and her thirty thousand seal skins.

A fur-seal family on St. Paul Island, Bering Sea.

From a photograph by D. W. Thompson and A. W. Marrett.

A Supply Ship Seized

The value of the prize is about six hundred thousand dollars, and will help the Government to pay damages if the arbitration goes against us. Captain Hooper, of the Corwin, carried out my instructions carefully and intelligently, and the result is a happy one. He found the Coquitlan at Port Etches, surrounded by thirty English sealers, and when he made the seizure all the Indians on the different schooners made for the shore, swearing that they were done with the sealing business. After a time they were induced to return on board, and the vessels put out for Victoria; so we are done with that lot, and the rest are so scared that I doubt if one of them will come into the sea. The Coquitlan had supplies for all the sealing fleet, and as they were captured with the vessel, of course the sealers must go home for more before they can go on with their work, and before they can get back the season will be over. I am quite satisfied with it all, and hope the Secretary may be the same.

" There has not been a sealer in the Bering Sea this season, and I am inclined to think they won't come.

" It is amusing to know the ferocious reputation I am getting up here. They seem to think I am going to eat all the sealers I catch, and I am held up as a terror to the crews of all whalers and other merchant ships. The effect is good, but it makes me laugh when I hear about it. There is one coal ship here with a union crew, and I am afraid I shall have trouble with them. The captain has appealed to me, and, on looking into the matter, I find that they won't work unless they have coffee at nine in the morning. I asked if they did not want tea and toast in the afternoon, and

335

told them that I would double iron the whole gang and put them on bread and water where the dogs wouldn't bite them, and if I heard another word from them I would stop the bread. The effect was good, and they are working very well.

"*Saturday, July 16th.*—I gave myself a holiday to-day and spent it in the open air catching trout. It has been a gloriously clear day—a thing seldom seen in this country, but now I have to face double work to make up for it. I am run down and can not sleep, and the doctor urged me to take a rest.

"*July 18th.*—The Danube has come in from Victoria with coal and stores for the English ships, and I see, from the Canadian papers she brought, that they are giving me a scoring for the capture of the Coquitlan. Well, we have the steamer, and Uncle Samuel is well ahead of the game. The idea of any one daring to execute our laws seems more than the Canucks can stand.

"*July 19th.*—Something has happened, I don't know just what; but the English captain is sending a ship at once to Victoria, and I have news that a sealer or two has come into the sea, and I am off after them. I don't know what may happen in the next month, but I shall keep my end up as well as I can.

"*At Sea, July 21st, 10* P. M.—Night before last, when the news was confirmed that a British sealer had come into the sea, I hurried out after her with two cutters, as soon as we could get steam, just at midnight, in the blackest fog I ever saw. One officer swears it was so dense that it slowed the vessel down running against it. All yesterday and part of to-day I have been searching for the sealer, but without success. This afternoon we landed an officer and a dozen men, armed and rationed for twelve days, with a good sailing launch, to guard the only pass he can get out of, and later on we shall probably catch him. Now we are on our way to the Seal Islands to look up matters there—so we go, always on the jump.

" *Friday Night, Island of St. George.*—This has been the devil's own day. I was called at half past three this morning by a message that a schooner was in sight, but when I reached the deck found that it was a whaling bark. But once awake I stayed up, having had about four hours' sleep. By noon it was blowing hard, and as thick as pea soup again, and in such weather we spent the day until 6 P. M., when we found this island and anchored with the sea breaking on the shore so heavily that no boat could land, and so we shall have to hang on here until morning to see what we can do. Just now the orderly comes to report that the officer of the deck says we are dragging anchor. The ship is most uneasy, and the seals are bellowing until I can't hear myself think. I must go on deck, where I shall probably spend most of the night looking after the ship.

" *Saturday Night, July 23d.*—I did spend most of last night on deck, and early this morning the sea ran down so that we could get a boat ashore with some mail; then we pulled out in another dense fog, and a fine day we had of it. However, one day up here is much like another—all fog and lookout. We certainly sha'n't get a foul bottom from lying still during these six months.

A Sailor's Log

"*Sunday, July 24th.*—We have seen the land occasionally to-day, or, rather, we have seen a white line of angry surf breaking on the rocks. No end of seals playing around and near the ship. They remind me more of a frolicking lot of school children than of anything else. I wish Russia had them all back again, and these blessed islands with their beastly fogs, too. We should probably have other nasty work to do, but nothing to equal this. Chile was worse, but there we had the possibility of a fight every day to make the time pass.

"*Unalaska, July 27th.*—Just out of a very bad gale, which has lasted since Sunday. Now I suppose I have raised the devil sure enough. The Rush found the British schooner Winifred, and I have seized her under our revenue laws, instead of under the *modus vivendi*, and shall send her to Sitka on Monday. Of course, the Canadians will raise a howl, and it may be that our own people won't sustain me. But I am right, all the same, and shall stand to my guns. The reason I have done this is because the captain of the Winifred commanded the Borealis last year and raided the rookeries on St. Paul Island, killing four hundred seals. The year before he commanded the Adele, raided the island, and killed three hundred and fifty seals. This year he transferred cargo in one of our ports without license, which renders him liable to imprisonment and forfeiture of his vessel. For raiding he is liable to ten years in prison. If I turn him over to the English, nothing will be done to him for raiding, so I determined to send him in and let our courts have a shy at him. The British finally yielded, and the sealer Winifred is mine. Her

338

captain, the most noted pirate in Bering Sea, will go to Sitka in her, and I shall be surprised if he does not spend the next ten years of his life in the penitentiary.

" We have also seized and sent to Sitka the Jane Gray, the American schooner we have seen before. In fact, we are raising considerable of a row, I am afraid, but we are stopping sealing in Bering Sea, which is what I was sent up here to do.

" *Friday Night, July 29th.*—No one who has not seized an English sealer under the guns of the English navy can know just how much writing that calls for— not to speak of the bluff—nor can guess what yesterday and to-day have been to me. I have convinced the senior English officer in Bering Sea that my course was the proper one, and he has so stated to me in his official letter on the subject; and now that it is all done with, I have fits of the shakes when I think of the volcano that was under us, and how close it was to the surface. A few more gray hairs in my head tell the story, and to-morrow I am taking the English officers out on a fishing picnic to show how friendly we are. 'Tis a funny world we live in, and I seem to strike many of the sensational snags. Of course, I have had to write some sort of an account of all the business to the Secretary of the Navy; but I have made it very short, for the amount of writing and work has been greater than could be imagined, and in addition I have taken in four hundred tons of coal since we came in here. But I shall go fishing to-morrow, and be ready for more work the day after. The Albatross will leave for Sitka on Monday or Tuesday, towing the sealer, and then we shall put to sea and try to find some more of the gang who have boasted in Victoria that 'no Yankee cruiser should ever overhaul them, for they had a strong Government back of them.'

"We all play a pretty strong hand sometimes. It may be that we shall come to grief for it. I hope not.

"*July 31st.*—We had a glorious picnic yesterday, and such fishing as I had never dreamed of; but on returning I found that I had been stung on the hand by some sort of a beast which had given me a fist as large as Sullivan's.

"Before leaving yesterday morning I had ordered the search of the American whaling bark Lydia, of San Francisco, suspecting that she had seal skins on board. On my return, the searching officer reported a barrel found marked 'Salmon,' and on opening it discovered fourteen salted fur-seal skins. The captain had tried to put them on board the whaling bark Northern Light, for 'Frisco, at midnight the night before, but our men were too much for him. Of course, we seized the Lydia, and have sent her to Sitka, which will raise a howl in the 'Frisco papers, and cause me to be called all the scoundrels on earth; but I don't care a sou. These whalers are a set of infernal pirates, and I shall run in some more of them if they give me the chance.

"The Adams came in this morning and reports the capture of the English schooner Mountain Chief, of Victoria, caught sealing in Bering Sea. Nelson put an officer and men on board of her, and she will be in to-morrow, when I shall turn her over to the senior British officer and ask him to keep her out of the sea in future, or we will blow the stuffing out of her.

A Nest of Pirates

"*At Sea, Two Hundred Miles Northwest of St. Paul Island, August 6th.*—As soon as our last mail closed we put to sea in a dense fog for the False Pass, to pick up the landing party, which had been on shore thirteen days. The distance was one hundred and forty-seven miles, and we ran it up without seeing anything but the fog, slowed the engines, got a cast of the lead, and in a few minutes made out breakers ahead and close aboard. I rang her full speed astern, and let go the anchor, and when the fog cleared in the night we were just one mile out of position, which I call the best piece of navigating I ever heard of, and I give the full credit for it to Conway, our navigating officer.

"At 10 A. M. day before yesterday the landing party got off the beach, through the heavy surf, and reported on board in excellent condition and having done good service. They had captured a number of small native boats engaged in sea-otter hunting against the law, taken from them their skins and guns, and released them with a warning. On the day of our arrival they had had a brush with a small steamer, which got away from them in the fog after they had fired five hundred rounds into her from their rifles and thought they surely had her. The whole place is a perfect nest of pirates; but I have not the time to treat them as they deserve, as we must keep constantly moving in order to prevent our Canadian friends from poaching in Bering Sea. The whole condition of Alaska, so far as the execution of the law is concerned, is a disgrace to our Government, and I shall so report; but it will not do any good.

"We are now on a trip of two thousand miles, covering the sea as perfectly as I can, but so far have seen nothing like a sealer. To-day we have seen more seals than during all the rest of our cruising away from the islands. They all seem to be feeding, and are probably the cows who have young on the islands. The water has been covered with a peculiar white, greasy-looking substance, and birds of all kinds are about in thousands —all of which may or may not have to do with the presence of the seals. There is much yet to be learned about these animals, and we are not going about it in the best way. The Government should send some hard-headed chap, with good common sense and no theories, to study them. One day, some time ago, a naturalist, sent by the Government, came to me and reported two dead cow seals on the beach. This looked as if there had been a raid on the rookeries, and I felt dreadfully. The man was closely questioned, and said he had examined them for sex, etc. Stanley Brown found the two animals, dead as reported, but they proved to be sea-lion pups—about as much like a seal as a black lamb is like a pig. So goes the Government money.

"*August 7th.*—I seem to do nothing these days but cruise around in the fog, which is black to-day. Even the seals seem to have had enough of it, and have disappeared. We shall get down to Attu in a couple of days, and if we find no sealers there I shall feel perfectly satisfied that there are none in Bering Sea; in fact, I am satisfied now that there are not enough to kill to any extent."

CHAPTER XXVIII

CRUISING IN HIGH LATITUDES

"*August 11th.*—We have to-day been to Uncle Sam's western limit, and I do not think much of it as a garden spot, though it was very pretty—what we could see of it through fog and clouds—beautiful green mountains above the nasty, rocky coast, streaked with snow and blurred over with fleecy clouds, and half veiled in fog. For the last three days we have had better weather—not a gale of wind in all that time, and no really bad fogs—most of the time rather clear, with smooth water.

"At daylight this morning we made Attu in a bank of fog, and had to lay off and on for two hours before we could make out anything to run for. About eight o'clock we 'caught on,' as the boys say, and soon had a boat on shore to learn if any sealers had been about. None had been seen, so we kept away to the east again and are now running for Unalaska, where we should be on the 13th. Up to to-day we have made, on this trip, thirteen hundred miles, and not a sign of a poacher, which leads to the conclusion that they are pretty scarce hereabouts. I shall be powerful glad when it is all over and we can see some blue sky and water again in place of this everlasting gray, which I am sure is hurting the eyes of all hands as well as our spirits. The little ship begins to show the effects of her twenty-five thousand miles since last October in the way of leaky tubes, and we shall have to lay up ten days to get things in first-class shape again before our next trip. If we had good coal we could do the work without the least bother, but the Department in its wisdom (?) has sent out cheap, nasty Nanaimo coal, which hurts everything—including my temper.

"*Friday, August 12th.*—We have been spinning along to-day, without the least trouble, at a good fast rate, and if nothing unforeseen happens we shall be at Iluiluik to-morrow before noon. We have to-day seen the sun set for the first time in Bering Sea, and it was a strange and beautiful sight. Maybe the sky was the same blue it used to be, but I had not seen it for so long it was very delightful to look at. Such a relief from the gray we have had for three months! Just before the sun set the fog lifted, and we saw a beautiful snow-streaked peak eighty-five miles away. It has been a wonderful day for this sea, and I fear we shall not have many more such. The orderly just comes to say it is very thick on deck, and that the officer of the watch wants me, so I will go and take my Scotch-mist bath.

"*Dutch Harbour, Unalaska, August 16th.*—I have had no time to write since we came in here, because of the vast amount of work on my hands; but now I begin to see daylight through it, and also see an end to our stay in Bering Sea. We came in here at noon on the 13th, and found no ships except the two Englishmen, who are always in port. The vessel that our landing party fired on at False Pass proves to be the American steam schooner Polar Bear, which put in here for medical aid, her chief engineer having a bullet through his forearm. The vessel was riddled with bullets fore and aft, showing that our boys shot pretty straight. The captain, of course, vows that he was fired on without provocation, and I have no doubt the newspapers will give me no end of a blackguarding about it. None of the Polar Bear's crew can explain why they neither showed their colours, nor answered the hail, nor stopped when fired on, except that they had a proper ' funk ' on, and ran below and hid themselves.

" On the morning of the 14th the Danube came in, bringing a large mail, and I have been so full of official reports that I can not think coherently of anything else. The Secretary sends me two long telegrams, neither of which has one word of reference to my actions up here, approval or otherwise.

" *August 17th.*—To-day Captain Parr, of the Melpomene, came for me to go fishing. The sport was such as one will only see in this region, I imagine— salmon-trout by the hundred, and the salmon so thick that every few minutes we had one hooked, sometimes in the mouth, but more often in the fins or stomach. The river was so crowded with them that we could have crossed on the fishes' backs if they had not been so slippery. I have often heard the stories of how these creatures crowd themselves to death in the shoal waters, and now I have seen it for myself. There were thousands of them pushing and wriggling up stream, where the water was only a few inches deep, until they were absolutely forced out on the dry ground, and there lay dead in heaps until the air was foul with the stench. When I came home the Ranger and the Mohican had arrived, and now, near midnight, I am just through with their captains and their numerous reports. All have been busily cruising, and no one has seen a sealer. I am convinced that we have captured the only ones that have come in to the sea.

"*Friday, August 19th.*—We had a jolly dinner in the wardroom last night—pork and beans the *pièce de résistance*. It blew a nasty southeast gale all day, and rained in true Alaska style, but the lads were glad to have me at their table, and the 'manner of them' took away all the discomfort of the southeaster. Captain Hooper, of the Corwin, was in the party, and proved a jolly companion. As we sat over our coffee and cigars, with the wind roaring and the rain pelting down, there came the flash of a signal outside; presently the Adams came pounding in against the sea, and, as Nelson came over the side in his dripping sou'wester, our wardroom party broke up, and we three commanding officers retired to my cabin to learn the news. 'Nothing in the shape of a sealer,' said Nelson, 'but plenty of wind, and as thick as pea soup.' The old chap was much cut up when I told him the orders had come that he had to stay in Bering Sea until December 1st, but he took it like the good seaman he is, and, after talking matters over, went to his ship apparently content. Hooper remained with me all night rather than face the gale for a mile or so.

"The Adams has something wrong with one of her bottom valves, and to-day our divers have been under her and made it right; but we are all more or less lame ducks from the miserable coal we have had to use. The Mohican and Ranger will not be able to cruise for four or five days, and I doubt if the Yorktown can get away for a week; but it fortunately makes little difference—there are no sealers to catch. They are scared stiff and couldn't be paid to come in— that is, not one of any size or value. Of course, small things, like those we have taken, will or may take the chance, because the vessels are not worth a thousand dollars, and, if they are lucky, they make six or eight thousand in as many days.

" To-day I have spent among the ships, hurrying the work and getting things in order as fast as I can. To-night I have spent several hours working on my reports to the Secretary, of which I have three in hand —all interesting and full of information. I hope he may publish them in full, for they show what we have been really doing.

" *August 20th.*—A cold, raw day, most of it spent over my reports and looking after our engines. The other ships are coaling as fast as they can, and in a few days we shall all be cruising again. The summer, if it can be so called, is over for us, and from now on it will grow colder and more boisterous. Berries and mosquitoes are now at their best. The salmon berries are only a large, watery kind of raspberry, but better than nothing, which is more than can be said of the whortleberries—they are blue and sour and full of seeds, and taste like a pinch of sour sand. This country produces nothing else in the way of fruit, but grows lettuce and radishes and very good turnips. I think they could grow a lot of things, but the natives only care for seal meat and dried, half-rotted fish. The few white people live on canned food almost entirely.

"*Sunday, August 21st.*—I have a very bad foot to-day, but must go on with my work, sick or well. The weather begins to tell on the men in the way of rheumatism, and some are pretty bad. The ships have been kept so 'on the jump' that all hands are getting tired; the duty is not so easy as it was, and the engines have a way of protesting that the severest orders will not affect. The Adams got out to-day, and I am driving the Mohican and the Ranger all they will stand. The Yorktown will be ready as soon as we can get to the coal pile, and in the meantime we are doing our target work as well as we can.

"*Tuesday, August 23d.*—A howling gale to-night, with much cold rain, and no doubt the Adams and Ranger are catching it in good shape. The coaling facilities are so miserable here that we can coal but one ship at a time, and that very slowly; otherwise the little white ship would be fighting the short chop-sea to-night instead of surging at her chains as she is doing. We shall be off before many days, and as gales are the rule now, I have no doubt we shall be sufficiently amused.

"*Unalaska, August 26th.*—Here we are, still in port when we should be at sea, but I am glad we are not, for the usual August gale has us in its grip, and we should be very wet outside. We are tied up to a coal wharf in Dutch Harbour, perfectly landlocked, and yet the sea finds its way in, and we are jumping and charging, to the great danger of the wharf. The Adams is dragging around the harbour in fine style, but as she has steam up I do not worry about her. In fact, I have learned not to worry about anything; but I shall be powerful glad when we are through with Bering Sea. The Adams came in two days ago, after picking up her landing party at the False Pass (where our men had been), and reports that the natives refuse to shoot any more sea otter for fear the Yorktown will come back and catch them. So we really did some good up there. It is a nest of pirates, and needs a firm hand and a lot of ball cartridge before the law will be respected.

"A schooner came running in before the gale yesterday, showing American colours, and I was afraid we had another prize on our hands; but she proved to be a fisherman from the outside in search of medical aid for one of her men, who had accidentally fired a charge of shot into his instep. The accident happened eight days ago, and the man is in a deplorable condition. Of course, the foot had to come off, and the chances are he will die. Day before yesterday our doctor was called on shore to attend a man who had shot his hand to pieces. He was going to shoot a sheep, and found the cartridge stuck in his Winchester. As he could not force it home he struck it with a hammer to drive it in. They have not found the hammer yet, nor some portions of his hand.

"The coaling arrangements here are causing us much delay and annoyance. When the coal was taken from ships we did very well; but now it has all been landed and piled in the open, so that it is soaking wet. I stopped taking it in this morning, as the rain was coming down in torrents and the coal bunkers were being flooded. I shall hold on here until the rain ceases before I take any more. The coal is of the poorest kind, and absorbs moisture like a sponge, so that in its present condition we are paying for over ten per cent of water. Of course, this pleases the contractor to death, and it would serve the Equipment Bureau rightly if I went on and paid for a hundred or two tons of water. But I don't want the bother of taking it in and pumping it out.

" The Daphne is ordered to Esquimault on her way home—sails on Monday; the Melpomene starts on a cruise as soon as this gale lets up, and will go to Victoria on September 14th, after which I shall have to look after the whole business. There is really no reason why we should not all clear out now, for there are no sealers in Bering Sea and it is too late for any more to come, and we are spending two thousand dollars per day for nothing; but our orders say we must stay, and stay it is. As I have the finest command in the navy at present, I ought to be satisfied.

" The wardroom of the Mohican gave me a dinner day before yesterday, which I enjoyed very much. There is a fine body of young officers aboard her. We had a good dinner for any place—soup, Little Neck clams, salmon trout, and roast ptarmigan are some of the things I remember. Everything except the soup was provided by the sportsmen of the mess.

" *August 28th.*—I dined yesterday on board her Majesty's steamer Daphne with Captain Wood, R. N., for whom I have great respect and esteem, and did not get home until midnight. The gale let up yesterday, and to-morrow I shall finish coaling and put to sea for a short cruise only, as we must be back here for the mails due after the 1st of September, and get the Corwin off on the 10th for Sitka.

"*Unalaska, September 6th.*—We started to sea on August 28th, but had only got outside when we made out the mail steamer coming in, so we returned for the night.

"After we had our mail we put to sea again the following morning, for a cruise to the westward, and by night were driving into a head sea that made things wet on board. We were in a nasty southwest gale, with a bad, heavy, breaking sea, and continued in it until we ran in here last night, and found the 'Frisco mail steamer in. The Department wires me that it approves of my doings up here, and also that the State Department commends me for something—I don't make out just what. This is the first word of approval or disapproval I have had from them since I left New York.

"*September 7th.*—I did not get over the shaking up we had in the last ten days, until yesterday, and now am pressed with official mail, added to the strain of constant work and worry, without proper assistants to relieve me of details. During the time of this last cruise I could not once write in my cabin; but we did catch a British sealer and brought him in safely, and will send him to Sitka by the Corwin as soon as the gale ceases.

"On Friday, when we were away off to the westward, steering north in a very heavy sea, the feeling suddenly came over me that we must steer east, and the impression was so strong that I sent for the navigator and told him of it, and said unless it left me we would steer east at noon. He was somewhat doubtful of what the sea would do with us on that course, but we steered it all the same. I felt convinced that something would come of it, and the sequel is extraordinary. On Sunday at noon I was on deck, as I usually am at sea, when the lookout aloft reported, ' Sail ho! ' and in a few minutes I made out a schooner, which proved to be the Henrietta, of Victoria, British Columbia, with four hundred and twenty seal skins on board. I had not changed the course at all, and yet we ran right up to her. It was curious. When we got near enough to throw a line on board the schooner, the sea was so nasty that her captain evidently thought we would not dare to lower a boat to send men on board of her, so he refused to make the line fast. We did lower the boat, however, much to his surprise, and in fifteen minutes an officer and six armed men had possession of his vessel, and his crew and all their arms were on board the Yorktown. The way the work was done and the boat handled was most gratifying to me—never saw anything better done. For some minutes my heart was in my throat for fear the boat would swamp; but she did her work, came back, and was hoisted without a scratch on her paint. Every man in the ship had his wits about him, and did what was ordered promptly and efficiently.

" Sunday night we kept the schooner in company, and on Monday, the sea having run down somewhat, we took her in tow and brought her here. She will be condemned and sold in Alaska for violating our revenue laws, and the Canadians will note another 'outrage' on their commerce.

"Upon our arrival I found the Oscar and Hattie, British schooner of Victoria, British Columbia, had been captured by the Mohican out at Attu Island, and sent in with a prize crew to report to me. She will come under the *modus vivendi*, and as soon as Captain Parr comes in with the Melpomene I shall turn her over to his tender mercies. We are really making it hot for the Canadian sealing fraternity. The gale in which we had been cruising calmed down somewhat on Monday, but yesterday the barometer began falling rapidly; last night a fearful southeast storm broke out on us, and to-day I have not been able to get a boat on shore. Of course, sealing is done for this year, as the weather from now on will probably be such that no seal can be taken; but we shall keep things on the jump until we start for home, and shall catch any vessel that breaks the law. It is the general opinion hereabouts that we have captured every vessel that has come into the sea.

"*Friday, September 9th.*—I was occupied every minute yesterday, until midnight. I was starting the Corwin home, *via* Sitka, with the Henrietta in tow, as soon as my despatches could be completed, only waiting for the gale to let up. At six I had finished, and went to dine with Captain Hooper before he sailed. Just as dinner was over a vessel was reported coming in, and at 9.30 the Mohican anchored, and Johnson and I talked until midnight. He had struck another rock, out at Attu this time. His ship was not injured, still he was worried over it. All things considered, the

Department has been lucky not to lose a ship this summer. We have cruised straight through, night and day, fog or clear, without decent charts, and not a single buoy or light in the entire country.

"The Corwin left at four this morning. I was sorry to see her go, for it is the first break in the fleet I have commanded, and I may never have such a command again. She takes a long report to the Secretary, which I should be glad to have him publish, and one to the State Department, which contains more information on seals and the Seal Islands than has ever been given in one report. I have been working all summer for three Departments—Navy, State, and Treasury—and I have had to make reports to each of them, which has vastly increased my labours; but I am thankful to say it is all now rapidly coming to an end, and in twenty days more we shall be ready to sail for home.

"*Monday Night, September 12th.*—We have improved the time to-day by having target practice; but the water was smooth, and the targets had no show against our six-inch guns, two of them being shot to pieces and finally utterly destroyed. The practice was excellent. To-night at eight, dark as a pocket and raining, I suddenly raised the alarm, 'Torpedo boats!' and turned the search lights on a target, which I had previously placed, and in two minutes we had fired sixteen hundred and ninety shots from small arms and machine guns, and the target was a sieve. We must have presented a beautiful sight from the outside, for we were a blaze of fire, fore and aft. If it had been a real torpedo boat coming at us, the man in command would have required a large head not to flinch, and a very small one not to have it shot off. There is not a place on the target as large as a man's hand unmarked by shot.

" To-morrow, weather permitting, we shall go outside and have a try at a target, running past it at high speed.

" *September 13th.*—The Melpomene has come in and is dumping in the coal as fast as she can, and hopes to get off for Esquimault day after to-morrow. Captain Parr will dine with me to-morrow, when he surely won't have much to eat and less to drink, as I am almost entirely out of all sorts of provisions.

" During his cruise he has been over to the Russian coast and back through Bering Sea and saw not a single sealer. The Russians have captured six schooners—one American and five Canadian—all of which have been condemned and burned. They have a good way of treating such chaps over there: the skins were taken out and sent to San Francisco to be sold for the benefit of the Russian Government, and the prisoners released, to find their way home as best they could. Next year the Russians mean to have more cruisers and really put a stop to sealing on that side, and then the whole gang will go for Bering Sea, and our commander commanding may have a real lively time of it. It may be that by that time the Department will awake to the fact that this is the command for an admiral or a commodore, at least, and send one up here.

" In a recent letter from Admiral Hotham, he says that the Coquitlan episode amused him very much. First, the Canadians wanted war—demanded that he should go to Sitka with the Warspite and tow the Coquitlan back to Victoria. When he would not do this, they accused him of having given me their place of rendezvous; but about this time, he says, the smallpox came along and the Canadians were so scared that he heard no more about war.

"Now, the smallpox having let up, they are after him again. They certainly are a miserable lot, and the admiral says they surely love me. When they hear of the Henrietta going to Sitka they will probably wish to embrace me. The admiral has been on the rocks with his flagship, which worries him, but he was in no way to blame for it—nor was any one else, except the people who made the charts and neglected to put the rocks on them.

"If I get my ship to 'Frisco without more damage I shall consider myself lucky. I do not expect to be detained here after the 1st of October, unless I hear of sealers being about, in which case I shall stay until I catch them, if I freeze for it; but I don't think they want to monkey with the Yorktown.

"*Unalaska, September 16th.*—The Melpomene left yesterday morning, the Mohican goes to-morrow, and the Elsie, a small mail steamer, the day after; but I hope to be in 'Frisco before either of them.

"My dinner to Captain Parr and the Canadian commissioners went off well. We had salmon, ptarmigan, and wild ducks among other things. Parr wrote me a letter before he left, which is a model of official sweetness, and in reply I applied sugar most artistically. And so Bering Sea has been freed of seal poachers, for one year anyhow, and no war has come of it. The summer has been one of hard work and much anxiety to me, and I hope to have some rest after it.

"*September 22d.*—Since I last wrote I have been 'down to the sea in a ship,' and, like all men who do that in a small ship, I have paid for it. On the 17th we put out in the beginning of a gale, as it proved, and when we came in this evening and dropped anchor I could for the first time sit down to write. When we left the harbour we found a fearful sea running, and it grew steadily worse until we came in to-day, when it blew with hurricane force; but through it all the little white ship grows better and better, and I am proud of her, in spite of the bad name she had when I took command of her. On this last cruise we ran about one hundred and fifty miles to the west of the Seal Islands, toward the Russian coast, when the sea was so tremendous that we were compelled to lay to for twelve hours, and as soon as we could we cruised off and on, looking for schooners, but none came in sight.

"Day before yesterday, still blowing a gale, we started back this way, intending to stop at the islands, but when we came near them the sea was breaking so viciously that we came on, and to-day saw the worst weather we have had since leaving New York. When we were about fifteen miles from Unalaska the wind attained hurricane force, blowing directly from the volcano of Makuslin, and we had a picnic. We were steaming twelve knots at the time, and tried to show some little canvas to steady the ship; but a piece as large as a tablecloth went like smoke, and we had to depend on the steam. The water was picked up in patches of twenty acres and carried off in spray two or three hundred feet, and the force of the wind was so great that the surface of the sea was cut down as level as a floor, and foaming white; but we made it somehow, and here we are safely at anchor, and the Bering Sea work is done, for this season at least.

" I am willing to admit that Bering Sea is the worst patch of water it has ever been my lot to tackle, and I sincerely hope I may never have it to do again. I find the Bear is in from the Arctic, and as she is to remain until December 1st, we are to give passage to the wife of Captain Healey and one other person. I shall give up my cabin to them, while I live as best I can. From now until the 1st of October I shall be hard at work getting ready for our trip down, and when once we start I shall make things ' hum ' if I can. I hope to sleep to-night for the first time in many nights.

" *Thursday Night.*—I have had a busy day of it, and wound up with dinner on board the Bear, and a very good dinner it was. Captain and Mrs. Healey, Captains Nelson and Nicols, Mr. Ware and son, who, with Mrs. Healey, are to be my guests to 'Frisco, composed the party. Ware and his son have this summer landed a mining party on the Yukon River, and are on their way home to Chicago. The Adams gets off to-morrow, and I shall not see her again, and in a week my command in Bering Sea will be a thing of the past. The summer seems short to look back at, but how the days drag now as the end approaches! If we get to 'Frisco, as I hope, on October 8th, we shall have steamed a little over twenty-eight thousand miles in one year. Certainly no one can say I have not been to sea sure enough.

"*Friday Night.*—One week more of Bering Sea and I am done with it for all time, I hope. It is perhaps this thought that makes these volcanic humps look very beautiful just now in the magnificence of their early winter coloring. This morning the mountains were clearly outlined against a cold steel-blue sky, the line of new-fallen snow, sharp and distinct, about one third of the way down the peaks, and the rest golden-red and green-brown, with here and there in the valleys, sheltered from the cold winds, a bright emerald-green spot. The Adams got away on time at nine o'clock, and one hour after the Rush came in, bringing the first of a southeast gale with her. Later on it came harder, and now it is nasty and cold enough to suit even the bears.

"Captain Coulson reports dreadful weather during the last ten days—just such, in fact, as I have had during our cruising. He is an old hand up here, and says he never knew it so bad before so early in the season, September usually being a fairly good month. No sealers have been seen, and only a few seals away from the islands, where the old ones are now busily engaged teaching the youngsters to swim and get ready for their long sea trip. It is a curious thing in Nature that these animals, which may be said to live entirely in the water, can neither beget nor bear their young except on land, and that the young one would instantly drown if put in the water within several weeks after its birth. A young seal is much more helpless in the water than a young kitten. But this is not more strange than that the mosquito, which is so plainly meant to live by sucking blood through its bill from a thin-skinned, hairless animal, is most abundant in the swamps of the tropics and the frozen regions of the Arctic, where no such animals can exist; nor why the leech, which lives by sucking warm blood, is found only in swamps where Nature forbids warm-blooded life.

"*Saturday Night.*—Finding this morning not too bad, we got under way and went outside for some great-gun target practice, of which we have not had time to do as much as I should have liked this summer. We found a moderate sea with squalls of rain and much wind. The target was soon placed, and running the ship by it at full speed, the six-inch guns opened in a way much to my satisfaction. Every shot was excellent until the eighth, which demolished the target and put an end to the practice.

"I have just now finished my table of distances made by the fleet under my command. The distance covered by all ships since leaving Port Townsend is sixty-one thousand four hundred and twenty-six miles, of which thirty-eight thousand three hundred and ninety-eight miles have been in Bering Sea. Nothing approaching this work has been done since the civil war closed, and I hope the Department may be as well pleased with it as I am.

"*September 30th.*—To-night is the end of this, unless the gale now blowing is too much for us to-morrow morning. Bering Sea has been policed in proper shape, according to my thinking; the job is finished, and to-morrow we are homeward bound. A happy lot we surely are. There is not a drop of anything to drink on board, not even a bottle of beer, so we are all very quiet and subdued in our happiness, and only hoping for a decent day to get well clear of these miserable islands. Yesterday daylight found us smothered in snow and hail, and since then it has snowed in real arctic style. Indeed, I never saw a snowstorm before—had no idea what one was like. I know now, and really don't care for any further knowledge on the subject. I know that I shall have to spend much of the next week on the bridge, but I don't care so long as we can make any way toward 'Frisco.

"*October 10th, 'Frisco.*—Just in, after awful trip down with gales and hurricanes all the way from Unalaska—the worst I have ever known. We were absolutely under water for five days, and I lived in wet clothing. Finally came a hurricane in which we were hove to for twenty hours."

I have made these extracts from my journal at length, since they give a much better idea of my life and doings in Bering Sea than I could possibly write now.

CHAPTER XXIX

IN COMMAND OF THE NEW YORK

The Secretary of the Navy and the President gave hearty approval for my successful work, and the President was good enough to mention me by name in his message to Congress. Few officers have had this honour in time of peace.

It had seemed to me from the time I first began to study the seal question that the easiest solution was for the United States to declare the seals a herd of domesticated wild animals owned by us and breeding on our territory alone, and after this declaration to state our intention to follow and protect them, no matter where they went. This would, at least, have brought the question to an issue, and a settlement would have had to follow very shortly. The theory of a closed sea did not appear to me consistent with our action in reference to the fisheries on the Eastern coast, where we denied to England the same contention.

A few weeks after my return from the Arctic I was detached from the Yorktown at San Francisco and ordered as naval secretary of the Lighthouse Board. When I reached Washington I found that the zealous watchdogs of the Treasury had checked against my pay the sum of three dollars and sixty-eight cents, because I had taken five days to reach my home instead of four. The checkage was the difference between duty and leave pay for one day. I had turned into the Treasury something over six hundred thousand dollars during the summer, and felt that this last contribution might have been spared me.

When the seal question again came up for consideration the conference was composed of very distinguished men—Secretaries Gresham and Carlisle on our side and Sir Julian Pauncefote and Sir Charles Tupper representing the Canadian side. I was requested to be present, and was very glad afterward to know that my practical knowledge of the subject had been of value in arranging the rules governing the taking of seals under the Paris award.

My second tour of duty as naval secretary of the Lighthouse Board was made more pleasant by the occasional trips of President Cleveland and members of his Cabinet, in one or the other of the lighthouse steamers which could be conveniently used for the purpose. I was usually with the President when health or recreation made such trips desirable, and took charge of all preparations and supplies. They were never allowed to interfere in the least with Government work, nor did they involve the expenditure of one cent of public money. They did, however, enable both him and the Secretary of the Treasury, who is President of the Lighthouse Board, to see the practical working of the service by contact with the keepers and inspection of the stations, and in this way were of great benefit. Many desirable changes can be traced to these outings, and it can be safely asserted that no more innocent or enjoyable form of recreation could have been devised.

During the summer of 1894 the fine, new, armoured cruiser New York was in need of a captain, and the Secretary of the Navy did me the honour to give me the command. I had been promoted to the grade of captain after my return from the Yorktown, and was one of the juniors on the list; hence the compliment was all the more marked. I was at Gray Gables making a visit to Mr. Cleveland when the time came for me to report, and he was good enough to take me down to New York with him and put me on board.

The New York was our only armoured cruiser, and at that time the flagship of Admiral Richard W. Meade, commanding the North Atlantic squadron. A few days after I had relieved Captain " Jack " Philip, the Department gave me additional orders as chief of staff to the admiral, in which capacity I served until he was relieved at his own request and placed on the retired list.

Admiral Meade was an able, courageous officer, and during our winter's cruise with the squadron, consisting of the New York (flagship), Columbia, Minneapolis, Cincinnati, and Raleigh, gave us admirable and sytematic drill. Modern methods and appliances were used in a modern way—torpedoes were run under service conditions, and search lights used to their utmost capacity as a means of communicating between vessels at sea at long distances from each other. The tone of the squadron was excellent, owing in a large measure to the personal character and bearing of the admiral. The war between Cuba and Spain, or, more

properly speaking, the revolution in Cuba, was in its
infancy, and the admiral was outspoken in his friendship for the Cubans—so much so that the Department
would not allow him to enter a Cuban port for fear
that his violent temper might involve us in trouble.
This was a source of much concern to him, and was
the beginning of the trouble that resulted seriously
to him later on. Upon our arrival at New York, early
in May, I was directed to fit out for a short cruise to
Europe to join in the ceremonies attending the opening
of the Kiel Canal.

Probably the most important work of Admiral
Meade's squadron during the West India cruise was
saving the city of Port-of-Spain in Trinidad. While we
were anchored there a fire broke out in the city, which,
owing to the strong trade wind blowing, soon made
great headway, and would have destroyed the entire
place had it not been for the work done by our men.
The squadron was anchored five or six miles from the
shore, and as the admiral refused to land men until
officially asked to do so, much property was lost that
otherwise might have been saved. When, however, the
request for assistance came, everything was ready, and
the fire brigades of the vessels were sent in at once under
command of the executive officer of the New York.
After four hours' very hard and dangerous work the city
was saved, and the men returned on board. I was sure
from the first that the fire was of incendiary origin, and
felt that a company of marines with plenty of cartridges would be needed before the job was finished;
but the admiral hesitated to land armed men in a foreign state. After some discussion he told me that I

might do as I pleased, but advised me not to take the responsibility of doing as I proposed. Without more delay I sent in forty men with two officers and plenty of ammunition. The moment they landed they were deployed through the threatened district, and soon put an end to the looting that was going on. Our men came back at midnight loaded with all sorts of things that had been given them by the people on shore, among others twenty young goats, which I promptly sent back in the morning. The Governor wrote a handsome letter of thanks, commending the excellent conduct of our men under most trying circumstances. He was particularly grateful for the marines, whose bayonets proved just the thing required.

The work of preparing for the Kiel cruise was rapidly done, and by May 18th I was ready for sea. Arrangements had been made for electrically illuminating the ship, and as she was the first of our new vessels to be shown abroad, and the occasion a notable one, it was decided to give as fine a display of fireworks as possible. I sent for the expert who attends to such matters in and about New York, and with him arranged the scheme that afterward astonished Kiel and the ships there assembled. When the various set pieces and the supply of bombs and rockets began to arrive I was at a loss to know what to do with them. After we had filled every available space below, there still remained a lot to be looked after. I had the boxes, which were very large, securely lashed on deck, covered with canvas, and painted. They were a source of great uneasiness to me until they were finally burned. If they got wet, of course they would not go off when the time came, and if some careless man dropped a spark from his pipe on them they would go off much too soon. Fortunately, I had no accident with them, and was well pleased when I saw the last of them.

The U. S. S. Columbia was also fitting out for Kiel, and was expected to beat us badly in the race across. My journal has the following:

" *May 22, 1895, at Sea, off the Banks.* — We got away on the stroke of twelve on Saturday in a most successful way, and apparently to the entire satisfaction of the navy-yard officials, who waved cordially to me as we straightened down the river. The mud bank tried to stop us, but I had said we would go at noon, and so we went. That is about the easiest way to manage: say you are going to do a thing, and then simply go ahead and do it. The ship behaved most beautifully, and the evolution was perfectly performed. Even the chaplain, dear soul! came and congratulated me, and said I must have a wonderful eye for distances, and no end of nerve.

" We came over the bar just behind the Lucania, and the way she ran us out of sight was amusing. If we had been using full power of steam we should probably be in sight of her now, but we had only three boilers, and were making but twelve knots and a half.

" Ice was reported well south of the Banks before we left New York, and not wishing any of that in mine, we came out on a course to keep us south of 40°; but the third day out, Monday, the temperature of the water suddenly fell 24° and the air 5°, so I knew who our neighbour was, and kept a bright lookout for icebergs. After an hour of most anxious watching the temperature again went up and all danger was past. Up to yesterday afternoon the weather was blowing, with rain and fog, but to-day is clear and beautiful and warm. To-night we shall be halfway over, and I shall treat the ship to another boiler, which should give us fifteen knots. I don't want the Columbia to catch us, and I do want to get in, take my coal and be cleaned up, when Admiral Kirkland puts in, in the San Francisco.

"Everything is quiet and lovely in the ship, but this morning, about four o'clock, I was nearly thrown out of my bed, by the engines reversing at full speed, and no end of a row lowering the lifeboat. A new landsman we had recently acquired had pulled the knob of the life buoy, just to see what would happen. He won't be so curious again, I think.

"*May 23d.*—After I wrote yesterday we came pretty near finding the ice again. The temperature of the water fell suddenly from 65° to 49°, and the air was bitter. I found on examining the last pilot chart that we were almost in the exact spot where a berg four hundred feet high had been seen less than a week ago. After half an hour we ran out of the cold into beautiful, clear, warm weather, which has continued ever since.

"Our extra boiler is helping, and we have been making over fifteen knots since eight last night. We shall be halfway across some time to-night, and the Columbia will have to 'hump herself' to sight us before we anchor. The doctor tells me to-day that, after carefully measuring the quantity of air pumped into the New York per hour, he finds that she is better ventilated out here on the sea than most of the large buildings in New York. Careful analysis shows that the quality of the air in the ship is as fine as the quantity is abundant.

"*May 27th, Two Hundred Miles West of Land's End.*—We are drawing up to the entrance of the Channel. We have made a lovely run—probably the quickest ever made by a man-of-war. The weather has been fairly good—a long swell from the northwest, which has cut our speed down somewhat, and a strong, steady southwest wind all the way. To-day is clear, and, if it continues so, we shall make the Bishop's Rock Light without trouble and be anchored off Netley Abbey tomorrow evening. We left New York in company with a large four-masted steamer, and for two days had her in sight all the time. Then she steered more to the north and we lost her. This morning at daylight she was in sight on our port beam, and it looks now as if we should run up the Channel side by side.

"*Off Netley, Southampton, May 29th.*—I stopped writing off the Scilly Islands, and yesterday afternoon the blessed fog caught us about two hundred miles off Land's End, but fortunately cleared as we came by Bishop's Rock, and so I entered the Channel knowing our position accurately. After passing Eddystone it shut in as thick as pea soup and I saw nothing up to Portland, when it cleared, and we ran for the entrance to the Solent, which we made night before last at ten, but no pilot could we get, so we had to anchor until six yesterday morning, thus losing valuable time. The run up past the Isle of Wight was exceedingly beautiful, as was the view of Cowes Roads; but the ship took most of my time and attention, and I could only glance at things as we ran by them.

"We found the San Francisco, Marblehead, and Alliance here, but not the Columbia. Admiral Kirkland will not take the squadron to Kiel, but orders us to meet him at Copenhagen June 12th, and from there we will go to Kiel for the show. After that is over, we are to be cut loose, as it were, to go where we please, and find our way back to New York when ordered.

"The Columbia came in last night at 9.30, having burned fourteen hundred tons of coal on the way over, as against eight hundred for us. We ran at half power, she at two thirds, so the New York is not a very slow ship.

"The admiral is to leave on the 5th, and we shall follow on the ninth; so we must hurry up the coaling that we may get cleaned up and ready. Yesterday afternoon I 'struck the beach' and had a delightful hour in the ruins of Netley Abbey, certainly one of the most beautiful spots I have ever seen. The lights and shadows were exquisite, and the air was filled with the songs of birds. Afterward I dined at the club for the sum of five shillings. I had soup, grilled mackerel, devilled kidney, three vegetables, cold roast beef and salad, cherry tart, cheese, a cup of coffee, and a pint of good red wine. No club in the United States can do anything like it for the money.

"Two Italian ships have come in to-day and more are expected to-morrow. I hear they are sending a fleet of ten vessels.

"*May 30th.*—Our flag was at half-mast yesterday, and the same to-day, for poor Mr. Gresham.

A Nigger Prince

"*Off Netley, June 5, 1895.*—I came back from London last night at midnight, after a most delightful visit. Met many friends there who gave me dinners, luncheons, drives, and made as much fuss over me as if I were named Mahan. Sunday we went into the park to see ' Church Parade,' and surely it was a sight. The Duke of Cambridge was walking slowly through the park and eying the dresses with apparent interest. After the park we drove to the zoo, where the Afghanistan prince was having an outing. All the royal carriages were out, and the Prince and Princess of Wales were showing him about. They call him a ' nigger,' and at the same time bow down to him and make much of him, for fear of what he may do in the East. Funny people! The nigger prince at a dinner party last week refused to enter the drawing-room because of the low dresses of the ladies, saying it was not decent. When he had to take out the lady of the house, he walked two yards ahead of her, and wouldn't look at her during the dinner. Funny nigger!

" This morning the admiral signalled for all commanding officers to repair on board. There he told us that we would have to be at Copenhagen on the 11th, and that he would then transfer his flag to the New York. Orders have come from Washington that we are to assemble at Kiel on the 15th—four days before we are wanted—and that the admiral, captains, and as many officers as the ship can hold, are to go by rail to Hamburg, and thence through the canal on board the Marblehead.

" *Copenhagen, Denmark, June 10th.*—Here we are, and if I am to do much of this sort of work I shall need

371

new eyes and new legs. We got under way from
Southampton at 3 A. M. Saturday, after I had slept just
two hours. Friday night I thought I would get some
sleep, but, as I was removing my coat, four English
officers came on board to say good-bye, and it was midnight when they left. At 3 A. M. I was on the bridge,
my clothes have not been off since, and my poor
legs and feet are very bad. When we got under way,
Saturday, the Columbia followed immediately, and we
had it 'nip and tuck' up the Channel. After three
hours we passed her, both of us going very fast, and as
we entered the Dover Strait we were leading about two
ships' lengths. Off the South Foreland we passed the
Spanish squadron—the Columbia on one side and we
on the other. It was coming on foggy, and at first the
Dons could not make us out, but as we ranged up
abreast of their rear ship they 'caught on,' and their
admiral, not wishing to exchange salutes, I suppose,
hauled down his flag until we had passed him. At the
same time he made signal for full speed, and it was
funny to see his efforts. We raced by them as if they
had been tied to a wharf. It was a beautiful sight—
what we could see of it for the fog. Shortly afterward
I slowed to half speed, as it grew so thick one could
'cut it with a knife.' The Columbia passed under our
stern, going full speed, and we saw nothing more of
her until we found her anchored here at noon to-day.

"*June 11th.*—Night before last, as we ran out of
the North Sea, the sun set at nine o'clock exactly, and
at half past eleven it was still light enough to read on
the bridge. The twilight gradually moved around to
northeast and the moon rose in the south. At 2 A. M.

the sun came up over the Swedish mountains, and the scene was worth coming all this way to look at. About 3 A. M. we passed a fleet of battle ships heading for Kiel, and soon after entered Skaw Sound without a pilot, and from there on I was kept busy."

The harbour is, comparatively speaking, a small one, and the channels narrow and very crooked; but we managed after a while to get a good berth near the San Francisco. Admiral Kirkland transferred his flag to me the following day with his staff and all their belongings, but, as he was only to remain on board a short time, concluded to mess with me rather than start his own mess.

CHAPTER XXX

THE KIEL CELEBRATION

Two days later we started for Kiel through the intricate waters of the Little Belt and arrived without accident. On the way we passed vessels of almost every nation, most of them at anchor putting the last touch of paint on before entering the harbour. When off the entrance to the port we were met by a torpedo boat, which put a German naval officer on board of each ship to show us where our buoys were. The one who came to us was from the Naval College in Berlin and was detailed for duty on the admiral's staff during our stay. He spoke English well and was a most accomplished man.

As we entered the harbour we found the German fleet drawn up in two long lines, and as we passed them each ship manned her rigging and cheered us. The cheering and the noise of the saluting guns made quite a Fourth-of-July effect. Before we reached our buoy the New York had fired one hundred and fifty guns in saluting the various notable persons in the harbour, though the Austrian fleet was the only one ahead of us. We took our buoys in a way to elicit the admiration of all who saw the evolution. As soon as we were fast to them, the telephone from shore was connected to our pilot house, and from that day until the day of our departure we had only to 'phone for anything that we wanted from a keg of beer to a brownstone front and it was furnished free of cost. The perfect way in which everything was arranged was a great credit to the emperor, who personally had his eye on every detail. Eighty-five buoys were laid down in the harbour, each one with the number of the ship that was to take it painted on it, and on top the flag of the nation to which she belonged. Each ship, as she took her buoy, was connected with the shore by telephone, as in the case of the New York.

In the space of two days all the fleets had arrived and were composed of the finest ships in the navies of the world. The question of the exchange of official visits under such circumstances was a most puzzling one, and here the good sense of the emperor showed out strongly. He designated one of his own vessels, a very large and roomy one, and invited all admirals and captains to meet him there at breakfast. With the invitation came a request that each would bring his orderly provided with a mail bag. After the breakfast was over, the orderlies were drawn up in line, and each admiral and captain dropped his card in all the bags except his own, and thus in a few minutes cards had been exchanged with all hands. After that, if one had the time, he could call on such officers as he had known before, or those whose acquaintance he cared to make. The New York was about the newest thing in the way of a cruiser, and everybody wanted to see her. She was also neutral ground, so to speak, where all could meet with a freedom not possible on other ships. We were not hunting for alliances with other nations nor they with us, and we could be and were as independent as was our far-away country.

The French and Russian fleets met outside the harbour of Kiel and came in together, showing in this, as in other actions, their strong desire to have the recent alliance between the two countries noticed. Both admirals declined the invitation of the emperor to land their crews and be entertained by the German naval contingent, and both fleets put to sea at the earliest possible moment permitted by the strictest etiquette.

The English squadron of four battle ships and two armoured cruisers seemed to me the most businesslike-looking outfit of the whole gathering. The ships were in perfect condition, and it was evident at a glance that they were not made so for the occasion, but that it was their usual condition, while in the case of the ships of some other powers the practised eye could see that "paint and putty covered a multitude of sins." I was particularly interested in the English cruiser from which the New York was supposed by many to have been copied. She was lying very near us, and her officers, as well as the British admiral in command, after looking us over carefully, admitted that the New York was far the better ship of the two. The admiral finally asked if I would object to the chief constructor of the British navy coming on board and having a look at us, and when I assured him that it would give me the greatest pleasure to show my ship to so distinguished a guest, he wired the admiralty, and I afterward, at

Opening the Canal

Gravesend, had the pleasure of having Mr. White on board for many hours.

The ceremonies attendant upon the opening of the Kiel Canal began at Hamburg, where the burgomasters gave a banquet to the emperor and his guests. Twelve hundred sat down to dinner, among them the most distinguished men in Europe. All military officers were in special full dress and the burgomasters wore their state robes. The emperor wore a gorgeous military dress with many brilliant decorations. After the banquet there was a fine display of fireworks on an island in the lake, which had been made for the occasion. Several thousand persons walked about on this island listening to the bands and enjoying the beer and other refreshments which were in abundance everywhere, and I doubt if any, except those familiar with the place, knew that they were on made ground, so perfectly had the work been done. In the midst of the banquet, which was most elaborate, schooners of beer were served. The idea of drinking mine was more than I could face, but the German officer who was looking after my comfort promptly disposed of it as well as his own. I had great admiration for his capacity.

Before this time the admiral commanding each fleet had sent a small vessel to Hamburg to convey the minister and other officials through the canal. After the fireworks display, we all got under way at 2 A. M. and started down the river according to rank, the emperor leading in the Hohenzollern. We, having the baby admiral, were No. 20, being near the tail end of the procession instead of near its head, where the importance of our country should have placed us. We ran down the Elbe sixty miles to Brunsbüttel, where we entered the canal, steamed through it a distance of about seventy-eight miles, and came out two miles below Kiel. At intervals along the line of the canal the emperor had massed bodies of troops, who were paraded and saluted the colours as each vessel passed. As the Hohenzollern, showing the emperor's flag, entered the harbour, there was a great outburst of cheering with the roar of salutes as the assembled fleets welcomed him.

For the purpose of entertaining his naval guests, the emperor had built on the land, near Holtnau, almost at the Kiel entrance to the canal, a large ship of the line. She was full ship-rigged, had all her yards across, and her gun deck was beautifully decorated for the dinner, which was given on the day following our arrival from Hamburg. When the banquet was over, souvenir medals were presented to all of us and we retired to the upper deck for our cigars, where all were presented personally to his Majesty and exchanged a few pleasant words with him. I stood near him during the time he conversed with the French admiral and his officers, waiting my turn to be presented, and could not help being impressed by his manner as well as by that of the Frenchmen. They were all ideally polite, but there was, in the bearing of the emperor, a hearty feeling of success which I did not observe in the manner of the distinguished officers who were saying good-bye to him. They were to sail in the early morning in company with the Russian fleet. When I was presented to him the emperor gave me a cordial hand-shake and kept others waiting quite five minutes while he talked to me in the most pleasant way. He had many questions to ask me, which he said he would expect me to answer before I left Kiel. His whole manner to the American officers was most pleasing and cordial.

I had arranged with the chief of staff to get rid of my fireworks on this occasion, that the emperor might witness them on his way back to the Hohenzollern from dinner. Certain signals had been agreed upon, and when these were made, indicating that his Majesty was in position to see, the New York cut loose. All the ships had been doing something in the way of fireworks, but it had leaked out somehow that the Yankees had something up their sleeve, and when we began, all the rest stopped to see what would happen. We started off with a set piece eighty feet long suspended between our military masts, a portrait of President Cleveland at one end and of the emperor at the other, and between them the legend in German script, "America sends heartfelt congratulations to Germany on the opening of the North Sea Canal." As this blazed out, the thousands of people massed on the shore only three hundred yards away broke into a great roar of cheers, which was taken up by the different ships, and gradually died out in the distance. Then the show went on with such bursts of rockets and bombs and mines as had never before been seen on a ship, and finally wound up with another set piece, the American shield at one end, the German double eagle at the other, and "Good-night" between them. The upper deck of the New York had been carefully covered with six inches of wet sand, but, notwithstanding many streams of water were constantly playing, I found that we were badly marked in many places. The carpenters were busy with their planes for several days before they were all removed. The German papers, as well as all the officers who witnessed the display, were unstinted in their praise. The feeling uppermost in my mind was one of thankfulness that it was all over without an accident.

At a reception given on board one of the German battle ships on the Sunday after our arrival I had an interesting experience. When I went over the side I found a large company, most of them dancing. As I was not a dancing man, I stood to one side to be out of the way, and entered into conversation with a young clean-cut-looking German captain who spoke English perfectly. It was soon evident to me that he was brilliant in his profession, and we engaged in a rather sharp professional talk. I did not agree with the captain, whose name I had not caught, and did not hesitate to speak my mind—nor did he. After a time he said he would be glad to present me to his wife, which he did, and I found her a very charming and attractive woman. Of course I had not caught her name either, and, after talking with her half an hour, I noticed that a good many people seemed to be waiting to speak to her, so I took myself off to the smoking apartment to enjoy a cigar. When I entered, Admiral Knorr greeted me and said, " Evans, the prince says you are a good fellow, and he wants the emperor to know you." I replied, " My dear admiral, I haven't seen the prince and don't know him." " Well," he said, " you ought to know him; you have been talking shop with him for half an hour, and I don't know what you have been saying to the princess during your conversation with her."

A Prince Unawares

I had been talking with two of the most delightful
people I ever met, Prince Henry and the Princess Irene,
without knowing in the least who they were, and I certainly told them both exactly what I thought about the
different things we discussed.   The prince was in his
uniform as a captain in the navy, and commanded the
vessel on which the reception was given.   I afterward
saw much of both of them and was indebted to them
for much courtesy, and the better I knew them the
more I saw in them to admire.   It was no doubt owing
to the courtesy of Prince Henry that his brother, the
emperor, gave me such marks of his distinguished consideration.   The Princess Irene came several times to
the New York, and seemed always interested and
pleased with her visits.

CHAPTER XXXI

THE GERMAN EMPEROR

THE racing spirit was rife at Kiel, and our men were delighted to have a hand in anything in that line. The San Francisco held the championship of the navy for twelve-oared cutters, and had on board the boat with which she had won it. We of the New York had a boat as yet untried and unnamed, which we thought well of, and I had given much time and care to the training of a crew, with the intention of winning the coveted prize if possible. When we met at Kiel we raced in the presence of all the foreign ships, and my men won by a good margin. This led to an interesting incident, which I shall record later on. We also entered our sailing launch for the regatta, which was arranged by the emperor for man-of-war boats under sail, and won the fifth prize, competing with thirty-six German boats of the same kind. It was generally admitted that we would have taken the first prize if there had been a bit more wind. When the race started, the breeze was very light and all German boats were well ahead of us, but later on it freshened up, and it was glorious to see the way our boat walked out to windward of them. At the finish we had done up all but five, and were so close to them that ten minutes more would have given

382

us the lead. We were the only outsiders in the race, and brought away two silver cups as our trophies.

In return for all the hospitality we had received we gave two entertainments of note. The officers of all the ships combined, and gave a dancing reception on board the New York, and I a dinner to the emperor and a party of his ranking officers. Of course, all the ships were constantly entertaining officers of various nationalities, and I doubt if there was a meal served in any mess of our fleet during our stay at Kiel, not even a breakfast, without the presence of guests. I can not do better than quote the following from my journal written at the time:

"*Kiel, June 28, 1895.*—The Kiel spree is a thing of the past, and we are now only waiting the arrival of our orders to be off. The whole business has been the most complete success possible, and when the last one of our nine hundred guests left, yesterday evening, I was gratified to think that we had not had a mishap of any kind except the explosion of the San Francisco's launch boiler, which was nothing. In order to wind up in proper shape, we gave a dancing reception on board the New York. All ships combined, and it was a magnificent success. All Kiel was invited, and all Kiel is talking of it to-day.

"Unfortunately, the empress was too ill to come, and the Princess Henry could not leave her, which was a disappointment to all hands. We had two bands and no end of dancing on both decks from three o'clock to 7.30. The flowers were beautiful, the women more so, and the food excellent—they drank nineteen kegs of beer and thirty gallons of punch.

" On the 26th Prince and Princess Henry came in
the afternoon with a party of ladies and spent two hours
on the ship, really enjoying themselves. When they
were about to go, the princess presented me with her
photograph, and I was ashamed to have to say that I
had not one of mine to give her in return. They are
lovely, refined, kindly people, and I am glad to have
known them.

" The evening of the 26th was the crucial test. I
had invited the emperor and Prince Henry and ten
admirals to dine, and they all accepted. When the
emperor came on board I had the men and officers
massed aft on the superstructure and in the gangways,
and as soon as Admiral Kirkland had welcomed him I
made him a short speech, reciting that we had the
champion twelve-oared cutter of the American navy,
and asked on the part of my crew the honour of nam-
ing her after his daughter Victoria Louisa. He was
really touched by the compliment, and, taking my hand,
granted my request most graciously. As soon as I
could, I turned to the crew and called for three cheers
for the Victoria Louisa, and then three cheers and a
tiger for the emperor. I don't think he ever heard such
cheers before. It was a very pretty episode and gave
our dinner a good start.

" As soon as we sat down the emperor said: ' How
pleased the empress will be when she hears of this! You
must have your boat and crew photographed and send
the empress one.' (This I did on my return to New
York.)

" The dinner was one of the most delightful I
have ever seen, a perfect success, and George, my

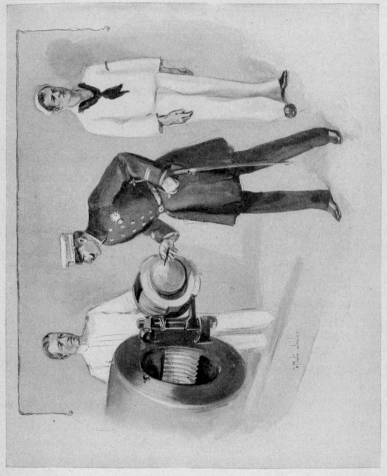

Visit of the German Emperor to the cruiser New York.

steward, who bossed the entire affair, is as proud as a
peacock.

"At 1 A. M. the emperor expressed a desire to visit
and inspect the engine room. And so we did. He
looked into every hole and corner, and even had us
disconnect one of the engines, marking time on us
himself. Then we went through the gun deck and out
on to the forecastle, where he asked how long it would
take to close all water-tight doors. I replied that in
the daytime we could do it in thirty seconds, but at
night it required about two minutes. Much to my surprise, he asked if I would mind doing it for him. Of
course I had to say yes, but when I tried to blow the
siren, the signal to close water-tight doors, there was
not steam enough, and the blessed thing would not
blow. The emperor thought he had me, and said,
'Now you see, captain, you can't close your bulkheads.' But he did not know everything. I said,
'You will see in a moment, sir,' and I touched one of
the general alarm buttons, which calls all hands to
quarters, and in a few seconds the men were swarming
up like rats.

"The emperor took the time himself, and in one
minute and a half the entire ship was ready for action with all water-tight doors closed. It was 2 A. M.,
the royal standard at our main and the search light of
the Columbia turned on it, the ship ready for action,
and the emperor complimenting the captain on the
forecastle. I find myself in some funny positions.

"When we went aft, where every one could hear
him, he said, 'Captain Evans, I can not imagine that a
ship could be in better condition'—very nice for all of

us. He left the ship just at 2 A. M., and all Germany has been reading accounts of it since."

I can recall very vividly how surprised I was when at five o'clock the same morning my orderly called me out of a sound sleep to report that the officer of the deck said the emperor was just then passing the ship, steering his own yacht. My only reply was, " For Heaven's sake don't stop him! " I managed to get one eye open, and, looking out of an air port in my cabin, discovered him, dressed in white flannels, steering the Meteor bound for an ocean race, and looking as if he had never taken a drink or smoked a cigar in his life.

People often ask me to tell them what impression the emperor made on me, and I always find it very difficult to answer the question. To say that he made a pleasant impression is simple and easy, but it means nothing. I found him one of the most magnetic and companionable of men—I should say, with one or two exceptions, the most magnetic. He knows more about more different things than any man I have ever met. When I was in Kiel my band was playing music composed by him, and on my cabin table was a book of poems written by him. He was the head and front of the finest army in the world, and at the same time giving his personal attention to what must some day be reckoned one of the leading navies. The Kiel Canal was of his creation, and his engineers told me that he was familiar with all its details, as well as with those of bridge-building in a large sense. The farmers informed me that he could instruct them in their business, and I personally saw him manœuvre a fleet at sea in the most creditable way. After luncheon at the

A Talk with the Emperor

palace one day, during a very interesting conversation, he described to me our first battle ship, the Indiana, which I afterward commanded, and his knowledge of her construction and details of armour and guns was perfect. He seemed to have the same knowledge of all foreign ships. When I gave him a Smithfield ham for dinner he even knew where Smithfield was.

On one occasion the emperor turned on me suddenly and said: " Captain, I understand you think I ought to have a strong navy. Will you tell me why you think so? " I replied that many of us who were interested in such matters had observed that the Jews had at one time made serious encroachments on English trade, but having no navy, of course they made no efforts to control the carrying trade; that then we had observed that the Germans had taken a hand in the game and had beaten the Jews, as they had the English, and that if I read the signs correctly, he, the emperor, meant with his cheaply built merchant ships to follow up this advantage of the German merchants and control the carrying trade of the world. I pointed out to him that a powerful navy was necessary to this scheme to protect his merchant fleet against the navies of those who might be disposed to contest this supremacy with him. He listened very attentively, and when I had finished he said, " Captain, unfortunately, my Parliament does not entertain the same view of the question." To which I replied, " If your Majesty will permit me to say so, I think you will eventually bring your Parliament to think as you do." I had many opportunities to see him among his people, and if he was not their idol, then they were certainly well up in the art of deception, for they seemed to worship him. To us, as representatives of our country, he was most cordial and considerate, and took no pains to conceal from others his strong friendship for the United States. I shall always remember him as I last saw him. He had given a splendid banquet in Kiel as a finish to his wonderfully successful opening of the canal. On one side of him sat the Grand Duke Alexis, on the other the Duke of York, while the lesser lights were seated according to rank. At the proper moment the emperor rose from his chair and, with a full glass of champagne in his extended hand, in clear, ringing tones that could be heard in every part of the room, said, in perfect English, " I drink to all the great sea nations who have sent their magnificent fleets to Kiel to join in the opening ceremonies of the North Sea Canal." He was to me the picturesque figure among all the ruling heads of Europe.

CHAPTER XXXII

BACK TO HOME WATERS

On June 30th I left Kiel with much regret and started on my return trip to New York, *via* England. The following extract from my journal is of interest.

"*North Sea, July 1, 1895.*—We left Kiel at 2 A. M. yesterday and had a beautiful run through the intricate channels of the Great Belt and out of the Skager Rack. The Columbia started with us and was in company until seven in the evening, when we ran her out of sight. The wind was fresh from the northwest, which was ahead, and the fleet of sailing craft beating out of the Baltic was beautiful to see, but I was glad when we were clear of them. We shall probably be in Gravesend at 8 A. M. to-morrow, weather permitting.

"*July 2d.*—An awful night! Up all night and most anxious. North Sea full of vessels, and the rain and fog nasty. Made the coast of England at 2 A. M. and found a pilot, but he was afraid to take us in, so away I went to Ramsgate, where we arrived three hours later, and soon had another pilot on board who brought us to this anchorage, six miles below Gravesend. Blowing a living gale all the way up, and my eyes fairly cut out of my head. As soon as the tide serves I shall go up to the town, make fast to a buoy, coal ship, and get ready for the trip to New York.

" *At Sea, Six Hundred Miles off New York, July 22d.* —We have had a real old-fashioned ' North Atlantic passage '—one gale following another in rapid succession. Until yesterday the shaking of the ship was so bad that writing was practically impossible, but now it has calmed down somewhat.

" Our last days at Gravesend were well filled with visits. Mr. White, chief constructor, came down from London, bringing some of his staff, to make notes on the ship, and the same day Admiral Morant came up from Chatham to spend the day, so we had a merry lunch party. On Sunday, Admiral Hotham and Captain Lambton came down from the city, and we had a long yarn over old times. In the meantime the ship was so crowded with all sorts of people that we had to stop them from coming on board. Everybody, from the member of Parliament for the district down to the servant maids, wanted to see the ship, and were, one and all, most enthusiastic over her condition. I never knew more hospitable people in my life—they wanted to do all sorts of things for us, from four-in-hand drives to dinner parties.

" On Monday, at 4 A. M., we left, and once being clear of the river and down as far as Dover, I let her go on her semiannual full-speed trial. We had a straight run in the Channel for it, and I was gratified to find that the engines and all their dependencies were in better condition than when we made our trial in January last. We had half a gale on our nose all day and all night, and when we cleared the Scilly Islands, at four the next morning, it turned into a whole gale from northwest with a nasty sea, and that state of things continued until yesterday afternoon, when it broke, and only the long, heavy sea remains. We should have made New York to-morrow evening if the weather had been halfway decent, but as it is we shall go in on Thursday—not a bad run, everything considered. Through it all the ship has proved herself wonderfully able and seaworthy, and I wish we had more like her, instead of the Columbia and Raleigh classes."

Upon my arrival in New York, July 25th, I was ordered to report to Admiral Bunce for duty as flagship of the North Atlantic squadron, which I did at the navy yard on the following day. I had carried the flag of two admirals, and now had the third, which was a rare experience for any captain, and one I imagine few captains would ever care to have. Flagship duty is not considered desirable as a general rule.

When the New York had had some small repairs made, we began cruising, and Admiral Bunce inaugurated the system of fleet drills which did so much to prepare the navy for its success in the Spanish War which came a few years later. I am sure that the feeling is general, among officers at least, that no officer ever did more conscientious work—work that led to more splendid results—than Admiral Bunce. He established two drill grounds, as they were called—one off New York and one off Cape Henry, Virginia—and when not coaling, the fleet could be found on one or the other of these grounds or cruising between them for months. We had constant torpedo drill, until each torpedo on board could be made to run with all the accuracy it was capable of. The firing was systematic and continued until the gun captains could hit the target with reasonable certainty; and the ships were kept under way in all kinds of fleet manœuvres at different speeds, until those in charge of them could handle them with confidence and without fear of collision. I am sure no such persistent work was ever before done by any fleet, and the good effects were most marked.

CHAPTER XXXIII

ON THE INDIANA

In October following my return from Kiel, I was detached from command of the New York and ordered to Philadelphia to fit out and command the Indiana, our first battle ship. She had been built at Cramp's shipyard, and was the heaviest armed and armoured ship in the world. The New York had seemed to me a complicated mass of machinery, but this new thing was a real machine shop from top to bottom. It required weeks of hard work and study after I joined her before I felt reasonably sure that I would not get lost, if I attempted to inspect her throughout; but when I did get the hang of her she certainly was a magnificent command. The Department had selected a very fine set of officers for her, and to them, particularly to the able executive officer, Lieutenant-Commander Swift, I owe all the reputation I made in her. After two months of constant work we got away from League Island, and, having taken in our torpedoes at Newport, joined the admiral at Fortress Monroe. Before reporting to him, however, the Inspection Board, presided over by Commodore George Dewey, took us to sea and gave us a thorough overhauling. Their report was very favourable, considering the short time

393

we had been in commission and the few opportunities
we had had for working the enormous guns of her battery.   She carried the first thirteen-inch breech-loading
rifles ever put afloat in our service; she had four of
them mounted in pairs in turrets, one forward and the
other aft.

During the winter it became necessary to clean the
bottom of the Indiana, and the so-called dock at Port
Royal, South Carolina, was the only one ready to receive her.   I was ordered to proceed to that point for
the purpose, and then return to my station with the
fleet.   I sailed from Hampton Roads with coal enough
to leave me with only two hundred tons on board when
I should reach my destination, hoping in this way to
reduce the draught of the ship as much as possible.
Everything went well with me until I had passed Cape
Hatteras, when I ran into a sudden terrific gale, which
soon produced a very ugly heavy sea.   I was naturally
desirous of testing the ship in such weather, as none of
us knew what a battle ship would do under such conditions, so I kept her going at full speed and drove her
hard into the seas.   We were soon battened down fore
and aft, and, despite our best efforts, much water found
its way below.   The waves were going clear over us
forward, at times completely covering our thirteen-inch
gun turret with solid green water and throwing heavy
spray over the upper bridge.   Having satisfied myself
that the Indiana could stand any amount of sea, so long
as she was kept head on to it, I changed the course and
brought the sea abeam, when to my surprise she rolled
very little and was entirely comfortable, except for the
water sweeping over her spar deck.   I then slowed her

From a copyrighted photograph by Enrique Muller.

Battle ship Indiana.

down to good steerage way, when she was as dry as a cork and looked like a small island surrounded by seething white breakers.

When the fury of the gale had passed I steamed on to the Port Royal lightship, and there waited for high water to help me over the dangerous bar. With a lighthouse tender sounding ahead of me I passed in on the very top of high water, and at the worst point in the channel had just one foot of water to spare. The least bit of a sea would have caused us to take the bottom, which is of hard sand. The risk was very great and the sensation anything but pleasant. Once inside, however, we were comparatively safe, and I steamed on to the so-called dockyard, hoping to dock the ship at once. When I arrived there, however, I found that nothing was ready for me. There was not sufficient water even if the dock had been ready. In the meantime the tide had begun to fall, and I was caught like a rat in a trap. It was impossible to take the ship to the lower bay again on that tide, so I had to remain where I was. The commanding officer of the station and the pilots came on board and pointed out to me a berth where the largest ship in the world could safely swing to her anchors. Indeed, according to their accounts, the only trouble with the place was that they had too much water and too much swinging room. However, I had my own views about all this; but as I could not get away, I had to make the best of it.

Half of South Carolina was on hand to see the first great battle ship placed in their beautiful dock, and as soon as I had anchored in the selected spot they crowded on board of me by thousands. The ship filled to suffocation with them, when at half tide she sat down on the hard bottom and remained there, much to my discomfort. I soon hustled the visitors out and then waited quietly to see what harm would be done before I could get out of the trap in which I was caught. It was impossible to move until daylight the following morning, when I hoped that Divine Providence would send in a tide sufficient for me to go into dock. As the flood made, it lifted the ship from her uncomfortable and dangerous berth and she swung with her stern up stream, in which position I attempted to hold her with heavy stern anchors, but it was no use. There was so little water under her that she practically formed a dam, and no power on earth could hold her. As the ebb tide again made, she swung to it, and I found myself with a wire hawser wound around our propellers to add to my comfort. The moment there was water enough I cleared out and anchored in the bay eight miles away from the bothersome dock.

Each high tide for a week I got under way and came up only to find that there was not water enough. Then I settled down to drill and target practice, determined to wait until an easterly gale or some other convulsion of Nature should send in the desired quantity of water. I waited, as I now recall it, nearly two weeks before I succeeded, and then only got into the dock by driving my engines at full speed. As we passed over the sill we had just five inches of water to spare. Once in and the gates closed, we were safe until such time as we wanted to get out again; but as there was no immediate prospect of water enough for that, I gave myself no concern about it. As the dock was being emptied, the powerful pumps gradually slowed down and finally stopped, choked up with shrimp. Cart loads of the finest shrimp I ever saw were taken out before the pumps were cleared and fit to run again. When the water was all out, I fed my crew of five hundred men on fresh shellfish the like of which they had never before seen. We had found one good thing at least in the Port Royal naval station, but I could not help thinking that it was a costly and dangerous way of getting shrimp.

Two days was all we required to do the necessary work, and after that we waited for water enough to escape. For nine days we watched the gauge, and then an easterly wind swelled the tide to the necessary point and we started. When about half of the ship was clear of the entrance the flood tide caught her stern and she started in the direction of a heavy stone structure, which was sure to crush her side in if she struck it. There was but one thing to do, and I did that as promptly as I could. I rang both engines full speed astern, and called out for all hands to stand clear of the lines and hawsers by which we were held. The engines responded promptly, the ship gathered way quickly, and, after a second or two of snapping lines, she shot out of the dock into the stream. For a few minutes it looked as if she must be seriously damaged, but she escaped the threatening stone structure by exactly eleven inches. We had a cork fender hanging over the side which was twelve inches in diameter, and she squeezed this against the blocks of granite as she passed. I lost no time in making my way to a safe anchorage, firmly resolved that if any more battle ships were to be docked at Port Royal some other captain would have to command them.

The Indiana was soon again with the fleet, and when the Massachusetts had been fitted out and commissioned, the two of them formed an excellent unit in the long months of drill which followed. Admiral Bunce kept us at it night and day, until the officers had become as familiar with handling battle ships as they had previously been with smaller vessels. We took them to the navy yard and berthed them without even the assistance of tugs, and the way we handled them in the narrow parts of crowded New York Harbour showed that some of us had mastered our job. And we had mastered it in the only way possible to seamen —by constant work and practice out on blue water. We all owe much to Admiral Bunce.

In the fall of 1896 the squadron started from Fortress Monroe for New York. It had been blowing hard for several days, and the admiral considered it a fit opportunity to test the sea-going qualities of the Indiana, and particularly the strength of the securing devices on her turrets. We found a heavy sea running before we were out of Chesapeake Bay, and when Cape Henry light was abeam I signalled that all my eight-inch turrets, four in number, were adrift, thinking that the admiral would direct me to return to port and secure them. On the contrary, we held on our course, and when the sun went down these turrets were securely lashed so that they could give no further trouble; but the sea in the meantime had increased very much, and the thirteen-inch turrets, each weighing five hundred tons, began to work loose, and by ten o'clock had destroyed their controlling devices and were free to do as they pleased. The after-turret was secured by lashing the muzzles of the guns to the towing bitts on the quarter-deck with hawsers. There was no great danger in this work, as I kept the ship as nearly head to sea as possible, but several times the men were almost swept overboard.

At midnight the gale was very bad and the sea coming on board in every direction. The night was as black as a pocket and the rest of the squadron out of sight ahead. I had been forced to slow down to protect the men and officers who were working on the forecastle in a desperate effort to secure the forward thirteen-inch turret, which was thrashing from side to side as the ship rolled and pitched. I stood by the wheel on the upper bridge, and frequently the whole forward end of her would go under water, men and all, and the sea would come up until I could easily have put my foot into it. At such times I held my breath as the water rolled off and the black heads of the officers and men, one after another, came in sight; I fully expected to see them swept overboard by the dozen. She was rolling forty degrees, and nothing I could do seemed to ease her. The sea was so irregular that I could not keep her bows on to it, and the night so pitch dark that I could not see where the heavy seas were coming from.

At 1 A. M. the ash-chutes on the gun deck had their covers torn off and the deck was flooded, and there was no way to get the water out except by bailing with buckets. The carpenter, who was in a great funk, came to me on the bridge, white in the face, and reported in a trembling voice, " Sir, the gun deck is full of water, and I can't see how we are ever going to get it out! " I replied, " Go down and drink some of it out, sir, and don't bother me again with your whining! " which sent him on his way and I saw no more of him. By the almost super-human efforts of the executive officer and the officer of the forward turret, assisted by one hundred or more men, the thirteen-inch guns were finally lashed securely to the eight-inch turret on the upper deck, and the forward turret thus secured. The work required four hours, and most of the time all hands engaged in it were under water. In the meantime the lifeboats, which were hoisted on the upper deck of all, were smashed by the sea, which came up under them and stove them against the davit heads. By four o'clock in the morning we had everything well secured and the water all cleared out, so that I felt no apprehension for the safety of the ship. Indeed, I had felt none after the first few heavy rolls she made with her gun deck flooded; then I did feel some doubt as to the result. I was soon satisfied that she would not capsize, and, later on, I made up my mind that she could do anything but climb a tree, and I thought she would do that if I gave her half a chance.

Between midnight and four in the morning one of the young officers lost his leg by having it caught by an armoured door weighing two tons, which, un-fortunately, carried away its fastenings at the wrong moment and closed just when the young man was thrown out of his bunk across the doorsill. This was the only serious accident we had, though many of the men were somewhat bruised. I was glad when daylight put an end to one of the worst nights I ever spent at sea, and thankful that I had escaped a serious disaster. The officers behaved, as they always do, perfectly, and the crew, many of them very young and new at the business, excited my warmest admiration. Not a soul on board, except the man who was advised to drink salt water, showed the least sign of fear or hesitation. I certainly had a crew full of sand up to their necks, and I felt like hugging every man Jack of them.

We landed our wounded officer in New York the following day, and then went to the navy yard for repairs. I was told that the ship had not rolled as badly as I thought she had by those who imagined that they knew many things which they really only guessed at. The fragments of the various gimcracks which had been intended to hold her turrets were taken out, in many cases with a dustpan and broom, and new and better things put in. We were getting experience in battle-ship fittings, but, like the shrimp-catching, it was costly and dangerous.

In fitting out the Indiana I was careful to see that she had, among other necessary things, a twelve-oared cutter, which I hoped some day might win from the cutter of the New York, which had done such good work at Kiel. I was careful in selecting the crew for her, and, after many months of faithful training, the race took place at Fortress Monroe. The distance pulled was six miles, in a rough sea, and the Victoria Louisa had to lower her colours to Uncle Sam, the name of our new boat. I think the same boats pulled several races after I gave up command, and honours were about even between them.

While refitting in New York, Mr. Rudyard Kipling breakfasted on board with me and seemed much interested, particularly in the machinery, which he examined very closely. Some weeks afterward he was good enough to send me a set of his books. On the title-page of Plain Tales from the Hills, facing a beautiful picture of Sergeant Mulvaney, done by my dear friend R. F. Zogbaum, he had written the following graceful lines, which I had hoped would always remain my personal property. But some one stole them and gave them publicity. For that reason I allow myself to put them in this book:

> " Zogbaum draws with a pencil,
>   And I do things with a pen ;
> And you sit up in a conning tower
>   Bossing eight hundred men.
>
> " Zogbaum takes care of his business,
>   And I take care of mine ;
> And you take care of ten thousand tons
>   Sky-hooting through the brine.
>
> " Zogbaum can handle his shadows,
>   And I can handle my style ;
> And you can handle a ten-inch gun
>   To carry seven mile.
>
> "' To him that hath shall be given,'
>   And that's why these books are sent
> To the man who has lived more stories
>   Than Zogbaum or I could invent."

During the fall of 1896 I was detached from the Indiana and once more ordered to duty on the Light-house Board, but this time as a member and not as naval secretary, where I had previously served. While on this duty I was detailed in addition as a member of the Personnel Board, which Secretary Long, of the navy, had ordered to consider some remedy for the controversy which existed between the line and engineer officers of the service. The board was composed of leading officers of the two corps, and ably presided over by Mr. Theodore Roosevelt, Assistant Secretary, to whom more than any other man belongs the credit for the remedy applied later in the shape of the Naval Personnel Bill. The scheme of amalgamation embodied in that bill was first proposed by me, and I wish to assume the responsibility which attached to my act. The entire board, of course, voted on the proposition and approved it as a body.

CHAPTER XXXIV

THE APPROACH OF WAR

In the early winter of 1897 I was honoured with the confidence of Mr. Roosevelt, and was frequently consulted by him about various naval matters. He saw clearly the approaching storm of war, and knew well how unprepared we were in many ways to meet it, and it was owing to his strong will and earnest recommendations to Mr. Long that many most important steps were taken. In making this statement I detract nothing from the wonderful ability shown by Mr. Long. He had a most patriotic and painstaking assistant in solving a problem, the solution of which has reflected great credit on the country for all time to come.

I left Washington in December, 1897, to make a trip of inspection of all the light stations on the South Atlantic and Gulf coasts in the lighthouse steamer Armeria. At Key West, Florida, I found the North Atlantic fleet under command of Admiral Sicard, and it was plain to me that that able officer expected war with Spain and was doing all he could to be ready for it when it came. The day before we sailed from the port the Maine was coaling preparatory to her visit to Havana. A large lighter was hauling out from the

404

coal dock and on her deck were a number of her men
who had been loading the coal, and it seemed to me
that I had never before seen a finer-looking lot of men.
Among them was an old shipmate of mine, William
Fuer, a boatswain's mate, who had served with me in
the Yorktown, and as he stood on the bows of the
lighter, directing her movements, he was the picture
of a man-of-war's-man—strong, handsome, and fearless.
I found his name in the list of those killed that awful
night in Havana, when, whether by accident or design,
Spain sealed her fate in the Western world.

A few weeks later I was in New Orleans, Louisiana,
where I had been enjoying the festivities of the carnival
season, when the news of the destruction of the Maine
shocked the civilized world. Men of all classes talked
to me on the subject and asked my opinion, and,
though I had a very decided one, I expressed none. It
seemed to me the time of all others for a man in my
position to hold his tongue and prepare for the serious
work I felt was in store for all of us. I begged them all
to await quietly the finding of the board that had been
ordered to investigate the whole matter, which I felt
sure would be painstaking and thorough. But I could
see, from the set faces of those Southern chaps, and the
quiet, determined way in which they spoke, that somebody was going to get whipped because the Maine had
been blown up. When I had visited Galveston and
found the same smouldering volcano there, I was
strengthened in my conviction that if the authorities
then in power did not declare war, they would be
turned out and others put in who would. I felt that if
the action of our admiral had been different—and it

probably would have been had he been younger and not so sick—time at least would have been saved. If he had gone into Havana the morning after the disaster with his whole fleet and said to General Blanco that he had come to find out why these American officers and men, the guests of Spain, had been foully murdered, it would, in my opinion, have produced immediate results and saved much time.

About the middle of March I again arrived at Key West on my way back to Washington, and was struck with the weakness of our fleet in the way of torpedoboat destroyers and guard boats. If war should suddenly come, and it looked as if it might at any moment, an enterprising enemy, with the Spanish torpedo vessels known to be in and about Cuba, could seriously damage if not destroy our entire force in a single night. I hurried on to Washington, determined to give Mr. Long my views on the subject. Fortunately, he sent for me the day of my arrival, and, having heard patiently and with deep interest what I had to say to him, at once, with the assistance of Mr. Roosevelt, proceeded to apply the only possible remedy. He ordered the purchase of a number of fast yachts and tugs in New York and other ports and directed that they be armed with all despatch and hurried off to Key West.

While I stood talking with him he gave directions to detach Admiral Sicard, who was condemned by medical survey, from command of the squadron, and order Captain Sampson to relieve him. Then, turning to me, he said, in his quiet, forcible way: " Now, captain, I have a surprise for you. I am going to order you to relieve Sampson in command of the Iowa. How soon can you start?" I had only arrived in the city five hours before, but feeling as I did the importance of not losing time, replied that I could leave for Key West at 4 P. M. that day, which I did. When trouble with Spain first threatened I had asked that if war came I might be ordered to command the St. Paul in case she was taken into the service. I was therefore much gratified to command the finest battle ship in the navy.

I arrived at Key West as soon as steam could get me there, and went at once to the Iowa, then lying with the other large vessels off Sand Key light, about eight miles from the town. It was a time of intense excitement. We all felt that war was sure to come, and we were anxious to have it done with, and therefore the sooner it came the better. That we were not as ready for it as we should have been was not our fault; what the navy itself could do we had done, and we felt confident that we could do the Spanish fleet up in an hour if it would come out in the open sea and give us a chance, but we knew it would never do that. It was borne in upon me that the worst use you could put a navy to was fighting, and the best, keeping the peace, yet we were about to be driven to the former because our naval force was and had been too small for the latter.

Admiral Sampson spared neither himself nor his officers and men in his preparations for the coming struggle—work was incessant day and night. Drills of all kinds were indulged in, but target firing was considered the most important one of all. Day by day we wasted Government ammunition, as some of the yellow newspapers had it, and no end of targets were destroyed. Night after night the torpedo boats had their try at us, that our men might know what the real thing would look like when it came. Coal bunkers and magazines were kept constantly full, as well as bread rooms and storerooms. In the meantime the admiral constantly conferred with his commanding officers, and with their assistance drew up a complete plan for the attack and capture of the city and defences of Havana. Our officers who had been in Cuba recently knew every fort about the city and the number and calibre of guns in each, and with this information in our hands, we knew just what we had to meet.

Sampson believed, and we agreed with him, that the thing to do, as soon as war was declared, was to strike quick and strike hard; but such was not to be our good fortune. The Secretary thought highly of the plans which were submitted to him, but, for reasons which he no doubt considered convincing, decided against them, in favour of a close blockade. I have always thought that we could have captured or destroyed Havana two days after the declaration of war, and it is my belief that this of itself would have ended the struggle in a very short time, and that Cervera's fleet would not have crossed the Atlantic. I make this statement with a full knowledge of what we had to encounter and after close study of the situation, which afterward changed very rapidly and was entirely different when General Blanco had strongly fortified the entrance.

In the early days of April the newly purchased

A Base Wanted

yachts and tugs began to arrive at Key West, and it would have been amusing, if the matter had been less serious, to see the value placed on these improvised guard boats. It was simply because we had no torpedo-boat destroyers, and officers of experience knew the danger of attack from the coast of Cuba. So these new arrivals were put to work at once, some of them on guard duty at night and others towing stores and coal from Key West, eight miles away, to the fighting ships, which were anchored in the open sea off Sand Key light. As a base of supplies, in a military sense, Key West was at this time an absolute and utter failure, because we had no supplies for war, either there or anywhere else, and the necessary shops and machines were not on hand. A few officers were working their hearts out over the same old impossible scheme of boring a two-inch hole with a one-inch auger, only in this case the auger seemed to all of us like a very small gimlet. However, we did manage somehow to keep the ships in a fair state of preparation, and as the days went by we felt that the important thing of all—our men—was most satisfactory. They were as fit and ready as men ever were, or could be, and only waited the chance to prove it to the country and the world.

CHAPTER XXXV

THE HAVANA BLOCKADE

THE tension grew greater and the excitement and strain harder to bear as the month advanced, until the 20th of April came, when we knew from the Washington despatches that the critical moment had arrived. During the evening of the 21st all the commanding officers of the outside fleet were summoned on board the flagship for consultation, and there we remained until nearly midnight, waiting for the message we felt sure must come before daylight. Some of us prepared to return to our vessels about ten o'clock, but Sampson requested us to remain. So over our fresh cigars we sat and listened to the quiet words of our clear-headed commander, while the wind howled and the ship pitched and rolled in the choppy sea. Just before midnight a naval cadet came to the cabin and reported a torpedo boat coming out at high speed, and in a few minutes a staff officer handed the admiral a telegram from President McKinley, which he immediately read to his assembled commanders. It said: "War declared; proceed to blockade the coast of Cuba," etc., etc.—Then, with serious, thoughtful faces, we said good-night to the admiral and each other, and returned

410

to our ships.   The expected had happened this time
at least.

When I reached the Iowa, about midnight, all of
the officers and most of the crew were on deck waiting to hear the news.   I told them in a few words, and
for half an hour I could hear the low hum of conversation among the men, then perfect silence fore and aft.
The signal lights of the New York glinted and winked
as the signal officers transmitted the order to be ready
to get under way at daylight.   The assistant chief of
staff was sent into the inner harbour with orders for
the vessels assembled there to come out as fast as possible, and by one o'clock they began to appear.   I say
they began to appear, but in reality we could only see
the long, ghostlike beams of their search lights as they
felt about for the buoys of the difficult channel.   Before daylight every vessel of the fleet was under way,
formed in double column, and headed for the coast of
Cuba.   In less than four hours from the receipt of the
order the navy showed its state of readiness by actually
starting for the enemy's coast.   Fortunately for the
country, we were in much better shape than the people
thought we were.

Everything was done to the ships in the way of protection that careful thought and long experience could
suggest.   Those of us who had been in battle before
were aware of the idiosyncrasies of shot and shell—how
they were apt to strike just in the spot where they
were most unwelcome—and we therefore protected the
soft places with such material as came to hand.   I had
taken on board the Iowa many tons of sand in bags, and
these I had used where I thought they would do the

most good. I had also unshackled our heavy sheet-anchor chains and wound them carefully around the exposed ammunition hoists, a job that took over a week of as hard work as I ever saw men do. In a word, everything had been done to make the ships ready for the ordeal they had to face.

At seven o'clock on the morning of April 22d, as we were standing on our course for Havana, a steamer was made out to the westward heading toward us with the Spanish flag flying. The Nashville was signalled to capture her, and in a few minutes that vessel had fired the first gun of the war and had taken the first prize. In the late afternoon the land about Havana was made out in the distance, and every preparation was made for battle in case the enemy fired on us. Shortly after we sighted the land, a vessel was seen well inshore attempting to escape to the eastward, and the New York left her place in column and gave chase, at the same time flying the signal, " Disregard movements of the commander in chief!"

I, as next in rank to Sampson, hoisted the guide flag, and, as senior officer present, held the fleet to its course direct for the Morro Castle at the entrance to the harbour of Havana. The New York soon ran out of sight, and I saw nothing more of her until about two o'clock the next morning, when she rejoined, having in the meantime captured the Spanish steamer Pedro and sent her into Key West with a prize crew. When we could make out clearly the lighthouse on the Morro, I formed the fleet in double column, with the lighter vessel double distance to the left, in order to bring them closer to the shore after I had established the blockade, and in this order continued on my course with all hands at the guns ready to return any fire that we might receive. We had orders not to bring on an engagement, but I did not consider that this order would apply in case the Spaniards fired on us. When the Iowa was about five miles from the Morro Castle, I made signal, "Head of columns right!" and, as the signal went up, I saw the flash of a gun on shore, and then others, until five had been fired. I gave the order to stand by to fire, and cautioned those about me to watch carefully for the splash of a shot; but, unfortunately, none came; they were only signal guns to announce our arrival. I continued on my way and established the blockade, and night settled down. General Blanco and the city of Havana were in a grip that was to make them very tired and hungry before it relaxed.

Our first night on the blockade was very exciting work. I had made up my mind that the Spaniards would attempt something in the way of a torpedo attack that night. It was the logical thing for them to do, and it is possible that they might have met with some success if they had been bold and daring. I was on the bridge during the entire night, and if I saw one torpedo boat I saw a thousand! Every breaking sea was to my imagination a torpedo boat. I had the fleet standing to the westward toward Mariel, and at one o'clock in the morning it became necessary to turn about and cruise slowly back toward the Morro. The night was intensely dark, and not a sound could be heard or a ship seen in any direction. As I made the preparatory signal from the bridge of the Iowa the answering lights flashed out, and there they were, the whole fleet in two long lines, as if tied on strings. They turned promptly at the signal and stood back in the direction indicated. Between two and three o'clock in the morning the New York rejoined, and the responsibility of command passed to the able shoulders where it belonged.

For ten days the Iowa, in common with the others, rolled and pitched in the trade-wind seas, watching the Spanish army, while new forts were built and new guns placed in position. At night we hauled off a few miles, so that our torpedo boats and guard vessels could have a fair chance at anything that came out. About daylight in the morning I steamed in and took my place in plain sight of the city and within easy range of the batteries, if any one wanted to try a shot at me; but the shot never came. It would not have been wise on the part of General Blanco to provoke the fire of the battle ships with their twelve- and thirteen-inch guns.

One afternoon, just before sundown, I saw with my glass two very trim-looking Spanish gunboats coming out of the harbour. They turned to the east and steamed along close to the shore, evidently much admired by the great mass of people I could see crowding the docks on the water front. After a short time the little chaps turned and steamed to the west toward Mariel. I signalled Mackenzie, who was near me in the Mayflower, to stand by to chase and at the same time gave orders to bottle up steam on the Iowa. When I thought there was a chance to cut them off, I made the signal to chase, and headed straight for the entrance at full speed. Mackenzie dashed in like a shot off a shovel, and for a few moments it looked as if

Battle ship Iowa.

we might nab them, but they saw us the moment we started and put for home with all the speed they could make. When they entered the harbour I could no doubt have reached them with my heavy guns, but they were not of much consequence, and I did not fancy the idea of sending a shell into the mass of women and children on shore. We were within easy range of the forts, and I did hope that they would give us a chance to pay our respects to them, but they remained quiet, though we could see the men about the guns. The gunboats never came out again while I remained on the Havana blockade.

During the early days of May I ran over to Key West, filled up with coal, and was back at my station during the night. The following morning at daylight I made out a tugboat coming out from the land with the signal flying, " Send a boat! " which was unusual if not cheeky. I examined her carefully with my glasses and discovered an officer on board in cavalry uniform. It turned out to be Colonel Dorst, of the United States army. He had landed some Cubans and a company of our men during the night, but the Spaniards had surrounded them, and the colonel explained to me that unless I went to their assistance his men would probably be killed or captured. While I was talking with him, the New York came in sight, steaming very fast, with the signal flying, " Iowa steer east by south, speed eleven knots! " I told Dorst that Sampson would no doubt send a gunboat to look after his party, which he did, and I started immediately in obedience to the signal, which I knew meant business of some sort. It was the starting of the expedition to San Juan, Puerto Rico.

CHAPTER XXXVI

THE CRUISE TO SAN JUAN

THE Iowa, Indiana, and New York ran all day to the eastward, and at sundown that evening met the other vessels that had been directed to rendezvous off Cruz del Padre light on the north coast of Cuba. News had come from Washington that Admiral Cervera had sailed with the Spanish fleet from the Cape de Verde Islands, and it was plain to all of us that Sampson's fleet should be well to the eastward to meet him if he attempted to pass through the West Indies, either to threaten our coast or enter a port on the north side of Cuba. The natural place for him to go to recoal and repair his ships was San Juan, Puerto Rico, where there were stores and machine shops, and Sampson had every reason to expect to find him there. It turned out afterward that Cervera was bound for San Juan, and had it not been for the unexpectedly low speed of his torpedo boats we should have found him there on May 12th. As it was, he received the news of the bombardment of San Juan when off Martinique and shaped his course for Curaçoa, and thus escaped. We all thought that we had given him ample time to reach his destination. Twelve hours more and we should have trapped him at San Juan instead of at Santiago.

When we reached the appointed rendezvous, late in the evening, we found there, among other ships, two monitors—the Terror and the Amphitrite. As they could not carry coal enough to steam to our destination, they were taken in tow. I was directed to tow the Amphitrite with the Iowa. The sea was very smooth, and we were soon pulling her along at nine knots, but before the job was finished I wished I had never seen a monitor. When once out from under the protection of the shoals the sea began to rise, and soon everything in the way of towlines had been parted, and it was only when we slowed down to seven knots or less that we could make anything hold. We found ourselves in the open sea looking for an enemy who could steam at the speed of sixteen to eighteen knots while we could barely maintain seven. The prospect of catching him was not very bright. However, we were doing our best with the tools the Government had given us to work with. After many vexatious delays, we arrived off the north coast of Puerto Rico on the afternoon of May 11th, and at sundown Admiral Sampson transferred his flag to the Iowa and notified me that I should have the honour of leading in the battle which we hoped would be fought the following day.

At daylight on May 12th the high land and forts about San Juan could be dimly seen. The fleet was in battle order and every ship ready to open fire. Slowly the Iowa steamed in until she was fairly within range of all the guns, when I stopped the engines and waited until we could see clearly everything in the harbour. The forts, as well as the city, seemed to be sleeping soundly, and there was nothing to indicate that the Spaniards expected or suspected our unfriendly visit. Our glasses soon disclosed the fact that Cervera was not there.

To give our men practice and season them a bit for what was to come, Admiral Sampson decided to bombard the batteries. I was standing by him on the bridge when he gave me permission to open fire. I stepped to the nearest six-pounder and ordered the captain of the gun to fire at the lighthouse tower with an elevation of twenty-six hundred yards, which he did, and I saw the shell explode near the base of the tower. I then gave the range to the whole battery as twenty-five hundred yards, with directions to fire at the Morro fort, and immediately ordered the bugler at my elbow to sound " Commence firing! " In a few seconds the whole starboard battery was firing rapidly, and, as the Indiana and other ships astern of us took it up, the roar became deafening. It was fully five minutes after we opened before any reply came from the shore, and during this time I could see the shells bursting and kicking up great clouds of dust and smoke as they struck or exploded in and about the batteries. Finally, when we were about one thousand yards from the Morro fort, a battery well back on the hill opened fire and several shells passed over us. I at once directed our guns on this battery, which did not respond so long as we were firing at them. In the meantime many other guns had opened on us, but those of the Morro fort remained silent, until two hours later, when we were hauling off. Our fire had been so severe that this particular fort could not respond.

In order to define our firing line, the admiral had ordered a boat anchored off the entrance to the harbour on the edge of the shoal to mark the point where we were to begin, and the Detroit was sent in to a point about eight hundred yards from the batteries to mark the edge of the shoal at that point, and between these two we were to steam, turning out as we passed close to the latter and coming on to the firing line again as we approached the former. Thus the fleet was to move in an ellipse until the signal to draw off was given. As we approached the Detroit for the first time the smoke was blinding, as there was no wind to blow it away. I ordered the rapid-fire guns to cease firing and continue to use the guns of the main battery, which eased the situation at once, and, as the smoke cleared, the sight was one long to be remembered. The Spanish batteries were all paying more or less attention to the Detroit, and the shells were cutting the water up all about her and bursting over her. Captain Dayton, who commanded her, was handling her beautifully, and her crew was making her five-inch rapid-fire guns roar and blaze. She was simply magnificent, a veritable spitfire. After we had passed over the firing line the second time she was signalled to change her position and draw off somewhat, but Dayton took a long time to answer the signal, and withdrew with great reluctance. We were much relieved when he signalled that he had escaped without injury. If I had had the power I would have changed the name of the Detroit that morning; I would have painted " Gamecock " on her stern, and kept it there as long as she remained afloat.

When the Iowa turned from the firing line for the second time, the Spanish fire became very steady and accurate. For a few minutes, until the Indiana and New York got to work on them, it was the best shooting I saw the Spanish artillery do during the war. Just after we turned and were steaming away from them I heard a shell coming, and an instant afterward it came into our upper deck and exploded with a sharp ringing report. The projectile, a Krupp armour piercer, passed through a steel beam and exploded under the boats, knocking the bottoms out of two of them and badly wrecking the third. The deck was filled with smoke, and I expected to find serious loss of life when it cleared up. The men to the number of one hundred or more were standing about in groups watching the fight when the smoke hid them from view. Many of them had their caps blown off by the explosion, and, as the smoke blew away, they were laughing and joking while they brushed the dust from their clothes. Everything about the deck was ripped and torn by fragments of the shell, but not a man was even scratched. The bottom of the sailing launch was badly wrecked, and a large fragment of shell completely destroyed the boat box, which contained an outfit of various articles. The small American flag belonging to the boat was blown out of the box and spread on the rail, it being the only thing left. It was not damaged in the least. I afterward gave it to President McKinley as a souvenir of the fight. Two more shells came in rapid succession, and both exploded in the superstructure. They were perfectly placed and showed that the enemy had our range accurately. Three men were wounded by the second, these being my only casualties during the day. We were much cut up and marked about the upper works, but no serious damage was done. The escape of our men was simply marvellous.

As we made the third round on the firing line, the return fire from the batteries was very weak, and it was plain to me that the city could be captured if we continued our bombardment a few hours longer. I counted nine places where fire had broken out on shore as the result of our exploding shells, and I felt sure that if we turned our guns on the city we could compel its surrender or destroy it in a short time. So far the only damage to the town was caused by a few wild shots due to the rolling of the ships in the trade swell. There had been no orders to fire at anything except the batteries, but, as they were very close to the town, some damage was unavoidably done to it. After we had been in action about two hours and a half, signal was made to withdraw; and as the fleet passed out of and beyond the range of the enemy's guns, Spanish flags were hoisted on all the forts and a furious but harmless fire kept up as long as we could see them.

Our men had received just what they most needed—practical demonstration of the fact that it required a great many shots to seriously injure a modern ship, and that every shell fired was not going to kill each individual man who heard it screaming over his head. Our experience that morning was of immense value to all hands, but particularly to those who were under fire for the first time. If we had had sufficient force to hold

San Juan, it would undoubtedly have been taken that day; but such was not the case, and we could not wait for the arrival of troops, even if they had been available for the purpose. Admiral Cervera was somewhere in the West Indies, and it was our business to get between him and our base of supplies at Key West as soon as possible. We knew that we had no time to spare, and I, as well as other commanding officers, advised Admiral Sampson to get to the westward with all possible despatch.

CHAPTER XXXVII

WITH THE FLYING SQUADRON

AFTER dark on the 12th of May I took my monitor in tow and we began our vexatious return trip to the Gulf of Mexico. Admiral Sampson was convinced that the Spanish fleet would make for Santiago or Havana, with chances in favour of the former place. When we had arrived off the north coast of Hayti a torpedo boat brought the news that they were at Curaçoa, and shortly afterward I was left in command of the fleet, with orders to get the ships to their various stations on the blockade as rapidly as possible, while the flagship hurried on to Key West with all speed. Had it not been for the monitors the problem would have been easy to solve, but with them to tow, and all hands short of coal, it was most difficult.

During the afternoon of May 17th, as we were passing in sight of Manzanillo lighthouse, I discovered two Spanish gunboats close inshore, evidently making for Nuevitas. As I could not go after them myself without casting off my monitor, and thus losing valuable time, I made signal to the Montgomery, Commander Converse commanding, to give chase. The way he made those two gunboats hunt a hole was beautiful to see. They disappeared behind the land, and to my great concern Converse did the same in hot pursuit. After a few minutes I saw him open fire with one battery and then with both, firing very rapidly. Fearing that he was in trouble, I signalled the Indiana, Captain Taylor, to go to his assistance. As the battle ship turned out of column to obey the signal, the Montgomery came out of the narrow channel stern first at full speed, having been handled from first to last in the most gallant and seamanlike way. I called Converse within hail and told him what I thought of him and his crew.

At eight o'clock in the evening, as we were entering the Bahama Channel, during a vicious black rain squall, the keen-eyed lookouts of the Iowa made out a torpedo boat coming toward us at top speed. She soon made her night signal and proved to be the Dupont, with Commander Kimball, commanding the torpedo flotilla. He had orders for me to cast off my monitor and get to Key West as soon as steam could take me there, as there was important work for my ship to do. I cast off the Amphitrite, signalled the Montgomery to take her in tow, and Captain Taylor to assume command of the squadron, and went below to my cabin with Kimball to read the despatches which he had in his hand.

We seated ourselves at the cabin table and I was deeply interested in Cervera's movements, when I heard a startled voice exclaim, "Look-out, captain!" I threw my head to one side to see what I was to look out for, when there was a tremendous crash and I was aware that I was hurt and more or less dazed. My first impression was that one of the Spanish gun-

A Singular Accident

boats had sneaked up on us and put a shell into my cabin. I had been thinking all the afternoon what a fine chance it would be for them that night; but when I was really conscious I saw that that was not the trouble. My cabin was full of men, all staring at me, their eyes fairly sticking out of their heads. They thought I was killed, and wanted to see the last of the " old man." I was soon aware that one of the doctors was feeling and twisting my right arm and that my right shoulder was in pretty bad shape. Through it all I was very sorry for Kimball, who, I thought, was surely killed, and I was greatly relieved when I heard his voice, which sounded a mile away.

The accident was soon explained. The men were running in the steel hawser, which we had been using to tow the monitor, and it had picked up the steel battle hatch, weighing something over four hundred pounds, which was lying on deck ready to be put on the cabin hatch when needed. The line had carried it along until it came directly over the hatch under which I was sitting, when it slipped off, came down edge first, and caught me on the shoulder instead of the head. The man who called to me to look out held on to it in his effort to stop it, and came down with it. My shoulder was badly mashed and dislocated, but the excellent medical men soon wiped the blood off, reduced the dislocation, bandaged my arm to my side, and turned me in with a stiff glass of grog under my belt. The only serious damage was to the cabin table, which was no longer fit for use. If my head had been four inches farther forward, I should never have had the pleasure of writing this book.

The Iowa arrived at Key West after sundown May 18th and anchored near the flagship New York. The flying squadron, Commodore Schley commanding, was at anchor in the immediate vicinity. Coal and ammunition lighters were brought alongside at once, and all night long my willing men shovelled away and stowed bread and powder. Sampson came on board to see me and urged me to my best efforts, as he wished the Iowa ready at the first possible moment to join Schley. Early on the 19th the flying squadron sailed for Cienfuegos and my men tugged away at the coal whips, scarcely taking time to eat. During the night of the 19th it was very rough, and by daylight officers and men were about worn out, but with a rest of only an hour we went at it again, determined to do all that men could do to carry out the wishes of our commander in chief.

At eleven o'clock Sampson signalled me, "You must go now, cast off lighters, show yourself off Havana before sundown, and then proceed with all possible despatch to Cienfuegos and report to Commodore Schley." At the same time he sent my written orders and official mail for the commander of the flying squadron. In ten minutes I was under way and standing out to sea with my decks piled waist-high with boxes of provisions and ammunition, while the whole ship was black with coal dust, and the officers and men looked like a gang of chimney-sweeps. Just as the sun was setting I slowed and stopped my engines about two miles from the Morro lighthouse, and remained in that position until it was fairly dark, when I rang the engines full speed ahead, and at twelve knots speed steered my course for Cape San Antonio at the west end of Cuba.

In the forenoon of the following day, when nearly up with the cape, I found the torpedo boat Dupont thrashing about in the heavy sea and her commanding officer unable to make out his position. I gave him his bearings, and he was off at once to deliver his orders to Commodore Schley. We had no despatch boats, properly speaking, and these delicate torpedo boats had to be used for the purpose. It was like ploughing a stumpy field with a carefully groomed and trained thoroughbred horse. On Sunday, May 22d, at 1.30 P. M., I stopped my engines two hundred yards astern of the Brooklyn, off Cienfuegos, Cuba, and, as my arm was still bandaged to my side, sent my executive officer on board to report the ship to Commodore Schley for duty in his squadron, and at the same time deliver him the official mail I had received from Admiral Sampson for him. I had, about 1.15 P. M., saluted the flag of the commodore. It was thus that I became a part of the much-talked-of and discussed flying squadron.

On May 23d I took in two hundred and fifty-five tons of coal from a collier between the hours of 10 A. M. and 6.30 P. M., besides giving coal to a torpedo boat. During the night it was reported to me that there were three white lights in line on shore, which I knew was the signal from the insurgents that they wished to communicate. I, of course, took it for granted that the commodore understood this signal as well as I did, otherwise I should have informed him of its significance. It appeared afterward that he did not;

and thus much valuable time was lost. On the morning of the 24th the Marblehead arrived, and the moment Commander McCalla heard of the three lights he went in and communicated, and in a few hours Schley knew that the Spanish fleet was not in Cienfuegos.

In the meantime I had received a draft of thirty-seven men from the Marblehead, most of them recruits from Detroit, Michigan. At 7.55 that evening the squadron got under way and went to sea, bound for Santiago. During the 25th and 26th we steamed along slowly, at times making as low as five knots in order to allow the Eagle, a small converted yacht, to keep company with us. She was bothered by the roughness of the sea, which did not trouble the larger vessels. The Brooklyn or Iowa could have towed her ten knots or more without difficulty. At times we steamed eight or nine knots, which was the greatest speed we made during the trip. At 5.25 P. M., May 26th, we stopped our engines at a point twenty-six to thirty miles to the south of Santiago, and there remained four hours or more in communication with the St. Paul, the Yale, and the Minneapolis. The air was very clear and the high mountains back of Santiago could be seen, but nothing else. No attempt was made, so far as I know, to determine whether the Spanish fleet was in the harbour or not. At 7.50 P. M. the commodore made the following general signal to the squadron: " Destination Key West, *via* south side of Cuba and Yucatan channel, as soon as collier is ready; speed nine knots." At 9.10 we went ahead at nine knots' speed, heading west, bound, as I supposed from the signal, for Key West.

Bewildering Orders

All hands on the Iowa were greatly surprised at this unexpected retreat, and I for one was absolutely in the dark as to its meaning. I felt reasonably sure that Cervera was in Santiago, but concluded that the commodore had better information than I on that point. My natural inference was that the Spanish ships had left Santiago and gone to the westward, and that we were going after them. This inference was completely wrong, for after two hours we stopped again and drifted about until noon of the following day, while some of the vessels took coal from the collier. Then we stood on to the west again, occasionally stopping, until 1.25 P. M., May 28th, when we were signalled to steer east, one half north, and steam six knots per hour. Thus we headed back in the direction of Santiago.

As there had been no conference of commanding officers, we were all completely bewildered as to what this peculiar manœuvring might mean. Some of us, remembering the fate of Admiral Byng, felt that if Cervera was really in Santiago and got one of his ships away and on to the coast of the United States, while we were tinkering at the machinery of a collier, the world might be startled by another dreadful court-martial sentence.

CHAPTER XXXVIII

FIGHTING AT LONG RANGE

AT 7.40 P. M., May 28th, the squadron stopped off
the entrance to the harbour of Santiago, distant there-
from about nine miles. During the night we steamed
slowly back and forth, closing in somewhat before daylight. At early dawn I was standing on the bridge
with the executive officer, Lieutenant-Commander
Rodgers, who had been our naval *attaché* at Madrid
and who knew every vessel in the Spanish navy. As
we stood straining our eyes for what we hoped we
might see, he suddenly turned on me and said, " Captain, there's the Cristóbal Colón!" In a moment
I caught her with my glasses lying moored in front of
the Punta Gorda battery in a position to command the
channel. The information was quickly flagged to the
Brooklyn, and in a second or two the answer came back,
" I understand." Then we made out another Spanish
ship and a torpedo boat and flagged this information
at once. Again the answer came back, " I understand."

In the meantime I had gone to general quarters
and loaded the heavy guns, hoping that we might
have a chance to use them on the Colón as she lay
helpless and at our mercy, but such was not to be

430

our luck. We steamed about in front of the harbour until a signal was made during the forenoon for commanding officers to repair on board the flagship. Then the fleet stopped while the commodore and his commanders discussed the situation. The details of this conference I am not at liberty to give, but I may say without impropriety that Commodore Schley was at last satisfied that Cervera's fleet was in Santiago Harbour and not in Cienfuegos. We continued to steam about in front of the place during Sunday, Monday, and Tuesday, while the Colón, with fires hauled and awnings spread, lay in plain sight, quietly watching us.

At 11.20 A. M., May 31st, Commodore Schley made this signal to the squadron: " The Massachusetts, New Orleans, and Iowa will go in after dinner to a distance of seven thousand yards and fire at Cristóbal Colón with eight- and twelve- and thirteen-inch guns. Speed about ten knots." At 1.25 P. M. the three ships mentioned formed column, the Massachusetts leading, showing the broad pennant of Commodore Schley; the New Orleans, a vessel purchased in England and with a new crew came second; and the Iowa last. The second-class battle-ship Texas, the splendid armoured cruiser Brooklyn, and the gunboat Marblehead, were spectators of the fight that followed.

The Massachusetts opened fire at 1.50, her first thirteen-inch shell striking the water outside the Morro, as I judged about two thousand yards short of the Colón. I therefore set my gun sights at eighty-five hundred yards and at 1.56 opened fire as soon as the Colón could be seen. All the projectiles fell short, though our guns were elevated to nine thousand yards. The harbour entrance was so narrow and our speed so great we could only fire a few shots before the Spanish ship was shut out by the land. At 2.01 I ceased firing. The Massachusetts in the meantime had turned with port helm away from the land, and thus materially increased the distance from the Colón. She opened fire again at 2.05, and the commodore made this signal: " Do not go in any closer." When I had turned the Iowa and could see the Colón, I decreased my speed and opened fire at 2.08, range ninety-five hundred yards, which I gradually increased to eleven thousand as I saw the shells falling short. At 2.16 the commodore signalled, " Cease firing," and the battle was over. Nobody had been struck, Spaniard or American. Two battle ships and a cruiser on our side had engaged one cruiser and a few guns mounted on shore on the Spanish side for about fifteen minutes and then drew off. The only cause we had for congratulation was the fact that nobody was hurt. I had all four of my twelve-inch guns disabled by damage to the dash pots from high-angle fire, but they were repaired long before we had any real necessity to use them.

Commodore Schley transferred his flag back to the Brooklyn at 2.50 P. M., the enemy ceased firing at 3.10, and we resumed our peaceful cruising up and down in front of the entrance to the harbour. Captain Moreau of the Colón told me weeks afterward that the last large shell from the Iowa struck about forty feet short of him, and when it exploded a small piece of it found its way into his cabin, and that he retained it as a souvenir of the day. This he said was the nearest any projectile came to striking his ship.

Volunteers Wanted

On June 1st Admiral Sampson arrived early in the morning, and after steaming well in toward the Morro made signal, " Come closer." From that hour the blockade of Santiago was so maintained that it was not possible for any vessel to escape. Orders were issued that if the enemy's ships attempted to escape we should close in at once and force them ashore or sink them; and these orders were posted on the bridge of the Iowa, and, I assume, on other ships also, so that even the signal boys knew what was to be done when we sighted them.

Preparations were at once begun for sinking the Merrimac in the channel, which was done in the most gallant and daring manner by Assistant Naval Constructor Hobson on the morning of June 3d, about half an hour before daylight. During the afternoon of June 2d Sampson had signalled me, " I want volunteers to sink the Merrimac." I gave the signal to the executive officer, with directions to read it to the crew and give me the names of those who wished to go. In a short time he came to me and said that all the officers had volunteered, and also the entire crew of six hundred men. It was something of a job to write down all their names, and, as I was sure only a few could be required, I signalled: " My entire crew has volunteered. How many men do you want? " The answer came back promptly, " I want one seaman from the Iowa." The question then was how to select one man out of six hundred good ones. I was naturally anxious to send a man who would die reflecting credit on the ship. I had no idea that any one would ever come out of the scrape alive.

Two men were selected, one by me and one by the executive officer. I took a petty officer named McLean, who had served with me in the Yorktown, a first-class man in every respect; the executive took a young seaman named Murphy, a native of the State of Maine, also first-class in every way. When told that I was going to sentence one of them to death in a few minutes, and being asked if they still wanted to go in the Merrimac, they both smiled and said " Yes." McLean offered Murphy fifty dollars for his chance, which was promptly declined, and the toss of a penny decided the case in Murphy's favour. Then McLean offered him one hundred and fifty dollars for his chance, which was also promptly declined, and the poor fellow went forward with the tears streaming out of his eyes because he had lost a chance to have his head shot off! They were fine fellows to tie to, those blue-shirted chaps of mine.

The position of the Iowa on the blockading line was directly off the entrance of the harbour, so that we could look straight up the channel as far as the Punta Gorda battery, and in this position I and my men lived from June 1st until July 3d. I was absent but one day, when I ran up to Guantanamo Bay for coal, and was back at my station at night. We took coal and food and ammunition on the blockading line, and, as I have said, did not leave it until the necessity for a blockade ceased to exist. The infernal place got to look like home to us; we almost knew the sharks and fishes that swam around us. Certainly we knew the batteries and just when we might expect to hear from them.

Hobson's Exploit

It was from this position that I watched the Merrimac make her last trip on the morning of June 3d. During the night of the 2d I caught sight of her several times, but it was nearly daylight when I saw her distinctly as she made for the entrance of the harbour. The Spaniards were on the alert, and just as the Merrimac turned into the channel I saw the flash of a small gun, and immediately afterward the firefly sparks along the shore indicated that the infantry had opened on her with their Mausers. Then the guns on Socapa began to blaze and were followed by those on the Morro and Esmeralda batteries and the Punta Gorda fort. Within three minutes the Reina Mercedes and other ships opened up, and, as their heavy guns flashed, the doomed ship stood out clear and distinct in the accumulating clouds of smoke. Finally the whole entrance to the harbour was a roaring blaze of powder smoke, and the Merrimac was shut out from our view. It was a dreadful sight—to my mind what hell might look like with the lid off! I had seen all I cared to look at, and, convinced that the gallant Hobson and his equally gallant men had gone aloft forever, I retired to the pilot house, where I consoled myself with a pipe. Slowly the clouds of smoke lifted and daylight disclosed the smokestack and masts of the sunken ship sticking out of the water.

As soon as it was fairly light I received a signal to stand in close and prevent any interference with the wreck of the Merrimac. I understood at once that Sampson wished me to see that dynamite was not used on her, and, having reached a point where I could command the channel with my guns, I stopped the engines

435

and waited for something to happen. All was as still as death, and there was no living thing in sight. I could see something swinging to a line from the mast of the Merrimac that looked like a life raft, but my strongest glasses failed to show anything like a man on or about it. Just at sunrise, as I stood on the end of the bridge watching intently, a white-covered navy steam launch came in sight steering down the channel, and, as she approached the wreck, the executive officer, who was by my side, said, " Captain, shall I open fire? " " No," I replied, " not yet." I meant to sink the boat, of course, if she showed any inclination to disturb the quiet of the scene. She stopped near the wreck for ten minutes or more and I could see a few men moving about on her rail, then she turned and went back up the harbour. I never knew until Hobson told me, weeks afterward, that Admiral Cervera was himself in the launch and that he (Hobson) was under the raft with his seven men, and that he surrendered to the Spanish admiral and was by him taken to the flagship. If I had opened fire on the boat, I should probably have destroyed her and killed the whole party, and two of the most picturesque figures in the Spanish war would have disappeared—Cervera and Hobson.

About three o'clock on the afternoon of June 3d Admiral Cervera did a thing that stamped him as the gallant Spanish gentleman we afterward found him to be. He sent out a vessel under a flag of truce with his chief of staff, Captain Bustamente, to communicate with Admiral Sampson and to say to him that Hobson and his men were well, had behaved most gallantly, and that he personally would see to their welfare; also that he would be glad to have us send in clothing or other things that would add to their comfort. There was never a more courteous thing done in war, and I am sure that every man in the American fleet appreciated it. That they afterward showed their appreciation and in a very substantial way is now a matter of history.

During the early days of June the bay of Guantanamo was seized, and, after a sharp engagement, the battalion of marines under Colonel Huntington and the force under Captain McCalla controlled the entrance to the harbour. The American flag was hoisted on the captured Spanish fort, and for the first time it flew over Cuban soil supported by American men. I, for one, hope it may never be hauled down. The possession of this beautiful landlocked water gave us a secure base where small vessels would be safe in storms, and all hands could coal in any kind of weather. A great load was lifted from the minds of all commanding officers, but the relief to the commander-in-chief was the greatest of all.

There had been rumours of the approach of the American army under General Shafter, and while we maintained our strict blockade we prayed that they would come soon, for the heat and strain of the work were hard to bear. We fired on the batteries frequently, more to give our men practice than for any other reason, for we all knew that it was impossible for any naval force to destroy them because of their location and commanding positions. We could and did drive the men away from the guns and keep them away from them whenever we opened on them, but the entire destruction of the works was beyond our power. The harbour and the ships it contained were inaccessible to a naval force, owing to the character of the channel and the mines planted in it. The capture of the forts was an army job, and we of the navy waited with absolute faith and such patience as we could command for the time when our brother arm of the service would come and do it.

At last the rumours took positive shape and we knew that General Shafter was on the way to Santiago with seventeen thousand of the best men in the world. On the afternoon of June 20th the great forest of masts and smokestacks off to the south of Santiago showed that the transport fleet had arrived. In a few hours orders came to send our boats, properly officered and manned, to a rendezvous off Baiquiri at a stated time to land the army and their belongings. This was a great surprise to us all, as we had been notified that this duty would not be required of us and we had left nearly all our boats at Key West. However, we were only too glad to do all and everything in our power to assist those who had come to help us to capture Santiago and its Spanish garrison. Our only regret was that they found us so badly prepared to do the work in the shortest possible time. Our officers and men were constantly employed night and day for three days landing the troops, and many of them for over a week more landing provisions and stores. In a word, we did everything that it was possible for us to do, and in return received the warmest thanks and the commendation of General Shafter expressed in official form.

From my position off the Morro I saw little of the

work of the army. Occasionally I could see small parties of men on the hills back of Siboney, and when the troops were seriously engaged I could judge their position by the clouds of smoke from the field guns, but of the actual fighting I saw nothing.

As time passed and the lines were established on the land side, Admiral Sampson drew in closer his blockading lines, so that we were always within easy range of the Spanish guns. At first our distance from the harbour entrance during the daytime had been four or five miles; now it was three, and during the night two miles and even nearer.

The plan of using search lights was perfectly carried out and originated, no doubt, with Sampson himself. I was the first one to carry out his orders in this respect, and I shall never forget my sensations as I did it. The Iowa was well in toward the land when the New York steamed in near me and the admiral hailed and said, "At dark, I wish you to go in and turn a search light on the channel." "How near shall I go, sir?" I replied. "Go in until you can detect a small boat crossing in front of the Punta Gorda battery," came back through the megaphone. "How long shall I remain there, sir?" I asked. "All night, sir." "Ay, ay, sir." The admiral certainly had given me a new sensation. The idea of deliberately placing a battle ship within a mile of two of the fastest torpedo boats in the world, and then turning on a search light to mark her position, was novel at least. All writers on the subject had advised sending such valuable ships to sea at night to keep the torpedo boats away from them; but Sampson had thought rapidly and accurately, and had gauged the features of this special case most admirably, as the result showed.

At dark that night I steamed the Iowa in for this new duty, and, when I reached what I supposed to be the proper position, turned on the search light and stopped the engines. All hands were at quarters, guns loaded, and everything ready to return the fire I felt sure would be opened on us. As the ship lost way and came to a standstill in the water, I examined carefully the channel with my glasses and concluded that I was not yet near enough to insure the work I was ordered to do. I therefore shut off the light and again steamed in, and when I stopped the second time, the beam of the search light showed up everything very distinctly. The sentries on the Morro could be seen plainly as they pulled their hats down over their eyes as a protection against the glare. The infantry fired spitefully with their Mausers without doing any harm, but the batteries remained silent, which has always been a great surprise and puzzle to all of us. They could have shot the search light out of us without doubt if they knew the first principles of pointing guns. Maybe they knew there were a lot of search lights in that fleet and it would be a hard job to put them all out.

After the first night, three battle ships—the Iowa, Oregon, and Massachusetts—were detailed to do search-light duty, and there was never a minute at night, until the Spanish fleet was destroyed, when the channel was not so lighted that it was impossible for anything to move on the water without being seen. The duty was well done, and only those who did it know how hard it was or how great the strain. As a rule the darkness was intense, and between the battle ships and the shore were guard boats and picket launches which would be endangered if their position were disclosed, and as a consequence the beam of the search light had to be accurately held on the channel. To do this when the heavy swell and the strong tide were cutting the ship about was more difficult than the average person would imagine. It was beautiful to see the accuracy with which these great ships were handled as they came in or went out of position with twenty-five or thirty vessels crowded about them and not a light on any of them. During all the time we were there the paint was not even scratched on one of them by collision.

On July 2d the long-looked-for attack on the shore batteries about Santiago was made, and the Spanish resistance found more stubborn than was anticipated. The fleet was much disheartened by the report that General Shafter intended to retire and fortify in a stronger position; but we all felt that, whatever he did, the Spanish fleet was doomed. None of us imagined for a moment that Admiral Cervera would attempt anything in the nature of a sortie, for that would be courting certain destruction. What we thought he might at any moment do would be to destroy his ships, land his men, and attempt to cut his way through our weakened lines. Toward evening on the 2d we discovered that several of the Spanish blockhouses to the west and northwest of Santiago were on fire, which indicated that the outposts on the mountains were being forced in by the insurgents and that they were destroying everything before retiring. Just at sunset

A Sailor's Log

Lieutenant F. K. Hill, who was the officer of the deck on board the Iowa, sent for me, and when I reached the bridge pointed out to me these fires, which presented a beautiful sight. He also called my attention to six columns of smoke near the entrance to the harbour which rose straight in the calm evening air. His opinion was that this indicated some movement on the part of the enemy's fleet, which was correct. It showed beyond a doubt that they had moved down from in front of the city; but, as they had often moved about the harbour, I did not consider it a matter of importance. I only said to Lieutenant Hill that we had the first search-light duty that night, and if they came out we should have a good chance at them, dismissed the subject from my mind, and went about my business. The incident, however, made a more serious impression on the mind of the signal quartermaster who was looking after the flags, and he, without orders to do so, bent on signal 250—"Enemy's ships coming out"—and had it ready to hoist. The flags remained bent on to the halliards all night, and were therefore ready to hoist on the morning of the 3d, when the fleet came out.

CHAPTER XXXIX

THE NAVAL BATTLE OFF SANTIAGO

About daylight on the morning of Sunday, July 3d, my son, Franck Taylor Evans, a naval cadet serving on the battle ship Massachusetts, came on board the Iowa. He had been on picket duty during the night of the 2d, and as his ship had gone to Guantanamo for coal, he brought his boat to my ship to remain until his own vessel returned. It was this lucky chance that enabled him to take part in the battle of that memorable day. The officers and men were about to be sent to quarters for Sunday inspection, all dressed in clean white uniforms, and I and my son were just finishing our cigars after breakfast when the alarm for battle sounded all over the ship. Both of us sprang to our feet and started for the deck, and as my head came above the hatch a gun was fired from the lower bridge of the Iowa, aimed in the direction of the Maria Teresa by Lieutenant Hill, who was again officer of the deck. Before this gun was fired, and immediately upon discovering the bows of the leading Spanish ship, the signal 250, which had been bent on the night before, was run up, and thus the Iowa had the honour of firing the first gun of the action, and first making signal that the enemy's ships were attempting to escape. When

I reached the bridge I found the engines set full speed ahead and the ship pointing straight for the entrance of the harbour. In about two minutes the guns of the starboard battery began firing—that is to say, the eight- and four-inch guns of the starboard battery and the forward twelve-inch guns. The crews of the rapid-fire guns were held in reserve until we should get to closer quarters.

As soon as I had a chance to look about me, I saw the New York about seven miles away off Siboney with her helm to port and turning rapidly in the direction of the fleet, and, judging from the great volume of smoke pouring from her smokestacks, her fires were being forced as much as possible. I could see distinctly the admiral's flag at her masthead, and with my glasses could have read any signal she had hoisted. She had started to the eastward a short time before, flying the signal, " Disregard the movements of the commander in chief," a signal that had been made whenever the admiral had for any reason been compelled to leave the blockading line. This signal indicated that we were not to follow the motions of the flagship, but, instead, close up somewhat so as to cover the interval caused by her absence, all of which was perfectly understood by the fleet. Before the firing began, my son asked me where he should take station, and I directed him to report to the officer commanding the division that corresponded to the one he served in on board of his own ship. I also directed that the men of his boat's crew should be stationed where they could render good service.

As the leading Spanish ship, the flagship Maria

The Spanish Fleet Appears

Teresa, swung into the channel leading out from the Punta Gorda, she presented a magnificent appearance with her splendid new battle flags and her polished brass work. Her bright new coat of paint was in marked contrast to the lead-coloured, iron-rusted ships that were rushing full speed at her. As she passed the Diamond Shoal at the entrance to the harbour she swung off to the westward and opened fire smartly with her port broadside and turret guns. From this moment the battle may be said to have been on, and the roaring of the guns was incessant. The Vizcaya came second, about six hundred yards astern of the flagship, followed by the Colón and then the Oquendo, bringing up the rear; the torpedo boats Furor and Pluton were not yet in sight. The speed I judged to be about eight knots as the ships came down the channel, which was increased to thirteen or more as they kept away to the westward in the open sea. They came at us like mad bulls, and presented a fine appearance as I caught sight of them occasionally through the dense smoke of our battery.

It had been my intention from the first to ram or torpedo the flagship if I could reach her, and to insure this, I remained, as much as I could, in the conning tower at the side of the quartermaster, who was steering, watching carefully every move of the wheel and directing the man just where to head. I kept the Maria Teresa open on my starboard bow, so that the guns could have a chance at her, until it became evident that I could not ram her or even get within torpedo range, when I swung off to port, gave her the full benefit of my starboard broadside, and then swung back

445

quickly and headed across the bows of the second ship, hoping to be able to reach her with my ram. The Maria Teresa passed me at a distance of about twenty-six hundred yards, and, as she crossed my bows, our forward twelve-inch guns were fired and I was confident that I saw both shells strike the Spanish ship. As I swung back for the second ship, my port battery opened on the Maria Teresa and the starboard guns continued to play on the Vizcaya and Colón, which were approaching us at great speed. The fire of the first ship had been very rapid and accurate when she opened, but it grew ragged and inaccurate as the range decreased. I soon found that the Vizcaya would also pass ahead of me, and that I could not reach her with ram or torpedo. I accordingly swung to port, gave her my broadside, and, as she passed at nineteen hundred yards, put my helm to port and headed in again to try for the next ship.

At this time the Colón came with a great show of speed, passing between the leading ships and the shore and much protected by their smoke. As she passed she struck me twice—two as beautiful shots as I ever saw made by any ship. I had been doing my best to fight the Iowa from the conning tower, but the temptation to see the fight was more than I could resist, and I frequently found myself on the bridge, deeply interested in the magnificent spectacle about me. It thus happened that I was on the end of the bridge when the Colón paid her respects to us. The first shell she fired at us, through a rent in the smoke, struck on the starboard side a little forward of the bridge, about four feet above the water line, passed through the cellulose belt, and exploded on the berth deck, demolishing the dispensary, breaking almost every medicine bottle in it, and doing great damage otherwise. The smells that came up in consequence of this explosion were variegated and intense, a mixture of medicine and mellinite. The second shell, of the same size as the first—about six and a half inches in diameter—struck just at the water line and about six to ten feet farther forward, passed through the side and into the cellulose belt, where it broke up without exploding. It however, made an ugly, jagged hole, eighteen inches long and eight inches wide, through which the water poured with great rapidity. The cellulose in the coffer dam, which was supposed to swell up and stop the shot hole, washed out and floated astern in a broad, brown streak. I think the Colón fired only twice at me, and, as I have stated, she did excellent shooting as far as I could see.

When the Oquendo approached me, I found that if I held on my course she would pass ahead of me, so I changed and ran parallel with her at a distance of about sixteen to fourteen hundred yards and opened on her my entire battery, including the rapid-fire and machine guns. At this time she was under the concentrated fire of several of our ships and the effect was most destructive. She rolled and staggered like a drunken thing, and finally seemed to stop her engines. I thought she was going to strike her colours, and was on the point of ordering the battery to cease firing, when she started ahead again and we redoubled our efforts to sink her. As I looked at her I could see the shot holes come in her sides and our shells explode inside of her, but she pluckily held on her course and fairly smothered us with a shower of shells and machine-gun shots.

In the meantime the Spanish flagship headed for the shore, in flames, fore and aft, and soon took the ground about seven miles to the west of the entrance to Santiago Harbour, and a few minutes later the Oquendo followed her, the flames bursting out through the shot holes in her sides and leaping up from the deck as high as the military tops. It was a magnificent, sad sight to see these beautiful ships in their death agonies; but we were doing the work we had been educated for, and we cheered and yelled until our throats were sore.

When we were hotly engaged with the last ship, two dense spots of black smoke and two long white streaks on the water indicated the positions of the Spanish torpedo boats as they made their gallant dash for liberty. We turned our rapid-fire guns and the after guns of the main battery on them, and at the same time other ships concentrated on the little gamecocks. In a very short time—not more than five minutes, I should say—a splendid column of steam mixed with coal dust sprang hundreds of feet in the air, and I knew that the boiler of one of them had blown up. A few minutes later the second one blew up, and the torpedo boats that had caused so much worry to friends and foes alike were things of the past. They had given us many sleepless nights, but when it came to the test of battle they had done just what many of us thought they would do. They had been disabled and destroyed in the shortest possible time. It was almost wicked to waste the lives of brave men in such an attempt.

About this time the flagship New York came racing back to join in the fight. As she passed the batteries they concentrated a heavy fire on her, to which she paid no attention, but fired three shots at one of the Spanish torpedo boats and then hurried on, coming up directly astern of the Iowa. She had the Vizcaya within range of her eight-inch guns for some time before that vessel ran ashore, but in order to hit her, would have had to fire over the Iowa, which I suppose was the reason why Captain Chadwick held his fire. Afterward, when she passed between me and the wreck of the Vizcaya, as I was hoisting out my boats to go to her relief, my men broke into cheers as they made out Admiral Sampson on the bridge.

The course of the Iowa had carried her inside of the rest of the American fleet, and, as I drew up abreast of the two burning Spanish ships on the beach, I could see their crews struggling in the water where the shells of our ships seemed to be bursting among them. The Maria Teresa had a white flag flying forward, which I was sure could not be seen by the vessels firing on them, so I hoisted the signal, " Enemy's ships have surrendered! " and the fire was at once concentrated on the fleeing Vizcaya. She was soon on fire, and off Accerraderos turned and headed for the shore, smoke and flames pouring from her ports and hatches. The Colón, the last ship of the splendid squadron, was standing to the westward, hotly pursued by the Oregon, Brooklyn, Texas, and New York. All the rest were shapeless wrecks on the Cuban shore, and nearly six hundred of their gallant officers and men had fought their last fight. God and the gunners had had their day.

At this point the battle of Santiago may be said to have terminated; at any rate I took no further part in it. I felt that I should be of no use in the chase of the Colón, as my speed was low, owing to the foul condition of the ship's bottom. She had been in the water seventeen months without docking, and her cylinder heads had not been off for six months. There was a duty for me, however, which I felt to be an imperative one, and that was the rescue of the brave but unfortunate men who had fought us so gallantly. Their wounded were in danger of burning to death, and those who had been fortunate enough to escape from the ships were in danger of death at the hands of the Cuban insurgents, who were willing, and I must say with ample provocation, to take the life of any Spanish officer or man. They were our prisoners, however, and I made up my mind that no harm should come to them if I could prevent it. I therefore ran in close to the burning wreck of the Vizcaya, hoisted out what boats I had and sent them to the rescue as rapidly as possible. I also directed the torpedo boat Ericsson and the converted yacht Hist to join in the work. The danger to our men and officers from exploding magazines was imminent, but they faced it with a courage and coolness that were habitual to them.

It was only a short time before the boat loads of dead and wounded began to arrive alongside, and then the ghastly, horrible results of our Sunday morning's work were apparent. I had made every possible preparation for the comfort of the wounded, and as the poor chaps were tenderly lifted over the side and handled by the men who, half an hour before, were anxious to kill them all, I could but be struck with this splendid phase of war. The beautiful white quarter-deck of the Iowa was soon stained with the blood dripping from the wet clothing of the wounded, and she looked as if she had been used as a slaughter pen.

Presently a boat came alongside bearing Captain Eulaté, commander of the Vizcaya. That was a sight I shall never forget as long as I live. In the stern, supported by one of our naval cadets, sat the captain, covered with blood from three wounds, with a blood-stained handkerchief about his bare head.. Around him sat or lay a dozen or more wounded men. In the bottom of the boat, which was leaking, was a foot or so of blood-stained water and the body of a dead Spanish sailor which rolled from side to side as the water swashed about. The captain was tenderly placed in a chair and then hoisted to the deck, where he was received with the honours due his rank. As the chair was placed on the quarter-deck he slowly raised himself to his feet, unbuckled his sword belt, kissed the hilt of his sword, and, bowing low, gracefully presented it to me as a token of surrender. I never felt so sorry for a man in all my life. Of course I declined to receive the sword, or rather I instantly handed it back to Captain Eulaté, but accepted the surrender of his officers and men in the name of Admiral Sampson, our commander in chief. My men were all crowded aft about the deck and superstructure, and when I declined the sword the brave hearts under the blue shirts appreciated my feelings and they cheered until I felt ashamed of myself.

As I supported the captain toward my cabin, he stopped for a moment just as we reached the hatch, and drawing himself up to his full height, with his right arm extended above his head, exclaimed, "Adios, Vizcaya!" Just as the words passed his lips the forward magazine of his late command, as if arranged for the purpose, exploded with magnificent effect. Captain Eulaté, a sensitive, passionate man, conducted himself in a way to elicit the admiration of all who saw him. After he had been attended to by the surgeons he occupied a part of my cabin, and did all in his power to aid me in making his officers and men comfortable.

The work of rescue was progressing rapidly; nearly three hundred prisoners—officers and men—had been received on board when the U. S. S. Resolute, Commander Eaton commanding, hove in sight, blowing her steam whistle, and with this signal at her yardarm, "Enemy's battle ship to the eastward." At first I thought that she had dressed ship in honour of our victory, and that the combination of signal flags was an accident, but as she drew nearer I knew this was not the case. A signal man was signalling that a Spanish battle ship was off Siboney, and Captain Eaton soon confirmed the news through a megaphone larger than any I had ever before seen. In reply to my inquiries, I was informed that the Resolute had been close enough to the newcomer to distinguish her colours, and that she was undoubtedly a Spanish battle ship, and probably at that moment was engaged in destroying our transport fleet at Siboney. After giving me this information, Captain Eaton continued his course to the westward in search of the admiral, who was out of sight, in chase of the Colón.

I felt absolutely confident that there was no Spanish

battle ship anywhere to the eastward short of the coast of Spain, but after a while I saw the Harvard, Captain Charles Cotton commanding, coming my way at top speed with a tremendous bone in her mouth and followed by a dozen or more army transports, all making the best speed they were capable of. Captain Cotton flew the signal, " Enemy's battle ship in sight to the eastward." The Harvard slowed and stopped quite close to me, while I hoisted in my boats and made ready to engage the new enemy. I asked Captain Cotton, who had assured me that he had been near enough to the stranger to make her out beyond doubt as a Spanish battle ship, why Captain Taylor in the Indiana was not knocking the roof off her. I could see the Indiana's smokestacks as she lay at her station off Santiago, where Sampson had sent her to prevent some Spanish gun vessels from doing the very thing this new battle ship was supposed to be engaged in. The answer to my question came back very promptly from Cotton: " Bob, he has fooled Taylor; don't let him fool you."

I could see the vessel referred to well out to sea, but standing in toward us, and I at once shaped a course to intercept her. My ship was cleared for action, the guns all loaded, and the men cheering wildly at the prospect of having a Spanish battle ship all to themselves; but the three hundred Spanish prisoners were a source of anxiety to me. To expose them to the fire of their own people would be barbarous, and to allow them to mix in with my men and go below in my ship during a fight would be tempting Providence. I decided at once on the only way out of the difficulty. I went to Captain Eulaté, explained the position to

him in a few words, and placed him, his officers, and
men on parole not to commit any act of violence
against the authority of the United States. Then I
put all his people where they would be reasonably safe,
and, with the Harvard and a score of transports following me, stood rapidly out to sink the approaching ship.
Most of the troop ships had stopped near me for protection, but some of them continued, I believe, as far
as Jamaica, ninety miles away. The stranger was now
in plain sight and my officers and best signal men declared her colours to be Spanish. I gave orders to
open fire at five thousand yards, and was rapidly approaching that distance when she made signal, " I am
an Austrian," and a few moments later hoisted her
number. She proved to be the Austrian armoured
cruiser Infanta Maria Teresa. One of that name was
a wreck on the beach a few miles away, and the second
would have gone to the bottom of the sea if she had
delayed her signal a few minutes longer. The Spanish
and Austrian flags were dangerously alike for such
manœuvring on that particular day.

A number of dead Spanish sailors had been brought
on board the Iowa from the Vizcaya while we were
rescuing her crew. They had either been taken dead
from the water or had died in the boats. I had had
them placed well aft on the quarter-deck and covered
with the Spanish flag. The time had now come to
bury them, and I therefore stopped my engines and
lowered my colours to half mast, and my motions were
followed by the Harvard and the troop ships. Then
all hands were called to bury the dead; the service was
read by their own padre in the presence of their own

officers and men, and the bodies were committed to the deep while my marines presented arms and my officers and men stood uncovered and silent as if we were burying our own people. I doubt if a more impressive funeral ever took place from the deck of a vessel of war, certainly not on the conclusion of a great naval battle before the combatants had had time to remove the powder stains.

As soon as the prisoners were received on board they were given all the coffee they could drink and all the hard bread and corned beef they could eat. Then they were scrubbed and fitted out with clean new uniforms, and it was hard to distinguish them from our own men. They were a fine, muscular lot of well-disciplined people. The officers, as well as the men, had lost everything except the clothing they wore, and this in many cases was very scant. Indeed, many came on board entirely naked, having removed all their clothing before attempting to swim ashore from their burning ships. The officers of the Iowa, from the captain down, gave up their quarters to the Spanish officers and supplied each one with a complete suit of clothing and as much champagne as they could be induced to swallow. We did all we could to make them forget their unfortunate surroundings, and their gratitude was what we expected from gentlemen of their profession.

When I had satisfied myself that the Resolute and Harvard had not seen a real Spanish battle ship, I directed the course of the Iowa to the eastward and resumed my station off Santiago, where I found the Indiana and Gloucester on guard. The latter was

about to transfer Admiral Cervera and some of his
officers to the Indiana, but, as I knew that Captain
Taylor had little if any spare room in his cabin, and I
had plenty, I offered to take them on board the Iowa,
which offer was at once accepted, and Captain Wain-
wright, who had that day made a name for himself
worthy the stock from which he comes, brought them
alongside in his boat. The full marine guard was drawn
up on the quarter-deck while the Spanish prisoners
were lined up on the opposite side, and the crew of
the Iowa, just as they came out of the fight, were
massed on the superstructure and after-turrets. I and
my officers stood near the gangway. As the brave
old admiral came over the side scantily clad, without
shirt or hat, yet an admiral every inch of him, the
officers saluted, the marines presented arms, and the
buglers sounded the salute for an officer of his rank.
As he bowed and extended his hand to me, my men
burst into cheers. For an instant it seemed to me
that Admiral Cervera misunderstood the demonstration; but then he realized its meaning, that it was the
tribute of brave men for a brave and gallant foe, and
he stood bowing his acknowledgment while the men
behind the guns made him understand what they
thought of him.

The meeting between the late commander in chief,
who had with him his son, acting as his flag lieutenant, and the commanding officers of the torpedo boats,
and Captain Eulaté and his men, was touching and
pathetic. After I had made him as comfortable as
possible, he asked to see the wounded Spanish sailors
who were crowded into our sick-bay. He had a word

Admiral Cervera's reception on board the Iowa.

of comfort and encouragement for each of them and they appreciated his visit. I gave him my cabin, where he lived until after sundown on the following day, when I transferred him to the St. Louis for passage North in company with the other captured Spanish officers. During the evening of the 3d of July he sat on deck under a small awning I had arranged for him, smoking and receiving the various officers who called to pay their respects. While he was somewhat depressed over the disaster that had befallen his fleet and his country, it seemed to me that he had anticipated it and bore himself with great dignity and courtesy. His conversation was most interesting, and I listened to him with great interest until he retired about eleven o'clock.

By that time Admiral Sampson had returned from the wreck of the Colón and we all knew of the complete annihilation of the Spanish fleet. There was a death-like silence over our fleet as the tired officers and men sought such rest as they could obtain. For me there was no rest, and I spent the night walking the deck, keeping a keen watch on the prisoners and occasionally visiting the wounded officers in my cabin to do what I could to add to their comfort. I felt that we had done a good, clean piece of work during the day, and was glad for the people at home who would be much relieved by our victory.

On July 4th we dressed ship, fired salutes, and conducted ourselves generally in a way befitting the day. When we had transferred our prisoners, we took our former blockading stations and fell again into our watchful routine. Toward midnight the Massachusetts, on search-light duty, discovered the Reina Mercedes, a Spanish cruiser of thirty-five hundred tons, coming out of the harbour. The Massachusetts opened on her at once and the Texas joined in the fight. The rest of us held our fire and watched one of the most beautiful engagements ever fought. The beams of the search lights showed up the Spaniard until she looked like a ship in a picture, and we could see the shells tearing through her and exploding all about her. Gradually she began to turn, then listed over to one side, and soon joined the Merrimac on the bottom and only a few hundred yards away from her. The batteries in the meantime opened up and for half an hour mortar shells and six-inch projectiles whizzed and roared over our heads. The Indiana received a mortar shell through her quarter-deck, and was the only ship struck. At midnight everything was quiet. The sea power of Spain had been destroyed in a manner which must bring great credit to the navy of the United States, and give us a standing as a naval power which we had never before enjoyed. And, beyond this, the war must speedily end.

During the evening of July 4th I wrote and submitted to Admiral Sampson my report of the engagement of July 3d. When I had about concluded it and was thinking of something good enough to say of the brave men who had fought under my command, my pen, without conscious effort on my part, wrote the following words: " I can not express my admiration for my magnificent crew. So long as the enemy showed his flag they fought like American seamen, but when the flag came down they were as gentle and tender as American women." I don't know whether it was the memory of the gentle American women, or the presence about me of the gallant American seamen that influenced my pen, but it certainly wrote exactly what I felt.

The blockade of Santiago was strictly maintained until the Spanish army surrendered, when we retired to Guantanamo, and a squadron of twelve ships, the Iowa one of them, was made ready to sail for the coast of Spain and call the bluff of Admiral Camara in passing his fleet through the Suez Canal ostensibly on his way to Manila to annoy Admiral Dewey. For several days we lay with steam up and everything ready to get under way on the receipt of telegraphic orders, but the orders never came. Spain was vanquished, Sampson at Santiago had completed the work so brilliantly begun by Dewey at Manila, and she sued for peace. When the protocol had been signed we received orders to proceed to New York.

CHAPTER XL

CONCLUSION

WITH men cheering and the bands playing " Homeward bound," we sailed from the island of Cuba, having wrested it from the nation that discovered it four hundred years before.

We reached New York August 20th, and there received a welcome which will never be forgotten by any one who witnessed it. The squadron, fresh from the enemy's coast and just as they had fought, steamed up the beautiful harbour, fired a salute of twenty-one guns off the tomb of General Grant, and returned to the anchorage at Tompkinsville. The hearts of officers and men were full to overflowing because of the kindly, patriotic welcome of their fellow-countrymen. The hardships we had endured were forgotten in the satisfaction we felt in having pleased our employers. There had been no time to advertise our coming or prepare for us a formal welcome; nevertheless New York city was one blaze of American flags, and every vessel that could steam or sail was crowded to suffocation with men and women and children from all parts of the republic to welcome our home-coming. It was a spontaneous outburst of patriotism and affection the like of which this country had never before seen.

Presentation of a Sword

Late in October the Iowa was ordered to be ready to sail for San Francisco and I was detached from her. I left her with great regret, much touched by the kindly feeling of her officers and crew.

From the day of my return I was generously treated by the people of all sections of the country. They showered invitations upon me for banquets and entertainments of all kinds. I could not accept many of them, but was, and am still, heartily grateful for the feeling that prompted them.

Some time after I left the Iowa I received a beautiful sword, which I value above all my earthly possessions, and the following letter:

"U. S. S. IOWA, FIRST RATE,
SAN FRANCISCO, CALIFORNIA, *February 14, 1899.*

"*Captain* ROBLEY D. EVANS, *U. S. N., Washington, D. C.*

"SIR: The members of this ship's company, who had the high honour of serving you from San Juan to Santiago, beg leave to present this sword as a token of our affection and reverence.

"It had been our intention to make this presentation when you relinquished command, but owing to the disintegration of the crew following our arrival at New York in August last, and our hurried departure, it was not done. Coming at this late day, it will show you, sir, that this action is not from momentary impulse, but that the affection and respect of this crew for you is deep-rooted and lasting, and that the men of the battle ship Iowa will ever cherish the memory of their beloved commander.

461

" And with this sword we send our wishes for your health and happiness always. It is an assurance from us that you are *more* than a hero to a *nation—you are a hero to your men.*

" Very respectfully,
" F. ZULCH,
" A. E. MOORE,
" J. COLLINS, *Chief M. A. A.,*
" E. McCORMACK,
" H. ENELS HOLT,
" *Committee.*"

My yarn of forty years of naval life is spun. I think I can not close it more appropriately than by repeating a remark made to me in Cincinnati. I was attending a reception in the Chamber of Commerce, where many people had assembled to greet me. A white-haired old gentleman stopped in front of me and, taking my hand, said, " Captain, I want to know how it feels when you are sure that there are seventy millions of people each of whom would like to look into your eyes and say, ' God bless you! ' " I could have told the kindly old man that it made me feel that fighting by day and watching by night, that danger in storm and suffering in tropic calm, were but " reasonable service " to such a country, and such fellow-countrymen as I am bound to by every feeling of my heart.

INDEX

A Sailor's Log

464

Index

Index

THE END